Vibes of Indian Economy-II
Focus on evolving economic Issues of Rajasthan

Anand Swaroop

BLUEROSE PUBLISHERS
India | U.K.

Copyright © Anand Swaroop 2024

All rights reserved by author. No part of this publication may be reproduced, stored in a retrieval system or transmitted in any form or by any means, electronic, mechanical, photocopying, recording or otherwise, without the prior permission of the author. Although every precaution has been taken to verify the accuracy of the information contained herein, the publisher assume no responsibility for any errors or omissions. No liability is assumed for damages that may result from the use of information contained within.

BlueRose Publishers takes no responsibility for any damages, losses, or liabilities that may arise from the use or misuse of the information, products, or services provided in this publication.

For permissions requests or inquiries regarding this publication,
please contact:

BLUEROSE PUBLISHERS
www.BlueRoseONE.com
info@bluerosepublishers.com
+91 8882 898 898
+4407342408967

ISBN: 978-93-5989-282-5

Cover design: Tahira
Typesetting: Tanya Raj Upadhyay

First Edition: February 2024

Morale Boosters

Suman
&
Lovely kids
Aman
Kabir

ABOUT THE BOOK

Chapter one provides progress and insight of the E-Way Bills system in Rajasthan. The total E-Way bill generation, value and volume of goods transported, sectoral analysis, inter - state, intra - state and analysis of export and import data of Rajasthan since the inception of GST.

The chapter two provides a brief description of major and minor mineral deposits and exploration in Rajasthan. It also provides detailed trends of E-Ravanna generation, royalty collection, mineral transported and mineral excavation since E-Ravanna was introduced in Rajasthan. The chapter also discussed top minerals and mines of the state from the perspective of E-Ravanna.

The chapter three analyzed cotton cloth bags industry in Rajasthan and the market trend of various types of cotton bags in Rajasthan. It also suggests the future prospects for cotton cloth bags industry in Rajasthan which holds immense potential for sustainable growth, environmental protection, and economic development.

The chapter four of the book described the data highlights of granite excavation in Rajasthan. It is found that there is a notable increase in both the net weight of granite extracted and the royalty revenue collected over the years in Rajasthan. This indicates a significant growth in granite mining activities and its demand in various industries and construction projects. It also describes District - wise granite mining extraction, royalty collection.

The chapter five examined the top five revenue earning major and minor minerals in Rajasthan. The chapter discussed the trends in terms of their production per hectare, sale value per ton and revenue per ton. It also discussed top districts of Rajasthan in terms of mining revenue and excavation of major and minor minerals.

The chapter six provides a basic understanding and overview of road accidents in Rajasthan. It covers almost all the aspects of road accidents in Rajasthan namely, profile & trends of road accidents, Accidents by Road categories, causes of road accidents, Road Accident Fatalities, information relating to road accidents, fatalities & causes. Chapter also provides remedial actions and the Government initiatives and implementing a multi - pronged road safety strategy namely Education, Engineering, Enforcement and Emergency Care.

The chapter seven describes the scope and prospects of ceramic based industries in Rajasthan. Chapter discussed strengths, weaknesses and opportunity for Rajasthan as the state has an abundant quantity of mineral deposits used for Ceramic industries.

TABLE OF CONTENTS

An overview of E-Way Bills – Perspective of Rajasthan 1

Mineral Deposits and Exploration in Rajasthan - Perspectives of E-Ravanna 38

Cotton Cloth Bags Industry in Rajasthan: A Step towards Environmental Sustainability and Economic Growth 72

Granite Industry in Rajasthan - Progress and Prospects 82

Top five major and minor minerals in Rajasthan - an outline............................109

Statistical Analysis of Road Accidents in Rajasthan..117

Preventive measures to mitigation Road accident 142

Ceramic Based Industries in Rajasthan 163

AN OVERVIEW OF E-WAY BILLS – PERSPECTIVE OF RAJASTHAN

GST network - Step forward

The introduction of the Goods and Services Tax (GST) was one of the milestones of the taxation which changed the whole indirect taxation process. By consolidating nearly all indirect taxes, with few exceptions, the implementation of GST is the major source of revenue collection in the country. The inclusion of the E-Way Bill system, E invoice and other online checks and balances in the GST framework ensure speedy, swift and evasion free indirect taxation. In April 2018 E-Way Bill system was established for inter - state transportation of goods, its purview was subsequently expanded to cover intra - state transportation in June 2018. To enhance its effectiveness in curbing tax evasion and preventing devious trading activities, the E-Way Bill System was seamlessly integrated with the VAHAN system governed by the transport department. Further, to make it more comprehensive and user friendly, this system was integrated with the e - invoice system of GST.

In January 2021, E-Way Bill system integrated with Radio Frequency Identification (RFID) technology, thus mitigating human intervention and unwanted abuse by unauthorized entities. This integration represents a significant stride towards minimizing the potential for fraud and streamlining the transportation of goods and thereby collection of Indirect taxes.

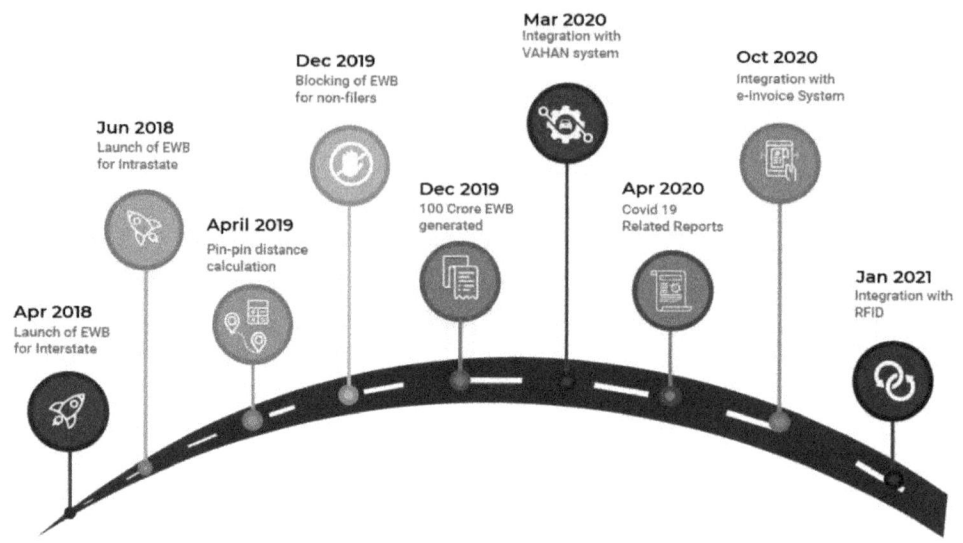

E-Way bills System – An introduction

E-Way bill is a mechanism to ensure that goods being transported comply with the GST Law and is an effective tool to track movement of goods and check tax evasion. E-Way bill is a permit needed for inter - state and intra - state transportation of goods worth more than Rs. 50,000. It contains details of the goods, the consignor, the recipient and the transporter. It can be electronically generated through the GSTN. The E-Way bill has been made mandatory for inter - state supplies from April 1, 2018 and for intra - state supplies from April 25, 2018. Primary Motive of introduction of E-Way bill system is to check evasion to keep the system perfect from the point of view of revenue leakages, to check unfair trade, curb unauthorized trade, helpful in policing of trade of illegal goods and introduce uniformity across the states for seamless generation of E-Way Bill.

The continuous evolution and integration of the E-Way Bill system underscores its pivotal role in ensuring seamless movement of goods while simultaneously fortifying the integrity and efficiency of the GST regime. Its integration with various technological advancements and systems has propelled it to the forefront of contemporary taxation practices, demonstrating the government's commitment to a robust and perfect taxation framework

Total generation of E-Way bills and Value of goods transported in Rajasthan

1. Total generation of E-Way bills in Rajasthan

The diagram conveys that the total number of E-Way bills generated is remarkable growth over the years accompanied by the corresponding percentage changes that demonstrate its successful trajectory.

Graph 1 - Generation of E-Way bill

(In Crores)

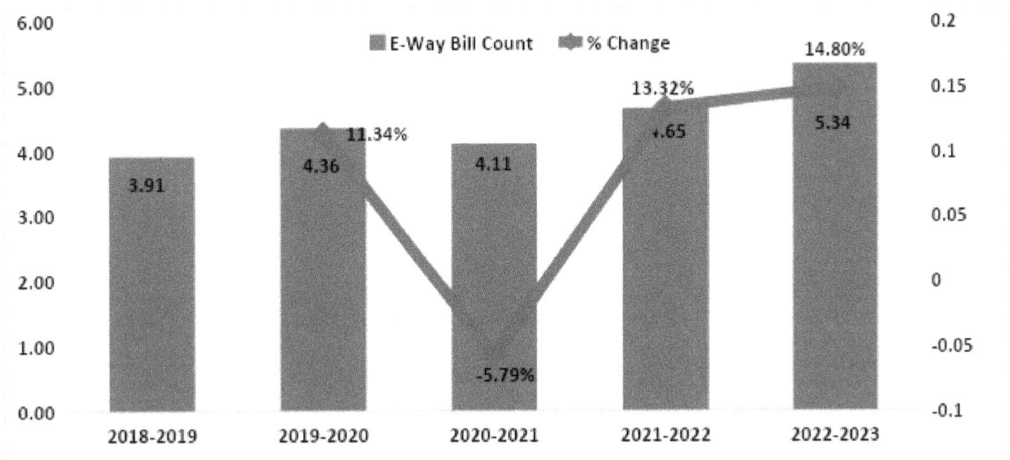

In the year of its inception in 2018 - 19, a total of 3.91 crores E-Way bills were generated by the traders of the country. Subsequently, in the year 2019 - 2020, this figure surged to 4.36 crores marking a growth of 11.34 percentage points. Come the Financial Year 2020 - 21, the whole world came to a halt due the lockdown imposed to prevent spread of CoronaVirus. This hampered the growth momentum of the E-Way bill generation as well. 4.11 Crore E-Way bills were generated during this year, resulting in a deceleration of the growth rate by 5.79 percent. The year 2021 - 22 marked the recovery phase of the entire taxation regime with a notable spike in generation of E-Way bills. An impressive total of 4.65 Crore bills were generated during 2021 - 22, representing a remarkable increase of 13.32 percent over previous year. Furthermore, the year 2022 - 23 witnessed the most substantial surge to date, with an outstanding generation of 5.34 crore E-Way bills, marking a remarkable growth rate of 14.80 percent.

Thus, except for the period of the lockdown, the figures for E-Way bill generation have persistently exhibited a trajectory of steady growth over the years. After integration of RFID and VAHAN the E-Way bill system is more robust and future growth of E-Way bill generation will reach a new high.

2. Total value goods transported through E-Way bills in Rajasthan

The diagram represents the cumulative value of goods transported through E-Way bills since its inception, alongside the relative percentage growth observed on an annual basis. The graph illustrates a consistent upward trend in the value of goods transported from the fiscal year 2018 - 19 to the fiscal year 2022 - 23. However, the growth rate experienced a slight decline in the year 2022 - 23.

Graph 2 - E-Way bills by total value of Goods

(In Crores)

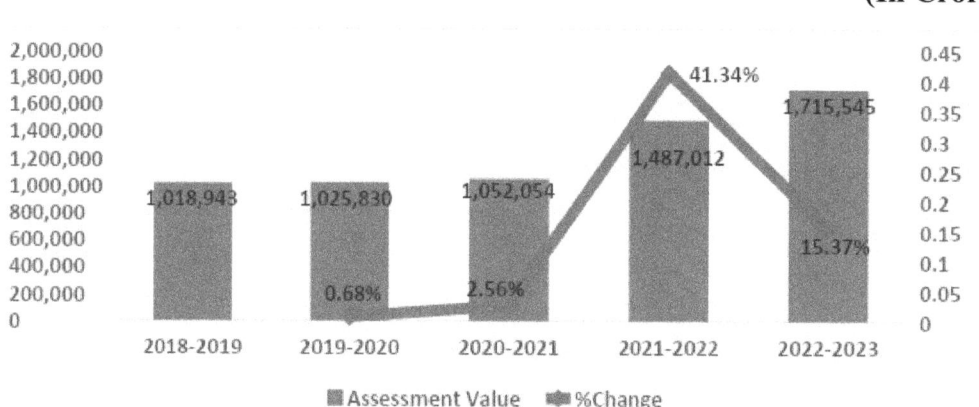

In the initial year of implementation i.e. the Financial Year 2018 - 19, goods with a total value of Rs. 1,018,943 crores were transported through E-Way bills. Subsequently, in the years spanning 2019 - 2022, this figure witnessed a marginal increase to Rs. 1,025,830 crores, signifying a growth rate of 0.68%.

The following Financial Year, 2020 - 21, exhibited a more substantial growth rate of 2.56%, as the total value of goods transported through E-Way bills reached Rs. 1,052,054 crores. Notably, the Fiscal Year 2021 - 22 marked a significant leap, with a growth rate of 41.34%. During this period, goods worth an impressive Rs. 1,487,012 crores were transacted through E-Way bills.

While the subsequent Financial Year, 2022 - 23, witnessed a decline in the growth rate to 15.37%, the total value of goods transported still reached a staggering Rs. 1,715,545 crores. This figure indicates the sustained growth and increased reliance on E-Way bills for the transportation of goods.

The graph and its corresponding data highlight the consistent rise in the value of goods transported through E-Way bills from FY 2018 - 19 to FY 2022 - 23. It demonstrates the importance of E-Way bills in facilitating seamless transportation and showcases the significant impact it has had on the economy.

3. Total value of goods transported through E-Way bills - sectoral analysis

Graph 3 illustrates the assessment value of goods for which the E-Way bills were generated over a period of five Financial Years, spanning from the financial years 2018 - 19 to 2022 - 23. The above data has been tabulated and presented in a graph based on different sectors, viz. Exports, Imports, Intra State supply of goods, Inter State Inward supply of goods and Inter State Outward supply of goods.

Graph 3 Total value of goods transported through E-Way bills

(in Crores)

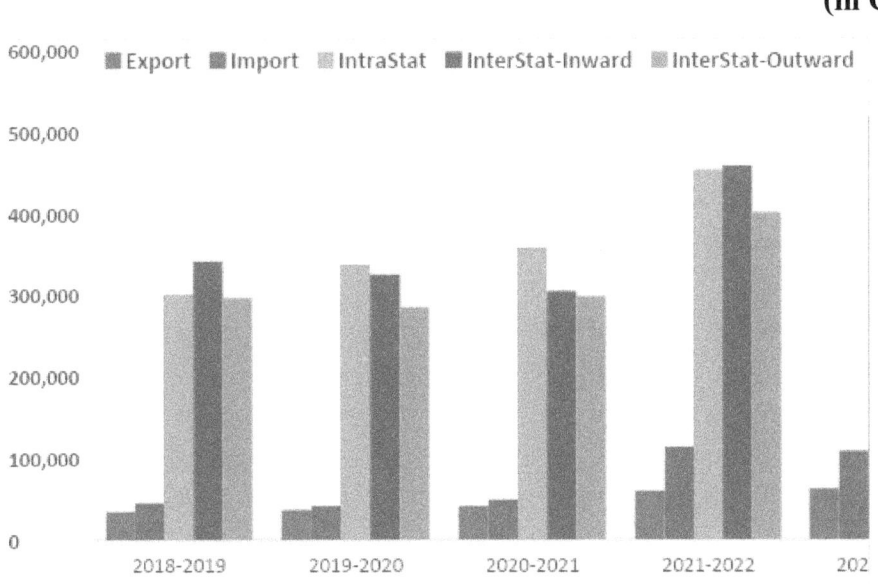

Upon analyzing the E-Way bill data for exports, it is evident that the value of goods supplied through the generation of E-Way bills has consistently increased. In the initial financial year of 2018 - 19, goods worth 34,366 crores were supplied through E-Way bills for exports. This figure witnessed a gradual increase, reaching 36,628 crores in 2019 - 20. Subsequently, in 2020 - 21, the value of goods meant for exports escalated to 41,256 crores. A substantial surge was observed in the following year, 2021 - 22, with goods worth 59,518 crores being supplied through E-Way bills. Finally, in the fiscal year 2022 - 23, the value of exported goods transported via E-Way bills reached 62,311 crores. These trends demonstrate a consistent upward trajectory in the value of goods intended for export, supplied through the use of E-Way bills

Turning our attention to the import of goods, the E-Way bill data reveals that in the financial year 2018 - 19, goods worth 44,626 crores were supplied using E-Way bills. However, this figure experienced a marginal decline in the subsequent year, with the value of goods supplied reducing to 41,257 crores in 2019 - 20. In the financial year 2020 - 21, the value of imported goods supplied through E-Way bills rose to 48,842 crores. Notably, in the fiscal year 2021 - 22, there was a significant surge as goods worth 1,13,423 crores were supplied through E-Way bills. Although there was a slight decline in the value of goods supplied in the fiscal year 2022 - 23, with the figure standing at 1,08,087 crores, the overall trend indicates substantial growth over the five - year period.

Shifting focus to the data concerning Intra - state supply of goods and the associated E-Way bills, it is evident that there has been consistent growth in the value of goods supplied. In the financial year 2018 - 19, goods worth 3,00,993 crores were supplied through E-Way bills for intra - state supply. This figure experienced a steady rise, reaching 3,37,510 crores in 2019 - 20. In 2020 - 21, there was further growth, with goods worth 3,58,403 crores being supplied via E-Way bills. Notably, the financial year 2021 - 22 witnessed a substantial leap in the figures, as goods worth 4,53,926 crores were supplied through E-Way bills. Finally, in the financial year 2022 - 23, there was a significant increment, and the value of goods supplied reached 5,18,824 crores through E-Way bills. These findings highlight a consistent and impressive upward trend in the value of goods transported through E-Way bills for intra - state supply.

Considering the data for Inter - state Inward supply of goods, it is evident that the value of goods supplied through E-Way bills experienced fluctuations. In the financial year 2018 - 19, goods worth 3,41,919 crores were supplied. The subsequent year, 2019 - 20, witnessed a slight decline, with goods worth 3,25,177 crores being supplied through E-Way bills. The fiscal year 2020 - 21 also experienced a minor deceleration, as goods worth 3,05,004 crores were supplied. However, the financial year 2021 - 22 marked a significant boost in the total value of goods supplied, with 4,59,049 crores transported through E-Way bills. Continuing this growth momentum, the fiscal year 2022 - 23 also observed a substantial increase, with goods worth 5,48,562 crores being supplied via E-Way bills. These findings indicate notable fluctuations in the figures, yet demonstrate an overall significant growth in the total value of goods transported through E-Way bills for inter - state inward supply.

Lastly, examining the data for Inter - state Outward supply of goods transported via E-Way bills, it is evident that the figures have displayed slight fluctuations. In the financial year 2018 - 19, goods worth 2,97,039 crores were transported through E-Way bills. This figure experienced a marginal decline, with goods worth 2,85,258 crores being supplied the following year, 2019 - 20. However, the financial year 2020 - 21 witnessed a recovery, with goods worth 2,98,549 crores being supplied through E-Way bills. The fiscal year 2021 - 22 marked a significant milestone in the growth story of E-Way bills, as goods worth 4,01,095 crores were transported through the generation of E-Way bills. Finally, in the financial year 2022 - 23, the growth momentum persisted, and the total value of goods for outward supply reached 4,77,761 crores. These findings highlight the fluctuating nature of the figures while indicating an overall growth in the total value of goods transported through E-Way bills for inter - state outward supply.

In conclusion, the analysis of the presented graph showcases a remarkable growth trend in the value of goods transported through E-Way bills over the span of five financial years. This growth is particularly notable in the sectors of exports, intra - state supply of goods, inter - state inward supply of goods, and inter - state outward supply of goods. The consistent rise in the value of goods supplied through E-Way bills signifies the efficacy and importance of this system in facilitating the smooth movement of goods across sectors while preventing evasion of taxes and duties across sectors.

3.1 E-Way bills - total value of goods transported inter - state outward supply

In regards to total value of goods transported in inter - state outward supply in Graph 3.1 presents an analysis of the assessed value of outward supply of goods transported through the E-Way bill system. This graph sheds light on the growth in absolute numbers, as well as the percentage change in figures, over a span of five years from the financial year 2018 - 19 to FY 2022 - 23.

Graph 3.1 - Total value of goods transported inter - state outward supply

(in Crores)

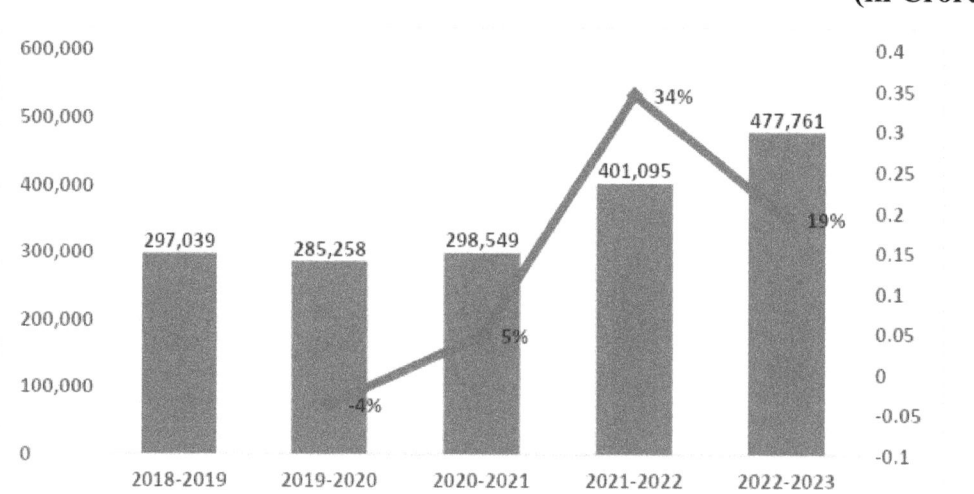

During the year 2018 - 19, the outward supply of goods through E-Way bills amounted to a substantial 297,039 crores. However, this figure experienced a slight decline in the subsequent FY 2019 - 20, dropping to 285,258 crores, which represents a decrease of approximately 4% compared to the previous year.

Nonetheless, the following financial year, 2020 - 21, witnessed a positive upturn, with the outward supply of goods reaching a value of 298,549 crores. This indicates a growth rate of 5% as compared to the preceding year, showcasing signs of recovery and resilience within the system.

The most significant surge in the growth of E-Way bills for outward supply materialized in 2021 - 22, when a remarkable total of 401,095 crores worth of goods were supplied. In percentage terms, this translated to an astounding growth rate of 34% in comparison to the previous year.

In the final year of consideration i.e. 2022 - 23, the figure soared to 477,761 crores worth of goods, indicating a growth rate of 19% over the previous year. This consistent expansion demonstrates the effectiveness of the E-Way bill system in facilitating the movement of goods and stimulating economic growth.

3.2 Total value of goods transported inter - state inward supply

In regards to Total value of goods transported in inter - state inward supply in Graph 3.2 illustrates the assessed value of the inward supply of goods from other states, as well as the percentage growth of this value on a year - on - year basis. The data presented in the graph provides valuable insights into the trends and fluctuations in the assessed value of inward supplies over the years, shedding light on the dynamics of inter - state trade.

Graph 3.2 - Total value of goods transported inter - state inward supply

(in Crores)

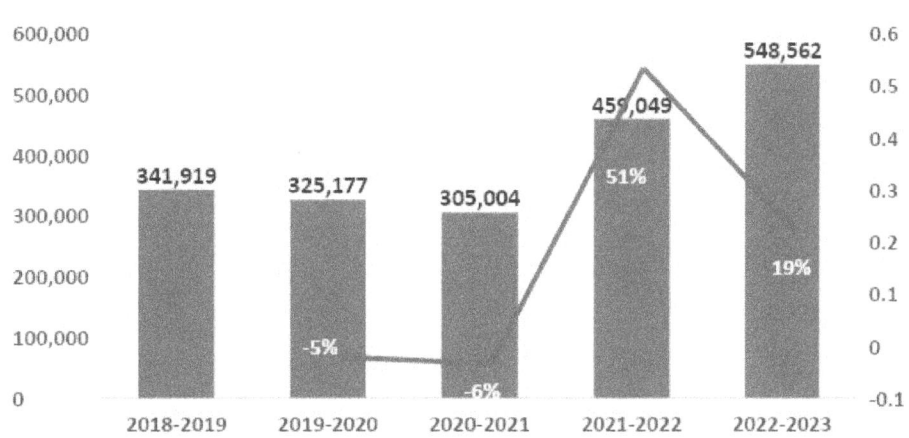

In the fiscal year 2018 - 19, the assessed value of inward supply of goods stood at 341,919 crores. However, this figure experienced a decline in the subsequent fiscal year, dropping to 325,177 crores in 2019 - 20. This decrease signifies a deceleration of 5 percentage points, indicating a contraction in the inter - state trade of goods.

The downward trend continued in the following fiscal year, with the assessed value of inward supply of goods further declining to 305,004 crores in 2020 - 21. This represents a 6 percent decrease compared to the previous year, underscoring a persistent decline in inter - state trade during this period.

Interestingly, the subsequent fiscal year, 2021 - 22, witnessed a remarkable shift in the trajectory of the assessed value of inward supply of goods. It recorded the highest - ever growth rate, with an impressive 51% increase. This substantial growth propelled the assessed value of inward supplies to reach a staggering 459,049 crores, signifying a significant rebound in inter - state trade.

Continuing this positive momentum, the fiscal year 2022 - 23 saw a further increase in the assessed value of inward supplies from other states, amounting to a noteworthy 548,562 crores. This growth represents a 19% rise compared to the previous year, highlighting a continued expansion in inter - state trade and a steady recovery from the previous downturn.

3.3 Total value of goods transported intra - state supply

In regards to Total value of goods transported in intra - state supply Graph 8 shows the assessment value of goods transported through the E-Way bill system. The data spans a period from the fiscal year 2018 - 19 to 2022 - 23, providing a comprehensive overview of the growth and fluctuations in the value of goods transported through this system.

Graph 3.3 - Total value of goods transported intra - state supply

(in Crores)

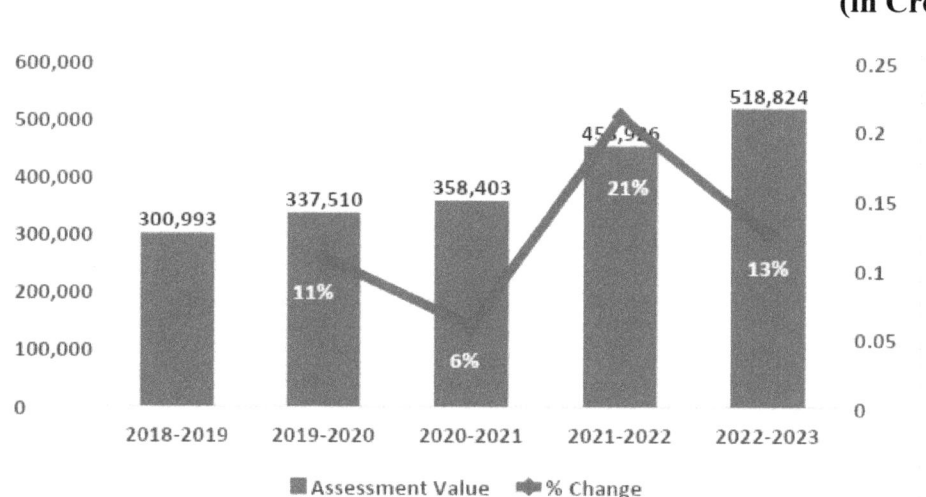

Graph 3.3 portrays the assessment value of goods transported through the E-Way bill system. The data spans a period from the fiscal year 2018 - 19 to 2022 - 23,

providing a comprehensive overview of the growth and fluctuations in the value of goods transported through this system.

In the fiscal year 2018 - 19, the E-Way bill system facilitated the transportation of goods worth a staggering 300,993 crores. Over the following fiscal year 2019 - 20, there was a notable increase in the value of goods transported through E-Way bills, reaching 337,510 crores effecting an increase of 11%.

As we progress to the financial year 2020 - 21, the graph reveals a continued upward trajectory, with the value of goods transported through E-Way bills escalating to 358,403 crores. Although the rate of growth in this year, at 6%, was comparatively lower than the previous year, it is still a substantial increase.

It was the financial year 2021 - 22 that witnessed the most significant leap in the value of goods transported through the E-Way bill system. The graph exhibits a remarkable surge to 453,926 crores, representing a staggering growth rate of 21% compared to the preceding year. This remarkable jump highlights the increasing adoption of the E-Way bill system by businesses.

Finally, in the financial year 2022 - 23, the upward trend continued, albeit at a slightly moderated pace. The graph shows a 13% growth rate, resulting in goods worth 518,824 crores being transported through the E-Way bill system. This figure solidifies the system's position as an essential tool for ensuring seamless movement of goods while also reflecting the sustained growth in trade and commerce.

3.4 Total value of goods transported as export supply

Graph 3.4 showcases the utilization of the E-Way bill system for the supply of goods intended for exports, presenting both the cumulative figures and the year - on - year percentage growth. The data encompasses multiple financial years, highlighting the evolving trends in the use of the E-Way bill system and the corresponding growth in the value of goods supplied.

Graph 3.4 E-Way Bill Value of export supply

(in Crores)

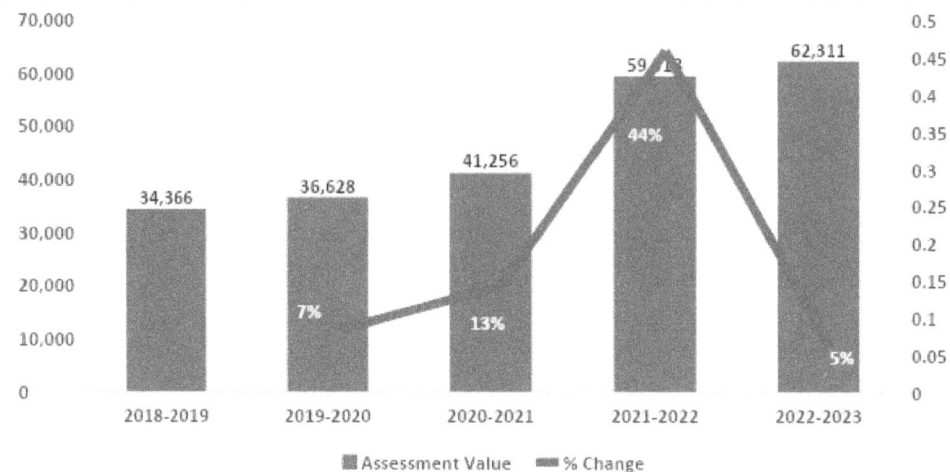

- There is 44% and 5% growth in export from last two financial year

Starting with the Financial Year 2018 - 19, the figures reveal that goods worth 34,366 crores, designated for exports, were supplied through the E-Way bill system.

In the following Financial Year 2019 - 20, there was a noticeable increase in the utilization of the E-Way bill system for exports, with the value of goods supplied escalating to 36,628 crores. This uptick represents a growth rate of 7% compared to the previous year.

The subsequent year, 2020 - 21, witnessed a more substantial surge in the usage of the E-Way bill system for exports, as the value of goods supplied climbed to 59,518 crores. This significant rise denotes a growth rate of 13% in comparison to the preceding year.

However, it is the Financial Year 2021 - 22 that stands out as the most remarkable period in terms of growth figures. The value of goods supplied through the E-Way bill system reached an impressive 59,518 crores, marking an astounding growth rate of 44%. This remarkable surge signifies a significant advancement in the utilization of the E-Way bill system for facilitating the export of goods.

In the final year under consideration, 2022 - 23, the growth rate moderated to 5%, albeit still showcasing a positive trend. Goods worth 62,311 crores were supplied using the E-Way bill system,

The analysis of the data from Graph 9 underscores the gradual and consistent growth in the usage of the E-Way bill system for the supply of goods meant for exports. The figures demonstrate an upward trajectory, with each financial year building upon the accomplishments of the previous one.

3.5 Total value of goods transported as import supply

Graph 3.5 - Total value of goods transported as import supply

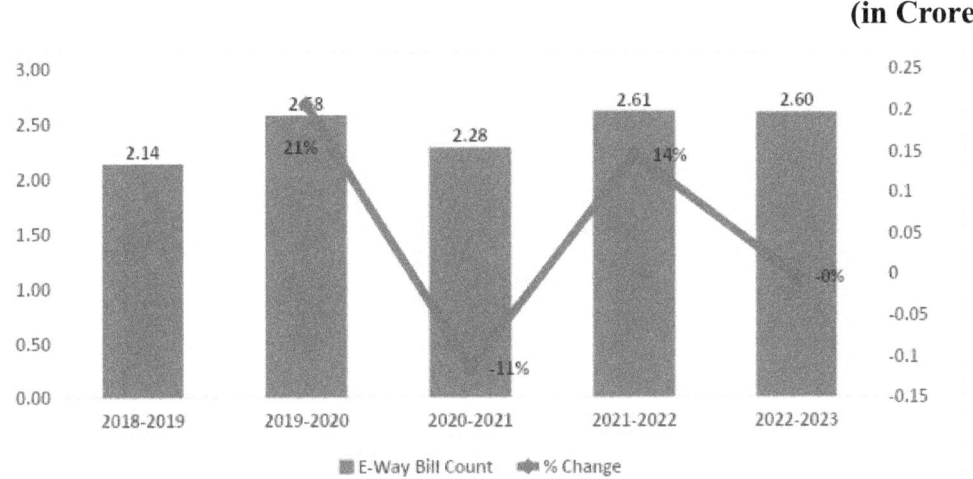

(in Crores)

4. Total generation of E-Way bills - sectoral analysis

Total generation of E-Way bills through E-Way bill Graph 13 depicts the number of E-Way bills generated over a period of 5 Financial years from 2018 - 19 till 2022 - 23 and the classification of the same according to sectors.

Graph 4 Total generation of E-Way bills through E-Way bill

(In Lakh)

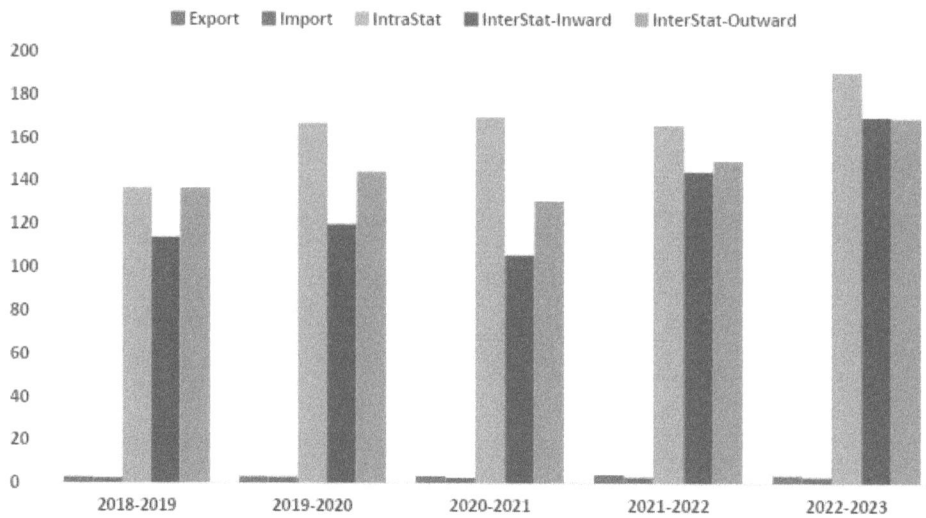

Graph 13 presents a comprehensive depiction of the number of E-Way bills generated over a period of five financial years, spanning from 2018 - 19 to 2022 - 23. The graph also provides a classification of these E-Way bills according to different sectors. By analyzing the data, we can gain valuable insights into the trends and patterns observed in the generation of E-Way bills for various categories, namely, exports, imports, intra - state supply, and inter - state supply of goods.

Focusing specifically on the E-Way bills generated for the supply of goods meant for exports, we can discern some intriguing patterns. In the Financial Year 2018 - 19, an impressive total of 3 lakh E-Way bills were generated. Surprisingly, in the subsequent Financial Year, namely 2019 - 20, the figure remained consistent at 3 lakh E-Way bills. Intriguingly, this trend continued into the fiscal year 2020 - 21, where again 3 lakh E-Way bills were generated for the supply of goods meant for exports. In the Financial Year 2021 - 22, we witnessed a marginal increase, with the generation of approximately 4 lakh E-Way bills. Surprisingly, in the year 2022 - 23, we observed a return to the earlier pattern, with approximately 3 lakh E-Way bills generated.

Turning our attention to the data pertaining to the supply of imported goods, a similar trend emerges. In the financial year 2018 - 19, a total of 2 lakh E-Way bills were generated for the supply of imported goods. This figure experienced a slight increase in the year 2019 - 20, reaching 3 lakh E-Way bills. However, in the subsequent fiscal year, 2020 - 21, the figure reverted back to 2 lakh E-Way bills. Remarkably, the trend persisted in the year 2021 - 22, with the generation of 3 lakh E-Way bills for the supply of imported goods. This positive momentum carried forward into the financial year 2022 - 23, with around 3 lakh E-Way bills generated for the supply of goods

Examining the data concerning the intra - state supply of goods over the five - year period, we uncover noteworthy insights specific to the state of Rajasthan. A staggering total of 137 lakh E-Way bills were generated for the intra - state supply of goods in the initial year. The subsequent year, 2019 - 20, witnessed a substantial growth of nearly 22%, as the number of E-Way bills escalated to 167 lakh. Maintaining an upward trajectory, the fiscal year 2020 - 21 observed a total of 169 lakh E-Way bills generated for intra - state goods. However, a slight decline was witnessed in the financial year 2021 - 22, with 166 lakh E-Way bills being generated. Fortunately, this decline was short - lived, as the subsequent fiscal year 2022 - 23, showcased a remarkable recovery, as the generation of E-Way bills rose to a total of 190 lakh.

Examining the inter - state inward supply of goods, it becomes evident that the number of E-Way bills generated fluctuated over the analyzed period. In the financial years 2018 - 19 and 2019 - 20, the generation of E-Way bills amounted to 114 lakh and 120 lakh respectively. However, in 2020 - 21, there was a marginal decline with a total of 105 lakh E-Way bills. The most notable observation emerges from the financial year 2021 - 22, wherein a substantial increment was recorded, as the number of E-Way bills generated reached 144 lakh. Continuing this growth trend, the subsequent fiscal year, 2022 - 23, witnessed the generation of 169 lakh E-Way bills for the inter - state inward supply of goods, indicating a consistent momentum in this category.

Lastly, analyzing the inter - state outward supply of goods, we observe slight fluctuations in the generation of E-Way bills. In the financial years 2018 - 19 and 2019 - 20, the figures stood at 137 lakh and 144 lakh E-Way bills respectively. However, in 2020 - 21, a marginal decline was observed, with 131 lakh E-Way bills generated. Subsequently, in the financial year 2021 - 22, a significant recovery was witnessed, as the number of E-Way bills surged to 149 lakh. Finally, in 2022 - 23, the inter - state outward supply of goods experienced its highest ever performance, with the generation of 169 lakh E-Way bills. This remarkable increase indicates a substantial growth and a positive trajectory in the inter - state outward supply of goods.

In conclusion, the analysis of Graph 13 allows us to discern various trends and patterns in the generation of E-Way bills across different sectors and time frames. Noteworthy observations include the stability and marginal growth in the generation of E-Way bills for exports and imports, the fluctuations and subsequent recovery in the intra - state supply of goods, and the fluctuating yet generally positive trends in the inter - state inward and outward supply of goods

4.1 Total generation of E-Way bills - inter - state outward supply of goods

In regards to **inter - state outward supply of goods** Graph 4.1 showcases a comprehensive representation of the absolute number of E-Way bills, along with the percentage change, pertaining to Inter - State supply of goods. The data depicted in this graph allows for a detailed analysis and commentary on the trends and patterns observed over the years.

Graph 4.1 - Generation of E-Way bills - Inter–State Outward Supply of goods

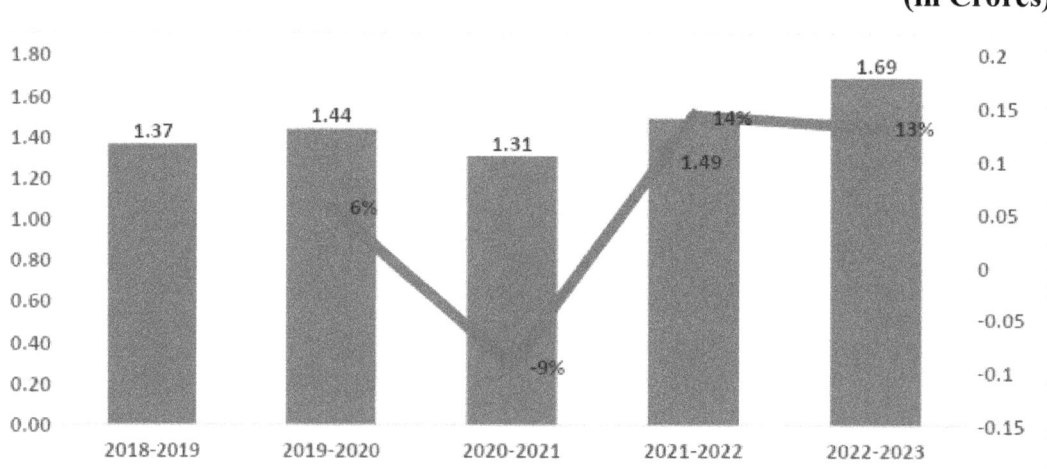

In the fiscal year 2018 - 19, the graph illustrates that a total of 1.37 crore E-Way bills were generated for the Inter - State supply of goods. This number experienced an upward trajectory in the subsequent fiscal year, 2019 - 20, reaching 1.44 crores. This indicates a growth rate of 6% compared to the previous year.

However, a deceleration in growth was observed in the following fiscal year, 2020 - 21. The number of E-Way bills generated decreased to 1.31 crores, signifying a slower growth rate of 9% over the previous year.

Nevertheless, the trend took a positive turn in the fiscal year 2021 - 22, as depicted in the graph. During this period, a notable surge in E-Way bill generation occurred, reaching 1.49 crores. This remarkable increase denotes a growth trajectory of 14% in comparison to the previous year, indicating a potential revival and a more robust market activity.

Continuing this positive momentum, the graph showcases further growth in the most recent fiscal year, 2022 - 23. A total of 1.69 crore E-Way bills were generated, indicating a growth rate of 13% compared to the preceding year. This sustained growth demonstrates the resilience and stability of the E-Way bill system for the Inter - State supply of goods.

In conclusion, despite a temporary setback in growth during 2020 - 21, the subsequent years witnessed a significant recovery and overall positive growth in the use of the E-Way bill system in the Interstate trade and supply of goods.

4.2 Total generation of E-Way bills - inter - state inward supply of goods

In regards **to interstate outward supply of goods** graph 4.2 presents a comprehensive analysis of the usage of the E-Way bill system for the Inward supply of goods, spanning from its introduction in the fiscal year 2018 - 19 to the most recent financial year, 2022 - 23. This graph not only depicts the growth trajectory in absolute numbers but also showcases the percentage change over the years, allowing for a nuanced understanding of the system's performance.

Graph 4.2 - Generation of E-Way bills - Inter–State inward Supply of goods

(in Crores)

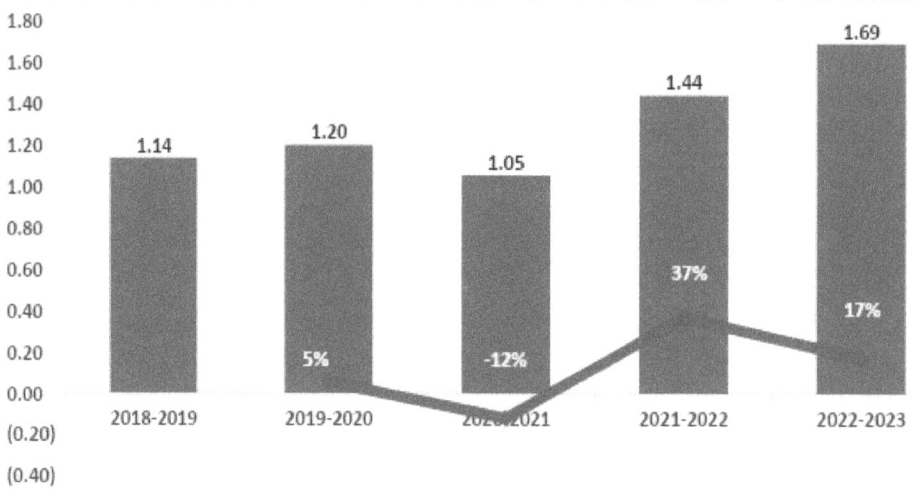

In the initial year of its implementation, 2018 - 19, the graph reveals that a total of 1.14 crore E-Way bills were generated for the Inward supply of goods. This figure experienced a modest increase to 1.20 crore in the following financial year, 2019 - 20, representing a growth rate of 5%.

However, as elucidated in previous graphs of this report, the outbreak of the COVID - 19 pandemic and the subsequent lockdown measures imposed to curb its spread had a profound impact on the growth trajectory. Specifically, in the year 2020 - 21, the graph illustrates a deceleration in the system's growth, with 1.05 crore E-Way bills generated. This marked a decline of 12% compared to the previous fiscal year.

Nonetheless, the graph showcases a remarkable resurgence in the subsequent year, 2021 - 22, characterized by the most substantial jump in growth. During this period, a total of 1.44 crore E-Way bills were generated, signifying a remarkable growth rate of 37%.

In the financial year 2022 - 23, there is further evidence of the system's sustained growth. The absolute number of E-Way bills generated reached a new high of 1.69 crore, The percentage change in figures for this year remained at 17%, reflecting a more moderate rate of growth compared to the previous year.

Overall, the data presented in Graph 4 demonstrates the evolution of the E-Way bill system for the Inward supply of goods over a span of several years. This analysis underscores the significance of the E-Way bill system as a valuable tool for regulating and facilitating the movement of goods for trade in the country.

4.3 Total generation of E-Way bills - intra - state supply of goods

In the regards to Total generation of E-Way bills - intra - state supply of goods in Graph 4.3 show the usage of the E-Way bill system for the intra - state supply of goods within the state of Rajasthan. The graph effectively illustrates the total number of E-Way bills generated over a span of five financial years, from 2018 - 19 to 2022 - 23, and also highlights the corresponding percentage growth.

Graph 4.3 - Intra - State E-Way Bill Generation

(in Crores)

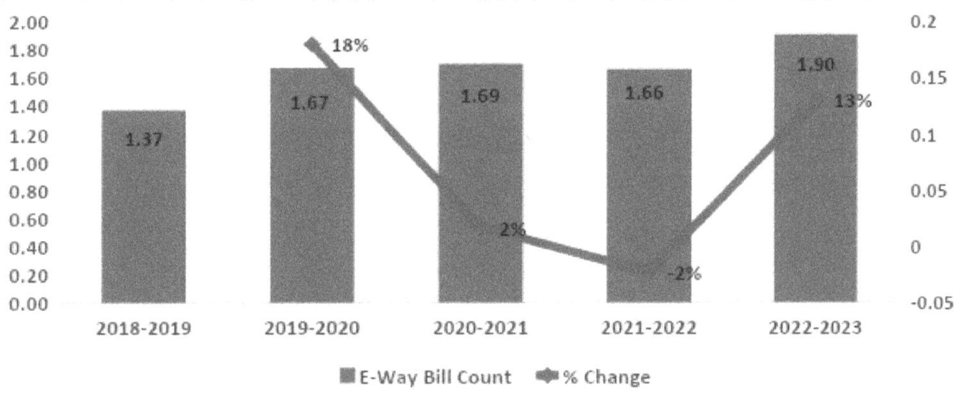

Year	E-Way Bill Count	% Change
2018-2019	1.37	
2019-2020	1.67	18%
2020-2021	1.69	2%
2021-2022	1.66	-2%
2022-2023	1.90	13%

In the initial financial year of 2018 - 19, the E-Way bill system recorded a total of 1.37 crore E-Way bills generated within Rajasthan. Subsequently, there was a significant increase of 18% in the number of E-Way bills during the following financial year, 2019 - 20, resulting in a total of 1.67 crore generated. This substantial growth demonstrates the rising adoption and effectiveness of the E-Way bill system in facilitating intra - state supply.

Continuing this upward trend, the financial year 2020 - 21 witnessed a further increase in the number of E-Way bills generated within Rajasthan, reaching a total of 1.69 crore. Although the growth rate during this year was relatively modest at 2%.

In the subsequent financial year of 2021 - 22, there was a slight deceleration, with the total number of E-Way bills generated dropping to 1.66 crore, marking a decline of 2% compared to the previous year.

Nevertheless, the graph concludes on a positive note, as the financial year 2022 - 23 witnessed a substantial rebound in the usage of the E-Way bill system. During this period, a remarkable total of 1.90 crore E-Way bills were generated, reflecting a robust growth rate of 13%. This growth rate signifies a renewed surge in the adoption and implementation of the E-Way bill system for intra - state supply of goods within Rajasthan.

4.4 Total generation of E-Way bills - for export of goods

In regards to Total generation of E-Way bills - for export of goods Graph 4.4 illustrates the number of E-Way bills generated over a period of five years, spanning from the fiscal year 2018 - 19 to 2022 - 23, along with the corresponding growth rates during these years. The data presented in the graph provides valuable insights into the trends and patterns observed in E-Way bill generation.

Graph 4.4 E-Way Bill generation for export supply

(in Lakh)

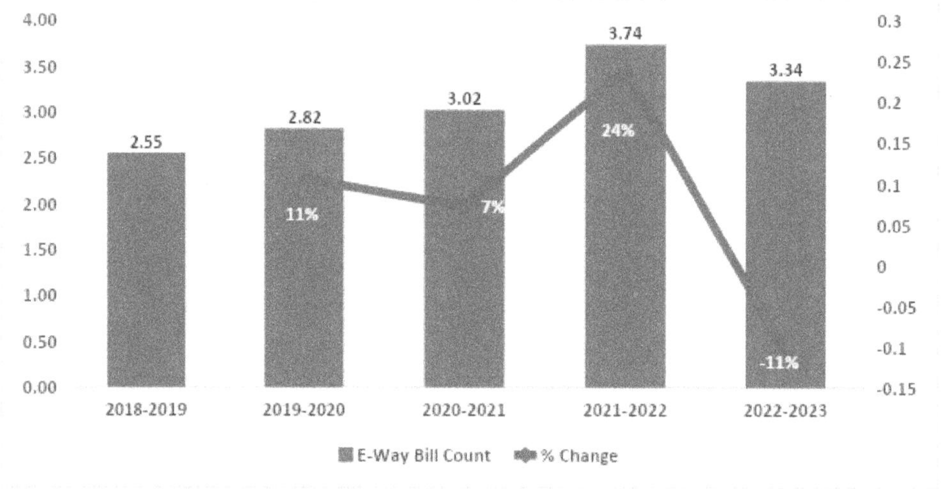

Year	E-Way Bill Count	% Change
2018-2019	2.55	
2019-2020	2.82	11%
2020-2021	3.02	7%
2021-2022	3.74	24%
2022-2023	3.34	-11%

In the fiscal year 2018 - 19, a total of 2.55 lakh E-Way bills were generated, serving as the baseline for subsequent analysis. The following year, in 2019 - 20, the number of E-Way bills rose to 2.82 Lakh, reflecting a commendable growth rate of 11%.

This growth signifies an increasing adoption and utilization of E-Way bills within the specified time period.

Continuing this upward trajectory, the number of E-Way bills generated further increased to 3.02 Lakh in the fiscal year 2020 - 21. Although there was a marginal decline in the growth rate to 7%, this figure still demonstrates a substantial expansion compared to the previous year. This steady rise in E-Way bill generation indicates a positive trend in compliance and adherence to regulatory requirements.

The subsequent fiscal year, 2021 - 22, witnessed a significant surge in the number of E-Way bills. The figures skyrocketed to 3.74 Lakh, signifying a remarkable growth rate of 24%. This substantial increment clearly indicates an accelerated adoption of E-Way bills, possibly driven by factors such as increased digitalization, ease of compliance, and awareness among businesses.

However, in the most recent fiscal year, 2022 - 23, a slight decline in the number of E-Way bills generated was observed. With a total of 3.34 lakh E-Way bills generated, there was a deceleration in growth by 11%.

Considering the cumulative analysis, it is evident that, except for the fiscal year 2022 - 23, there has been a consistent and substantial rise in the number of E-Way bills generated over the five - year period. This trend indicates an encouraging level of compliance and adherence to E-Way bill regulations among businesses, fostering a transparent and efficient system of goods transportation.

4.5 Total generation of E-Way bills - for import of goods

Graph 4.5 provides a comprehensive analysis of the E-Way bills generated for the Import Supply of goods from the Financial Year 2018 - 19 to the Financial Year 2022 - 23. This graph not only presents the actual number of E-Way bills generated during this five - year period but also highlights the growth rate associated with this data.

Graph 4.5 E-Way Bill generation for import supply

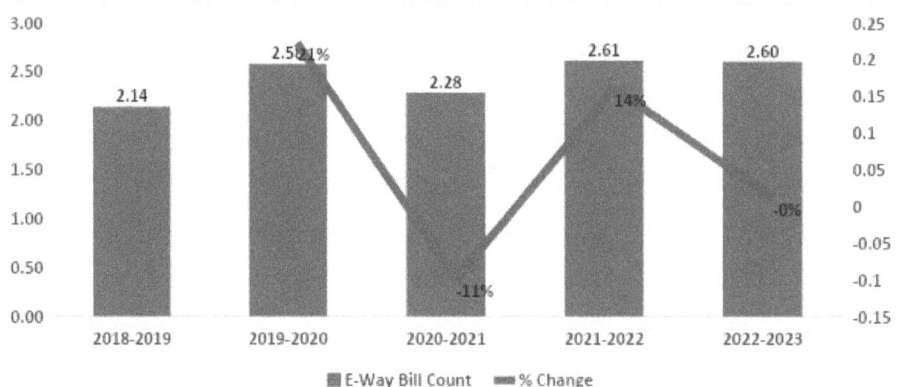

(in Lakh)

In the Financial Year 2018 - 19, the supply of imported goods necessitated the generation of a total of 2.14 lakh E-Way bills. Subsequently, there was a notable increase in the number of E-Way bills generated in the following year, with 2.58 lakh bills recorded in 2019 - 20 growing at a substantial growth rate of 21%.

However, the Financial Year 2020 - 21 witnessed a slight decline in the number of E-Way bills generated, with the figure falling to 2.28 lakh marking a decline of 11% compared to the previous year.

The subsequent Financial Year 2021 - 22 experienced resurgence in growth, with a notable 14% increase in the generation of E-Way bills for imported goods. This increase propelled the cumulative figure to 2.61 lakh, demonstrating a recovery from the previous year's decline and reaffirming the upward trajectory of the usage of E-Way bill system for imported goods.

Finally, in the Financial Year 2022 - 23, the number of E-Way bills generated for the import supply of goods remained consistent with the preceding year, registering almost identical figures at 2.60 lakh bills.

The presented data and its analysis provide valuable insights into the trends and patterns observed in the E-Way bills generated for the Import Supply of goods over the specified time frame. Despite the slight decline in 2020 - 21 and the subsequent stagnation in 2022 - 23, the overall growth rate stands at an impressive average of 7.25% over the five years.

5. Inter - state industry wise analysis of E way bills - Value of goods transported

5.1 Inter - State outward supply of goods - Top five industry

In light of the data pertaining to the Outward supply of goods originating from the state of Rajasthan, an analysis of **Pie Chart 5.1** offers a profound insight into the five most prominent categories of goods that have been dispatched outside the state.

Graph 5.1 - Top five Inter - State outward supply of goods

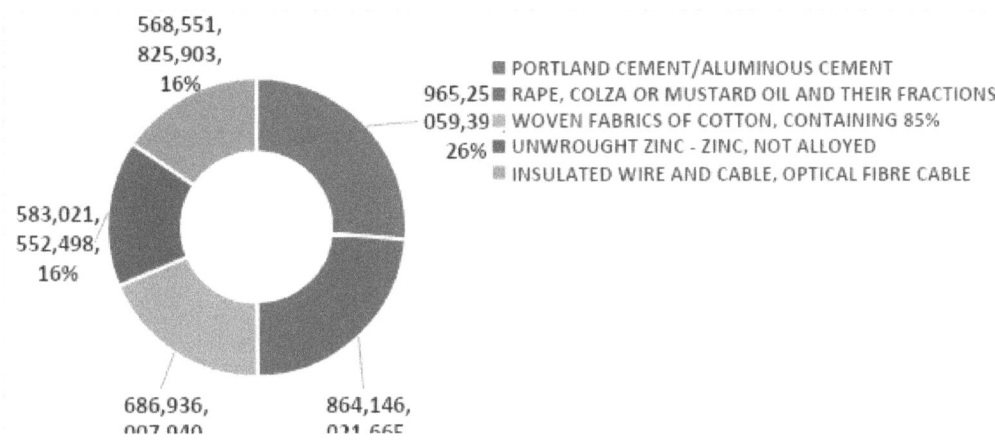

In light of the data pertaining to the Outward supply of goods originating from the state of Rajasthan, an analysis of **graph 5.1** offers a profound insight into the five most prominent categories of goods that have been dispatched outside the state.

Remarkably, the category of 'Portland Cement/Aluminous cement' claims the lion's share, accounting for a substantial 26% among the top outward supplies. This striking statistic serves as a testament to the paramount significance of the cement industry within the economy of Rajasthan.

Following closely behind is the category of 'Rape, Colza or Mustard Oil and their fractions,' which commands a significant 24% share among the top five commodities transported beyond the state borders. The remarkable prominence of this category underscores the crucial role played by the oil sector in Rajasthan's outbound trade activities.

Another noteworthy observation is that 'Woven Fabrics of Cotton, containing 85%' constitutes a considerable portion of the overall share, holding 19% among the top five goods dispatched from Rajasthan. This statistic underscores the substantial contribution of the textile industry, particularly cotton - based fabrics, to the state's outward trade.

Furthermore, 'Unwrought Zinc – Zinc, not alloyed' holds a notable 16% share among the top five goods supplied by Rajasthan. This figure highlights the significance of the zinc sector and its significant presence in the state's outbound trade.

Lastly, 'Insulated wire and cable, Optical fiber Cable' emerges as a noteworthy category, accounting for a commendable 15% share among the top five commodities supplied by Rajasthan. This finding emphasizes the state's prowess in the production and export of high - quality wire, cable, and optical fiber products.

The data analysis presented in Pie Chart 2 provides valuable insights into the composition of Rajasthan's outward supply of goods. By identifying and delving into the top five categories, we gain a comprehensive understanding of the economic sectors that drive the state's trade activities.

5.2 Inter - State inward supply of goods - Top five industry

Data analysis reveals fascinating insights into the inward supply of goods in the state of Rajasthan, as depicted in graph 5.2. This chart provides a comprehensive overview of the top five categories of goods that dominate the inward supply landscape.

Graph 5.2 - Top five Inter - State inward supply of goods

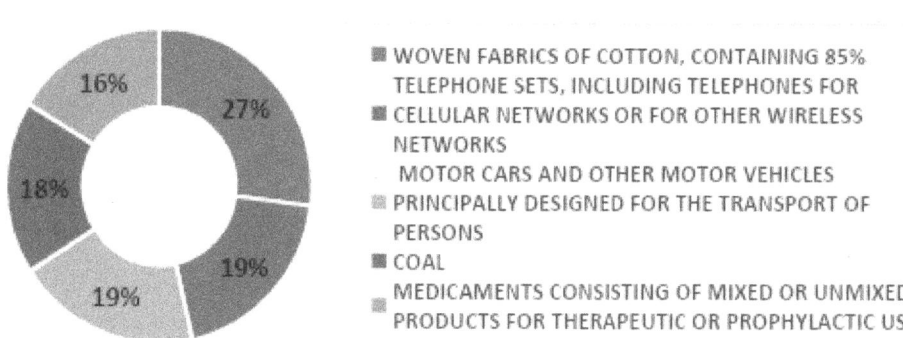

Among the top five inward supplied goods, the category 'Woven Fabrics of Cotton containing 85%' commands a significant share of 27%. This highlights the potentially high demand for cotton - based woven fabrics in the state.

Another notable category is 'Telephone sets including telephones for cellular networks or for other wireless networks,' which captures a substantial 20% share among the top five inward supplied goods. This observation suggests a significant reliance on telecommunications infrastructure and the widespread adoption of modern communication technologies within the state.

'Motor cars and other motor vehicles principally designed for the transport of persons' hold a notable share of 19% within the top five goods supplied inward to Rajasthan. This statistic reflects the significance of the automotive sector, indicating a strong demand for personal transportation means.

Furthermore, 'Coal' emerges as another important commodity, accounting for 18% of the top five commodities supplied inward. This finding underscores the reliance on coal as an energy source within Rajasthan and its contribution to power generation and industrial activities.

Finally, 'Medicaments consisting of mixed or unmixed products for therapeutic or prophylactic uses' represent a noteworthy category, holding a 16% share among the top five commodities supplied into Rajasthan. This statistic highlights the importance of healthcare and medical services.

In summary, the analysis of graph 5.2 emphasizes the significant role played by various goods in the inward supply dynamics of Rajasthan.

5.3 Export supply of goods - top five industries

Data analysis of goods meant for exports, specifically those transported through the E-Way bills system, reveals a compelling and intriguing pattern, as illustrated in graph 3.3. In this analysis, we have categorized the data into the top five commodities, each offering unique insights into the export trends.

Graph 5.3 - Top five export supply of goods

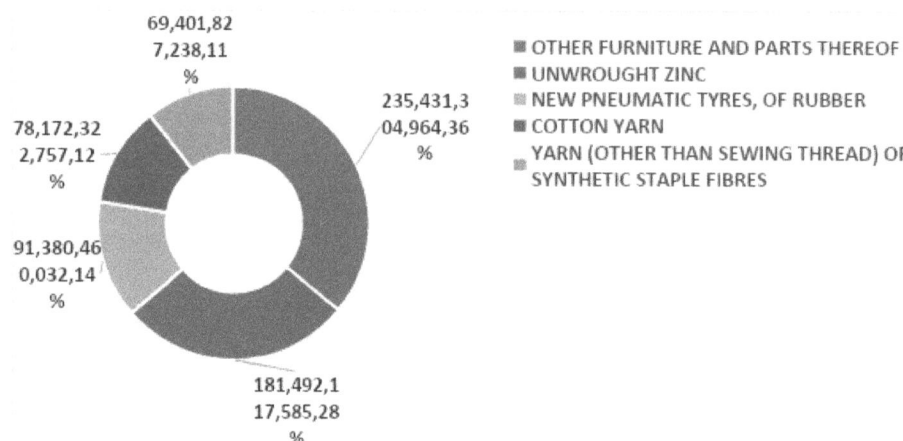

Remarkably, the category of 'other furniture and parts thereof' dominates the chart with a staggering 36% share, indicating its significant presence in the exports facilitated by the E-Way bills system. This substantial contribution underscores the importance and demand for such furniture in international markets.

Following closely is the commodity of 'unwrought zinc,' constituting 28% of the top five commodities. This notable proportion suggests a relevance of unwrought zinc in the global trade landscape.

Another noteworthy inclusion among the top five commodities is 'new pneumatic tyres of rubber,' which commands a significant 14% share emphasizing the economic significance of this commodity.

Additionally, 'cotton yarn' holds a considerable 12% share within the top five goods meant for exports, utilizing the E-Way bills system.

Lastly, the category of 'yarn (other than sewing thread) of synthetic staple fibers' emerges as a noteworthy commodity, accounting for a commendable 10% share among the top five commodities exported by Rajasthan and transported by using the E-Way bills system.

These findings from the data analysis shed light on the key commodities that drive Rajasthan's economic growth.

5.4 Import supply of goods - top five industries

An in - depth analysis of the data pertaining to imported commodities for which E-Way bills were generated reveals significant insights into the top five categories of goods. This analysis is presented in graph 5.4, which provides a visual representation of the distribution of these commodities.

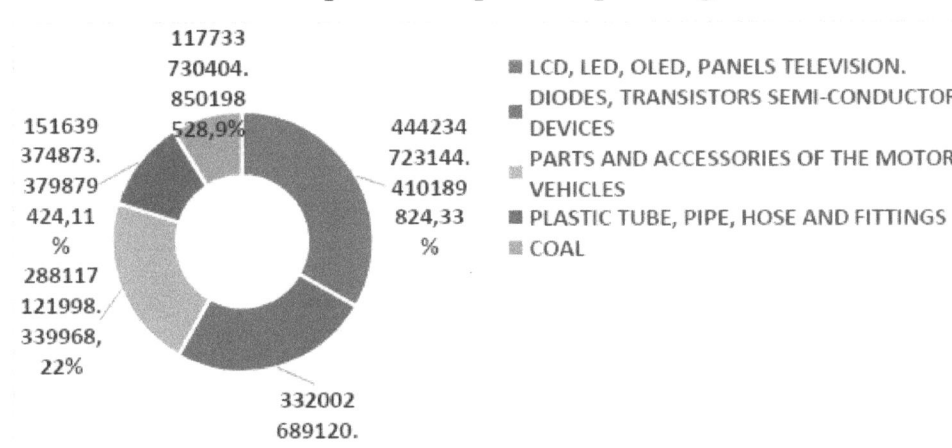

Graph 5.4 - Top five import of goods

The largest portion of the imported commodities is dominated by the category of 'LCD, LED, OLED Panels Television,' accounting for a substantial 33% share. This indicates a strong demand for advanced television technologies within the region.

The category of 'Diodes, Transistors, and Semiconductor Devices' holds a notable 25% share among the top five commodities. This highlights the significance of electronic components in the import landscape. The presence of such a substantial share further emphasizes the importance of the electronics sector in driving economic growth and technological advancements in Rajasthan.

Additionally, 'Parts and Accessories of Motor Vehicles' constitute a commendable 22% share among the top imported commodities for which E-Way bills were generated. This highlights the region's reliance on imported components to support its automotive industry.

Next in line, 'Plastic Tubes, Pipes, Hoses, and Fittings' account for 11% of the total share among the top five commodities. The demand for such items may be driven by various sectors, including construction, infrastructure development, and manufacturing.

Lastly, 'Coal' constitutes 9% of the share among the top five commodities imported into Rajasthan. Although relatively smaller in percentage, this category is significant as it represents the region's reliance on coal for energy generation and industrial purposes. This data suggests that the energy sector and associated industries play a notable role in Rajasthan's economic landscape.

In conclusion, the analysis of imported commodities, as indicated by E-Way bills generated, provides valuable insights into the top five categories of goods in Rajasthan. These findings serve as a foundation for further analysis and strategic decision - making in the realms of trade, industry, and economic development in the region.

6. Intra - state Industry wise analysis of E way bills - Value of goods transported

6.1 Intra - State outward supply of goods - Top five industry

Upon conducting a comprehensive analysis of the data concerning the top Inter - state Outward Supply of Goods sector, a wealth of fascinating insights have emerged. Delving into the statistics, it becomes evident that certain categories of goods have notably excelled in terms of inter - state outward supply from the state of Rajasthan through the utilization of the E-Way bill system.

Graph 6.1 - Industry wise - top five Intra - State Outward supply of Goods

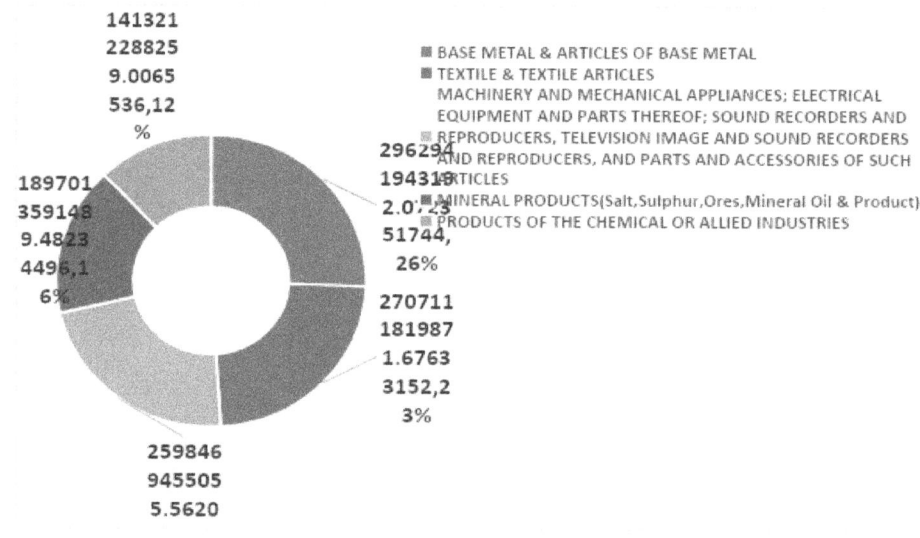

The most prominent category among the top five commodities is 'Base Metal & Articles of Base Metal,' which captures a substantial 26% share. This data underscores the significance of the metal industry within the inter - state supply chain originating from Rajasthan.

Following closely is the 'Textile & Textile Articles' sector, commanding a significant 23% share among the top five commodities. This observation reflects the prominence of Rajasthan's textile industry in the inter - state supply dynamics. The state's rich heritage and expertise in textile manufacturing contribute to its remarkable position in this sector, as evidenced by the substantial volume of outward supply.

Moreover, the category encompassing 'Machinery and Mechanical Appliances; Electrical Equipment and Parts Thereof; Sound Recorders and Reproducers; Television Image and Sound Recorders and Reproducers; and Parts and Accessories of Such Articles' also claims a noteworthy 23% share among the top five commodities supplied from Rajasthan.

Furthermore, 'Mineral Products' such as salt, sulfur, mineral oil, and their related derivatives, hold a commendable 16% share among the top five commodities. This finding underscores the state's significant presence in the mineral resources sector, which contributes to its outward supply. Rajasthan's abundant mineral reserves and the subsequent extraction and distribution activities play a vital role in the inter - state trade landscape.

Lastly, 'Products of the Chemical or Allied Industries' encompass 12% of the share among the top five commodities. This data highlights the state's involvement in the production and distribution of chemical products and allied goods. Rajasthan's contribution to the chemical industry, including the manufacturing and supply of diverse chemical products.

These findings offer valuable insights into the state's strengths and areas of expertise in inter - state trade, highlighting its pivotal role in the national supply chain

6.2 Intra - State inward supply of goods - Top five industry

Data analysis of the Inter - state Inward Supply of goods into Rajasthan, facilitated by the E-Way bills system, reveals noteworthy insights regarding the state's indirect taxation system and the functioning of the E-Way bills mechanism. Expert commentary on these findings underscores the significance of specific commodities in the state's inward supply chain.

Graph 6.2 - Industry wise - top five Intra - State inward supply of Goods

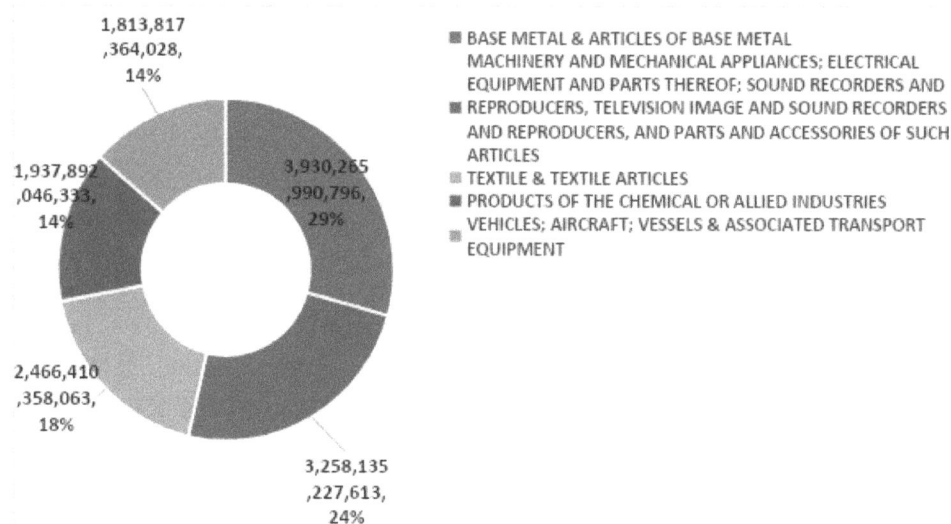

One of the most striking observations is that the category of 'Base Metal & Articles of Base Metal' commands an astounding 29% share among the top 10 commodities. This statistic highlights the importance of this commodity group in Rajasthan's economy and its significant contribution to the state's overall inward supply dynamics.

Furthermore, the category of 'Machinery and Mechanical Appliances; Electrical Equipment and Parts Thereof; Sound Recorders and Reproducers; Television Image and Sound Recorders and Reproducers; and Parts and Accessories of Such Articles' occupies a significant share of 24% among the top five commodities. This finding underscores the crucial role played by these commodities in Rajasthan's economy and the state's reliance on machinery, electrical equipment, and related components for various sectors.

Another notable share of 18% is held by the 'Textile and Textile articles' category, indicating its significance in Rajasthan's inward supply system. The prominence of this commodity group reflects the state's strong textile industry and the considerable volume of textile - related transactions conducted through the E-Way bills system.

Moreover, among the top five commodities transported inward into Rajasthan via the E-Way bills system, the 'Products of the chemical or allied industries' category takes precedence by holding 15% share.

Lastly, the presence of 'Vehicles; Aircraft; vessels & associated transport equipment' holding a 14% share among the top commodities highlights the significance of the transportation sector in Rajasthan's inward supply network.

These insights serve as a foundation for evidence - based policy formulation and informed decision - making to strengthen Rajasthan's economic growth and optimize its indirect taxation system

7. Analysis of E-Way bills generation and value of good transported (outward) by Rajasthan with top five State

7.1 Outward Supply of goods by Rajasthan to top five state - Generation of E way bills

Analysis of the data pertaining to the inter - state outward supply of goods reveals significant insights into the generation of E-Way bills, shedding light on the top - ranking states and the quantum of such E-Way bills. This analysis provides valuable information that can inform policymakers, economists, and businesses alike.

Graph 7.1 - Top five State Outward Supplies - Generation of E-Way bills

(E-Way bills in Crores)

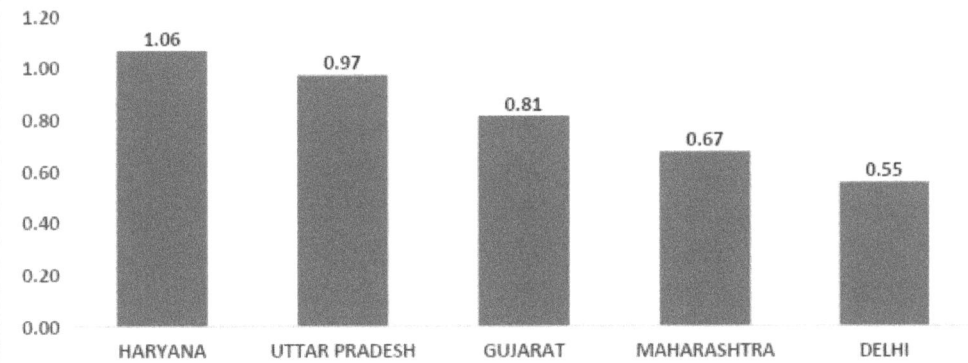

Haryana emerges as the state with the highest number of E-Way bills generated, establishing its dominance in inter - state trade. A staggering 1.06 crore E-Way bills were generated for Haryana, indicating a robust flow of goods to this state. This

substantial volume underscores Haryana's position as a key player in the interstate trade ecosystem.

Uttar Pradesh secures the second position, with 0.97 crore E-Way bills generated. The state's remarkable performance in terms of E-Way bill generation highlights its dominance in the inter state trade activities with Rajasthan.

Gujarat stands firmly in the third position, with 0.81 crore E-Way bills generated. The state's strong presence in the inter - state outward supply of goods is evident from this figure. Gujarat's strategic location, well - developed infrastructure, and favorable business environment contribute to its prominence in facilitating trade transactions.

Occupying the fourth pedestal is Maharashtra, with 0.67 crore E-Way bills generated. This data underscores the state's importance as a major hub for inter - state commerce. Maharashtra's economic significance, coupled with its industrial capabilities, positions it as a key partner in inter state trade activities with Rajasthan.

Lastly, Delhi secures the fifth position, with 0.55 crore E-Way bills generated. Despite being a relatively smaller geographic area, the high volume of E-Way bills for Delhi showcases its prominence as a key center for trade and commerce with Rajasthan. The capital city's role as a gateway for goods distribution and its strategic location make it a vital participant in inter - state trade activities.

These findings demonstrate the significance of these states in terms of inter - state trade and provide valuable insights into the quantum of E-Way bills generated.

7.2 Outward Supply of goods by Rajasthan to top five state - Value of Goods

Through a meticulous analysis of the data pertaining to the inter - state outward supply of goods, an intriguing picture emerges, highlighting significant insights into the E-Way bills system. This system serves as an invaluable source of information, allowing us to comprehend the magnitude of goods transported between states. By examining the total value of goods supplied through the E-Way bills system, we can discern remarkable patterns and draw meaningful conclusions.

Graph 7.2 - Top five State Outward Supplies - Value of Goods

(in Crores)

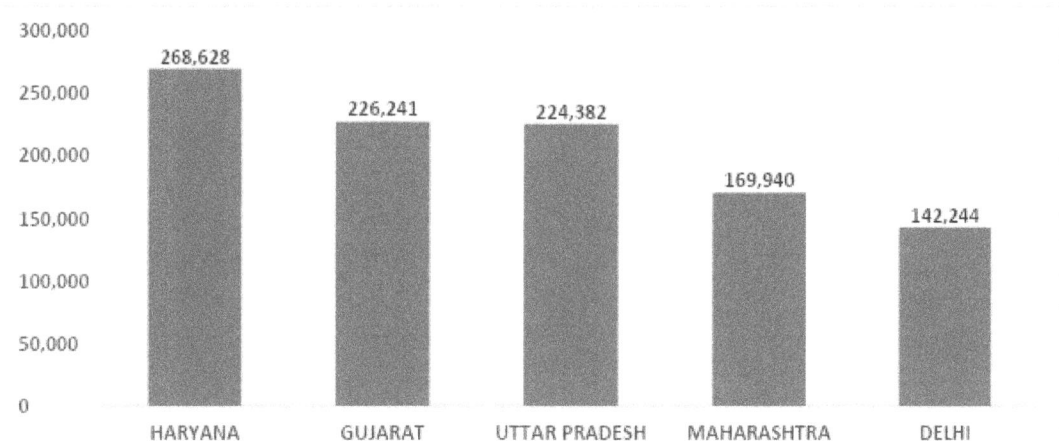

First and foremost, when considering the monetary value of goods, it becomes evident that Haryana claims the leading position, having received a staggering 268,628 crores worth of goods through the E-Way bills system. This figure exemplifies the tremendous economic activity and exchange transpiring within the state, making Haryana an essential hub for the movement of goods.

Following closely behind Haryana, the state of Gujarat emerges as a formidable contender, as it secured the second position in terms of value, with goods amounting to 226,241 crores being supplied through the E-Way bills.

Capturing the third spot is Uttar Pradesh, which received goods worth 224,382 crores through the E-Way bills system, originating primarily from the state of Rajasthan. This inter - state dynamic between Uttar Pradesh and Rajasthan exemplifies a symbiotic relationship between the two states. Consequently, both states play instrumental roles in driving economic growth and trade.

Moving forward, Maharashtra holds the fourth rank in the hierarchy, with goods worth a substantial 169,940 crores being supplied from Rajasthan through the E-Way bills system.

Lastly, we come to the fifth position, with Delhi as the recipient of goods worth 142,244 crores that were supplied through the E-Way bills system.

In summary, the analysis of inter - state outward supply of goods, taking into account the total value of goods supplied through the E-Way bills system, showcases a fascinating landscape of economic activities. Haryana, Gujarat, Uttar Pradesh, Maharashtra, and Delhi emerge as significant players, showcasing their respective strengths in facilitating trade and economic growth. This comprehensive analysis not only provides a snapshot of the inter - state dynamics but also underscores the crucial role played by the E-Way bills system in enabling seamless and efficient movement of goods across state boundaries.

8. Analysis of E-Way bills generation and value of good transported (inward) to Rajasthan by top five State

8.1 Top five inward Supplier States to Rajasthan - Generation of E way bills

By analyzing the data pertaining to the inward supply of goods and the corresponding E-Way bills generated, we can gain valuable insights into the economic dynamics and regional trade patterns. This analysis focuses on the top five states in terms of the maximum number of E-Way bills issued, shedding light on their prominence in facilitating trade activities.

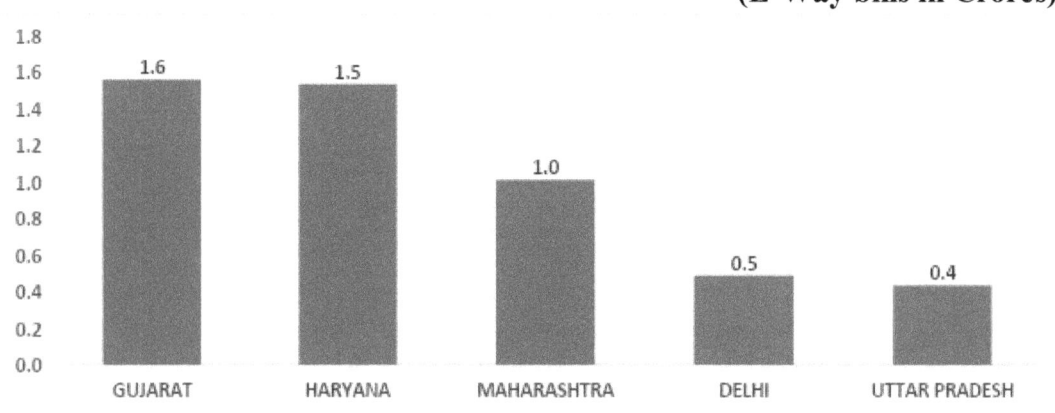

Graph 8.1 - Top five inward Supplier States

(E-Way bills in Crores)

Among the top five states, Gujarat emerges as the leader in generating E-Way bills for inward supply of goods. Astoundingly, a staggering 1.6 crore E-Way bills were generated from Gujarat alone, highlighting its significance as a key trade hub.

Securing the second position is the state of Haryana, which exhibited remarkable performance by generating 1.5 crore E-Way bills for inward supply into Rajasthan.

Taking the third position in this analysis is Maharashtra, with 1.0 crore E-Way bills generated for inward supply of goods into Rajasthan.

Delhi, the capital territory of India, secures the fourth position in this analysis with 0.5 crore E-Way bills generated for inward supply. Despite its relatively smaller geographical area, Delhi's strategic location and status as a major commercial hub make it a significant player in the supply chain ecosystem.

Finally, Uttar Pradesh contributes to the analysis by issuing 0.4 crore E-Way bills for inward supply into Rajasthan. Uttar Pradesh's adjacency to Rajasthan and its large consumer base make it an attractive choice for businesses seeking to reach the markets of Rajasthan efficiently. This demonstrates the interdependence and synergistic trade relationships between neighboring states, emphasizing the importance of seamless interstate trade for overall economic growth.

The presented data on the top five states for which maximum E-Way bills were generated offers valuable insights into the regional dynamics of the inward supply of goods in India.

These states serve as beacons of progress, showcasing the potential for further development and collaboration to fortify India's position as a thriving economic powerhouse.

8.2 Top five inward Supplier States to Rajasthan - value of goods

Upon conducting a meticulous analysis of the data pertaining to Inter State inward supply of goods accompanied by the generation of E-Way bills, an array of significant insights emerge regarding the top five states that serve as major suppliers of goods to Rajasthan, as well as the voluminous quantity of goods they have provided. The findings shed light on the prominent role played by these states in fostering the economic ties and trade dynamics between Rajasthan and its counterparts.

Graph 8.2 - Top five inward Supplier States to Rajasthan

(in Crores)

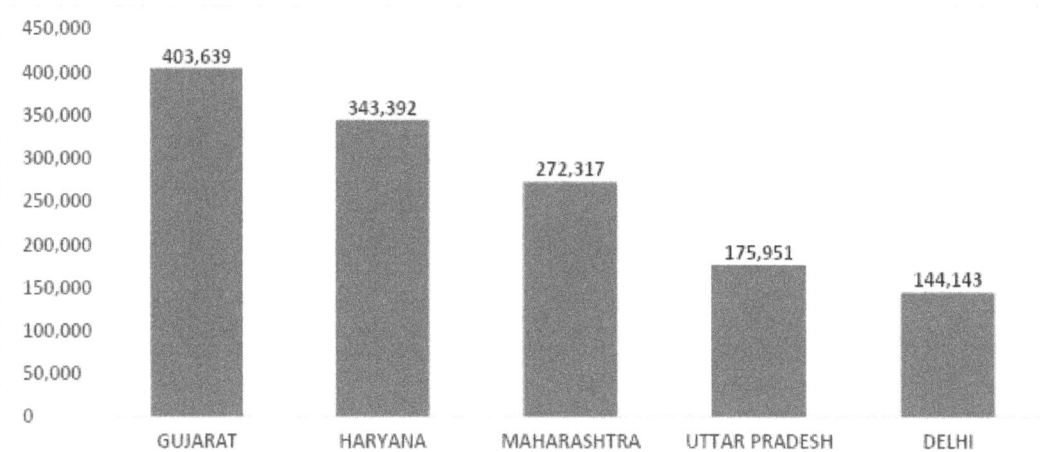

At the pinnacle of the list, we find the state of Gujarat, which emerges as the foremost contributor, having supplied goods amounting to an astounding value of 403,639 crores through the utilization of the E-Way bill system under the Goods and Services Tax (GST) regime. This remarkable figure underscores the pivotal position held by Gujarat as a key trade partner.

Securing the second position, we encounter the state of Haryana, whose contribution to Rajasthan's supply of goods via the E-Way bill system reaches an impressive valuation of 343,392 crores. This substantial amount highlights the noteworthy role played by Haryana in sustaining the inflow of goods to Rajasthan.

Taking the third rank is Maharashtra, which has delivered goods worth 272,317 crores to Rajasthan, further reinforcing its position as a significant contributor to Rajasthan's economic growth. The substantial value of goods supplied by Maharashtra underscores the state's prominence in Rajasthan's supply chain.

Occupying the fourth position is Uttar Pradesh. The total worth of supplies made by Uttar Pradesh to Rajasthan amounts to 175,951 crores. While the volume of goods is relatively lower compared to the top three states, Uttar Pradesh's contribution remains noteworthy.

Finally, we find Delhi at the fifth position, having provided goods worth 144,143 crores to Rajasthan via the E-Way bill system.

In summary, the meticulous analysis of data related to Inter State inward supply of goods, with a specific focus on E-Way bill generation, yields crucial insights into the top five states that supply goods to Rajasthan. These findings emphasize the economic significance of these states in bolstering trade and commercial ties between Rajasthan and its neighboring regions.

MINERAL DEPOSITS AND EXPLORATION IN RAJASTHAN - PERSPECTIVES OF E-RAVANNA

Brief outline of mines and minerals in Rajasthan

Rajasthan, the largest state in India, is known for its rich and diverse mineral resources. With approximately 81 varieties of minerals, the state holds a prominent position in terms of mineral availability and variety. Mining activities in Rajasthan cover 57 different minerals, making it a significant contributor to the country's mineral production. The mining sector plays a crucial role in the state's socio - economic development, providing employment opportunities to rural and tribal communities and contributing substantially to the state's revenue.

Major Minerals and Their Deposits:

Lead, Zinc, and Silver: Rajasthan boasts the largest lead - zinc ore deposit in India, with a total estimated reserve of 629.92 million tonnes. Significant lead - zinc - silver deposits are found in Zawar (Udaipur), Rajpura - Dariba - Bethumi, Sindesar Kalan - Sindesar Khurd (Rajsamand), Rampura - Agucha, Pur - Banera (Bhilwara), Dehri (Sirohi), Kayer - Ghugra, Sawar (Ajmer).

Limestone: The state is abundant in limestone resources, with reserves totaling 21,660 million tonnes of all grades. Jaisalmer district is known for SMS grade limestone, while cement - grade limestone is found in 25 districts, including Chittorgarh, Nagaur, Jaisalmer, Pali, Jhunjhunu, Sirohi, Ajmer, Banswara, and Udaipur. Rajasthan ranks first in cement production in India.

Copper: Rajasthan holds 54% of the total copper resources in the country, amounting to 809.09 million tonnes. Copper deposits are available in various districts such as Jhunhunu, Sikar, Sirohi, Udaipur, Bhilwara, Ajmer, Alwar, Bharatpur, Chittorgarh, Rajsamand, and Dungarpur. The state is the second - highest producer of copper concentrate, contributing 41% to the country's production.

Gold: The state has estimated resources of 118.88 million tonnes of gold ore, with major deposits in Banswara and Khetri Copper - Belt (district Jhunjhunu). Gold is also extracted as a by - product in the Khetri Copper - Belt.

Iron Ore: Rajasthan possesses significant iron ore resources, totaling around 2,621 million tonnes of both hematite and magnetite deposits. Iron ore deposits are found in Morija - Neemala (Jaipur), Lalsot (Dausa), Rampura, Dabla (Sikar), Taonda (Jhunjhunu), Pur - Banera, Bigod (Bhilwara), Nathara - Ki - Pal, Thur (Udaipur), Indergarh, Mohanpura (Bundi), Dedrauli, Liloti, Todupura, Khora (Karauli).

Manganese: The state contains estimated manganese resources of 5.78 million tonnes, mainly concentrated in the districts of Banswara. Small deposits are also present in Rajsamand and Udaipur.

Tungsten: Rajasthan possesses about 23.92 million tonnes of tungsten ore resources, accounting for approximately 27% of the country's total. The important tungsten deposits are available in Nagaur and Sirohi districts.

Lignite: Large lignite deposits occur in the Barmer - Sanchore, Jaisalmer, and Nagaur basins in districts like Barmer, Jaisalmer, Bikaner, Nagaur, and Jalore. The state has around 5,720 million tonnes of lignite resources utilized for lignite - based power plants and captive use.

Barytes: Rajasthan holds 2.99 million tonnes of barytes resources, with important deposits occurring in Udaipur and Alwar districts.

Calcite: The state has an estimated 10.39 million tonnes of calcite resources, with deposits located in Sirohi, Udaipur, Jaipur, and Sikar districts, as well as Bhilwara district.

Fluorite: Deposits of fluorite are found in Dungarpur district, with proven resources of 0.7 million tonnes and 2.5 lakh tonnes with CaF_2 content of 17% and 20%, respectively. Jalore district also contains 0.07 million tonnes resources with CaF_2 content ranging from 20% to 80%, and Sikar district with 0.35 million tonnes resources containing 8% to 15% CaF_2.

Wollastonite: Extensive deposits of wollastonite are found in Pali, Sirohi, and Udaipur districts, with lower - grade deposits present in Ajmer.

Potash: Rajasthan has significant sub - surface halite - bearing evaporite occurrences over an area of 30,000 sq.km., covering parts of Shri Ganganagar, Hanumangarh, Bikaner, Churu, and Nagaur districts. This offers an opportunity for establishing fertilizer industries based on Potash.

Rock Phosphate: The state is rich in rock phosphate resources, with a total estimated reserve of 98.64 million tonnes. Deposits are primarily located in Udaipur, Banswara, Jaisalmer, Jaipur, and Alwar districts. The Jhamar - Kotra rock - phosphate deposit is the largest in the country.

Minor Minerals and Their Deposits in Rajasthan

Dolomite:

Rajasthan has estimated resources of 599.40 million tonnes of dolomite. The important dolomite deposits are found in various districts, including Ajmer, Bhilwara, Chittorgarh, Jaipur, Jaisalmer, Jodhpur, Udaipur, and Rajsamand.

Feldspar:

The state is a major producer of feldspar in India, with approximately 87.94 million tonnes of resources. Ajmer district is the leading producer of feldspar in Rajasthan. Other important feldspar producers include Bhilwara, Rajsamand, Pali, Tonk, and Sikar districts. Minor productions come from Dungarpur, Sirohi, Udaipur, Chittorgarh, and Jaipur districts.

Garnet:

Rajasthan was a significant producer of gem and abrasive varieties of garnet until 2004 - 05. Garnet deposits are located in Udaipur, Ajmer, Bhilwara, Rajsamand, and Tonk districts, covering a strike length of 250 km. The most important gem variety is found in Tonk, while the abrasive variety is found in Bhilwara and Rajsamand districts.

Gypsum:

Rajasthan accounts for 82% of the country's gypsum resources, with a total reserve of 1055.55 million tonnes. The state remains the leading producer, contributing 99% of the total output. Gypsum is found in various districts, including Bikaner, Nagaur, Barmer, Hanumangarh, Jaisalmer, Shri Ganganagar, and Jalore.

Silica Sand:

Rajasthan has assessed resources of about 332.46 million tonnes of silica sand. The important deposits of silica sand are located in Bundi, Bikaner, Sawai Madhopur, Kota, Baran, Jaisalmer, and Jaipur districts.

Clay:

The state holds known resources of ball clay, fire clay, and china clay, amounting to 31.81 million tonnes, 66.42 million tonnes, and 432.51 million tonnes, respectively. The important locations of clay deposits are in Bikaner, Pali, Jaisalmer, Nagaur, Badmer, Bhilwara, Chittorgarh, Jaipur, Bundi, Karoli, Sawai Madhopur, Sikar, Ajmer, and Jodhpur.

Emerald:

Emerald deposits are found in a 221 km - long belt stretching from Rajsamand district to Ajmer district. Important localities include Rajgarh, Tikhi, and Kalaguman (Rajsamand). However, emerald occurrences in the region are highly sporadic and variable.

Siliceous Earth:

Siliceous Earth is found in Barmer and Jaisalmer districts, with estimated resources of 10.000 million tonnes.

Soapstone:

Important deposits of soapstone are located in Udaipur, Dungarpur, Dausa, Bhilwara, and Sawai Madhopur districts.

Marble:

Rajasthan is the richest state in India in terms of marble deposits, both in quality and quantity. The state is the most important center for marble processing in the country, with about 95% of the total processing units. Rajasthan possesses large reserves of about 1,231 million tonnes of good - quality marble. The significant marble deposits are found in various districts, including Makrana, Nagaur, Jaipur, Alwar, Dausa, Jaisalmer, Rajsamand, Pali, Banswara, Udaipur, Bundi, Sirohi, Dungarpur, Ajmer, Sikar, Jodhpur, Bhilwara, and Chittorgarh. Marble is classified into 10 groups by the Bureau of Indian Standards (ISI) based on color, shade, and pattern.

Granite:

Rajasthan is richly endowed with large reserves of different varieties of granite spread over 23 districts. More than 200 localities of granite have been identified in various districts, including Jalore, Sirohi, Bhilwara, Pali, Barmer, Jhunjhunu, Tonk, Alwar, Ajmer, Banswara, Jaipur, Jodhpur, Sawai Madhopur, Sikar, Udaipur, Rajsamand, Chittorgarh, and Dungarpur. Granite has a 95% share in India's dimensional stone export. The export of high - value - added items like tiles, polished slabs, and monument stones has seen an average growth rate of over 50% per year.

Slate and Phyllite:

Slates and phyllites are low - cost decorative stones that can be split into slices with thickness ranging from 8 to 14 mm. These stones find wide applications in interior and exterior decorations, roofing, paving, shelves, and flooring purposes. They are found in parts of Ajmer, Alwar, Jaipur, Sawai Madhopur, Bharatpur, Bundi, Pali, Tonk, Udaipur, and Chittaurgarh districts.

Sandstone:

Rajasthan is the largest producer of sandstone in India and an important sandstone producing state. Sandstone is an excellent building stone with various uses like roofing, flooring, paving, beams, pillars, arches, doors and window sills, wall facing, fence posts, mile markers, etc. Rajasthan sandstone is mainly found in the area of Dholpur, Bharatpur, Karauli, Sawai Madhopur, Bundi, Jhalawar, Kota, Bhilwara, Chittorgarh, Jaisalmer, and Baran districts in eastern Rajasthan, and in scattered form in Jodhpur, Nagaur, and Bikaner districts of the western desert plain.

Future Prospects:

For future mineral development, Rajasthan is focusing on exploration programs in five key areas: ferrous metals, limestone, industrial minerals like fluorite, lithium, asbestos, mica, cobalt, etc., dimensional and decorative stones, and general exploration encompassing minerals like limestone, sandstone, and quartz in different districts.

The state plans to identify and explore new areas for minerals like marble, granite, masonry stone, phyllite/schist, quartz, and feldspar. The delineation of suitable areas for carving blocks of these minerals will lead to auctions, boosting revenue and curbing illegal mining activities.

Rajasthan's mineral wealth is a crucial asset for its economic growth and development. The state's diverse mineral deposits present immense opportunities for industrial development, job creation, and revenue generation. With a strategic focus on exploration and sustainable mining practices, Rajasthan can continue to be a major player in India's mineral sector while ensuring the responsible utilization

E-Ravanna System - An Introduction

"Ravanna" means the Ravanna or E-Ravanna duly issued by electronically generated from the departmental web portal and includes any other system notified by the Government for dispatch, consumption or processing of mineral or overburden from a specified area granted under any mineral concession or permit.

"Transit Pass" means a pass including e - transit pass duly issued by the Department or generated online, to the lessee, stockiest, trader, dealer etc. for lawful transportation of royalty paid mineral.

There were high incidences of illegal mining of minerals in the State. In 2017 Rajasthan government introduced a new system for online generation of Ravanna/transit pass through departmental web portal. From November 2017 for dispatch of minerals with the aim to check evasion of royalty, to enhance transparency in the system and to facilitate paperless environment friendly work.

1. Primary Motive to check evasion, i.e. to keep the system perfect from the point of view of revenue leakages
2. To check unscrupulous(unfair) trade, curtailing unauthorized trade also helpful in policing of trade of illegal minerals
3. Introduce uniformity across the states for seamless generation of E-Ravanna

1. Total Generation of E-Ravanna, Royalty collection trough E-Ravanna and mineral transported through E-Ravanna

Table 1 - Executive Summary

FY	Royalty (Cr)	Net Weight MT(Lakhs)	Rawanna (Lakhs)
2017-2018	1,187	1,427	48
2018-2019	2,009	2,770	96
2019-2020	2,911	2,545	102
2020-2021	3,918	2,600	106
2021-2022	5,058	2,965	117
2022-2023	6,088	3,427	128
Grand Total	21,170	15,734	596

1.1 Total E-Ravanna generation - Regarding the figures for Ravanna generation presented in table 1 column 3, a total of 48 lakh Ravannas were generated in 2017 - 18. This figure almost doubled to 96 lakh Ravanna generation in the year 2018 - 19. Subsequently, the figures increased slowly but consistently year - on - year, with 102 lakh Ravanna generated in 2019 - 20 and 106 lakh Ravanna generation in 2020 - 21. The figures for the financial years 2021 - 22 and 2022 - 23 stood at 117 lakh Ravannas and 128 lakh Ravannas respectively.

Graph 1.1 - Generation of E-Ravanna

(Lakh)

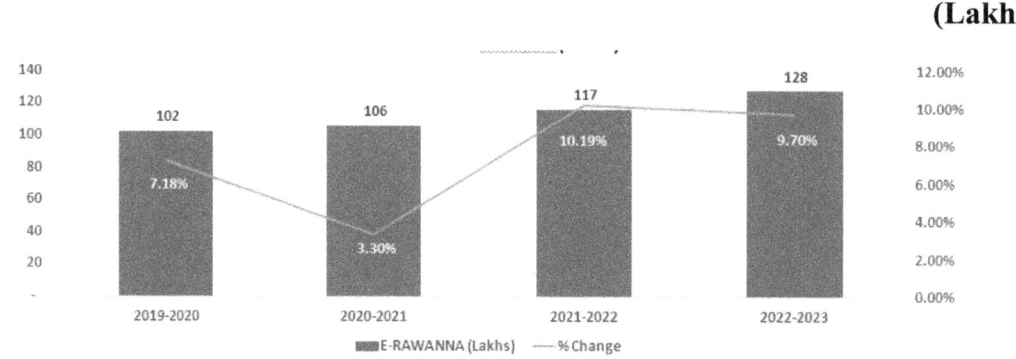

Graph 1.1, providing a visual representation, indicates a consistent growth in Ravanna generation with varying growth rates each year since 2017. In 2019 - 20, there was a 7.18% increase in Ravanna generation figures compared to the previous year. The growth rate dropped to 3.30% in the year 2020 - 21 due to COVID 19. Notably, there was a significant jump in the growth rate in 2021 - 22, which reached 10.19%. Furthermore, in 2022 - 23, there was a growth of 9.70% in the number of Ravanna generations.

1.2 Royalty Collection - It is evident from the table that since 2017 royalty, mineral transported and E-Ravanna are in increasing trend. In the Financial Year 2017 - 18, the total Royalty collection for minerals excavated in the state was Rs.1,187 crores which increased to Rs.2,009 crores in the year 2018 - 19. The amount for royalty collection further increased to Rs.2,911 crores in the year 2019 - 20 followed by Rs.3,198 crores in 2020 - 21, Rs.5,058 crores in 2021 - 222 and Rs.6,088 crores in the year 2022 - 23 as presented in Table 1 Column 1.

Graph 1.2 - Royalty Collection

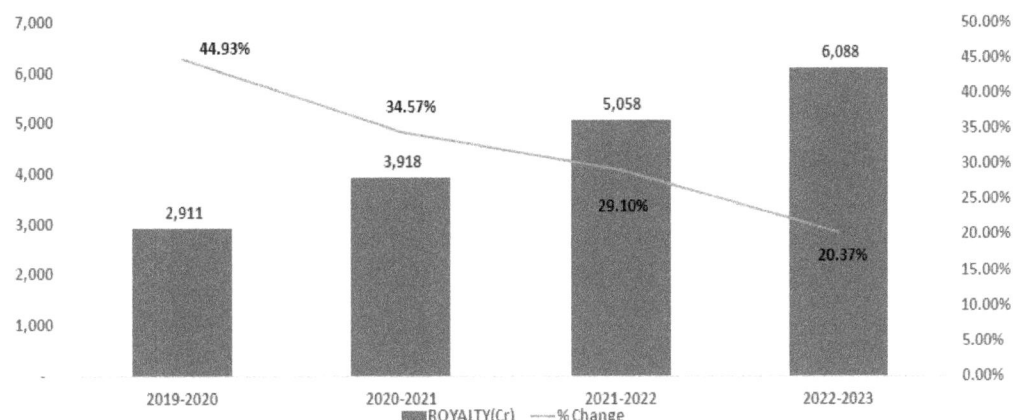

(in Crores)

Graph 1.2, depicting the Royalty Collection and the consequent year - on - year growth rate, demonstrates a consistent increase in royalty collection. However, on deeper analysis, it can be observed that the growth rate has steadily declined from 44.93% in 2019 - 20 to 34.57% in 2020 - 21. It further decreased to 29.10% in 2021 - 22 and the latest figure for the financial year 2022 - 23 indicates a growth rate of 20.37%.

1.3 Mineral Quantity Metric Tonnes (Lakh) - Regarding the Quantity of Mineral excavated (Net Weight MT – Lakh   ), as shown in Table 1 Column 2, a total of 1,427 lakh metric tonnes was excavated in the fiscal year 2017 - 18. This quantity increased to 2,770 lakh metric tonnes in the year 2018 - 19 which is a significant growth when compared with previous year. In 2019 - 20, there was a slight decrease, with the quantity reaching 2,545 lakh metric tonnes. It then increased to 2,600 lakh metric tonnes in 2020 - 21, 2,965 lakh metric tonnes in 2021 - 22 and finally, 3,427 lakh metric tonnes in 2022 - 23.

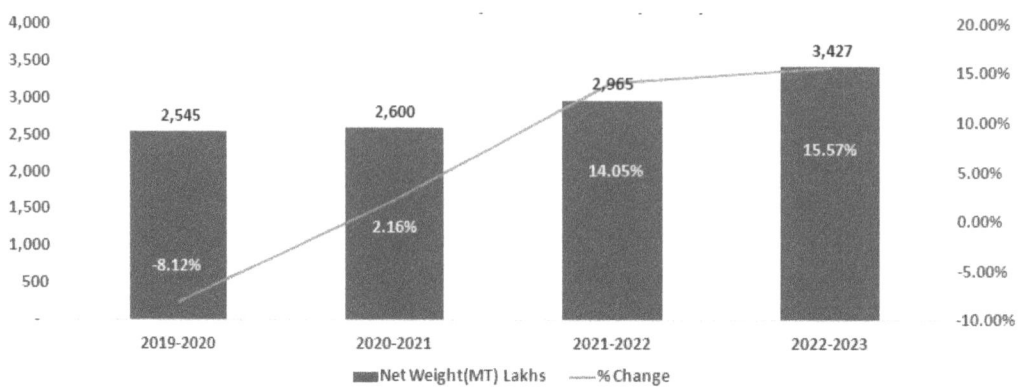

Graph 1.3 - Mineral Quantity Metric Tonnes (Lakh)

Graph 1.3 illustrates the Data for Quantity of Minerals excavated in Metric Tonnes (Lakh), exhibits a consistent growth rate, year - on - year, from the financial year 2019 - 20 to 2022 - 23. The growth rate stood at 2.16% from 2019 - 20 to 2020 - 21. In 2021 - 22, there was a significant leap with a growth rate of 14.05% compared to the previous year of 2020 - 21. Additionally, in 2022 - 23, there was again a noteworthy growth rate of 15.57%.

2. Growth Trends of Ravanna Generation, Royalty Collection and Mineral Excavation

Growth trends in three key parameters: Ravanna Generation (in Lakh), Royalty Collection (in Crores), and Quantity of Mineral Excavation in Metric Tonnes (in Lakh) in the state of Rajasthan are supporting each other. Graph 2 examines and depicts the growth trends in three key parameters. The analysis focuses on the period spanning from the financial year 2018 - 19 to 2022 - 23 and aims to identify consistent trends and notable developments in these parameters. Notably, there has been a consistent increase in Royalty Collection, which has tripled in the last 5 years. In 2018 - 19, the total collection was Rs.2,009 crores which increased to Rs.6,088 crores in 2022 - 23. Furthermore, the number of Ravanna Generations have demonstrated gradual but consistent growth. The number of E-Ravanna generations increased from 96 lakh Ravanna generations in 2018 - 19 to 128 lakh Ravanna generations in 2022 - 23. Same is true for Quantity of minerals excavated in metric tonnes (in Lakh). Barring the FY 2019 - 20, there is a gradual but consistent growth in minerals excavated in the state of Rajasthan.

Graph 2 - Growth Trends Across Ravanna Generation (Lakh), Royalty Collection (Cr) and Quantity Metric Tonnes (Lakh)

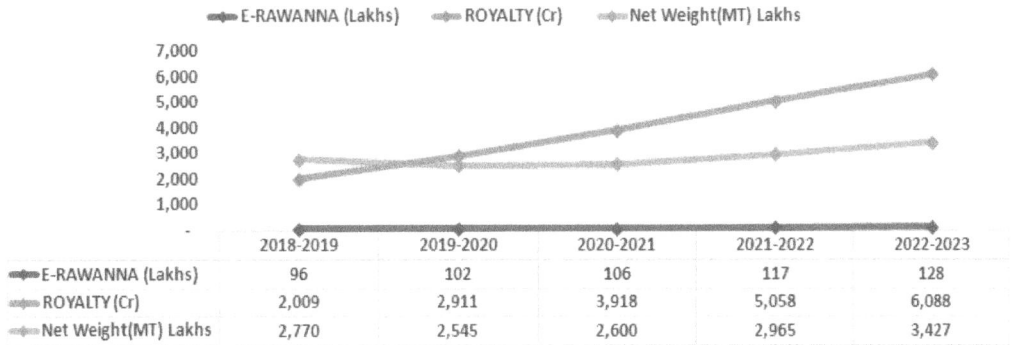

	2018-2019	2019-2020	2020-2021	2021-2022	2022-2023
E-RAWANNA (Lakhs)	96	102	106	117	128
ROYALTY (Cr)	2,009	2,911	3,918	5,058	6,088
Net Weight(MT) Lakhs	2,770	2,545	2,600	2,965	3,427

The above graph shows that since the introduction of the E-Ravanna system, royalty collection in absolute terms increased by three fold whereas E-Ravanna generation and mineral transported are way behind with 0.33 and 0.25 fold respectively.

3. Analysis of E-Ravanna top five minerals

3.1 Royalty Collection - Top five Minerals

Graph 3.1 highlights the top five minerals contributing to royalty collection, namely Zinc, Limestone, Lead, Masonry Stone, and Marble. These minerals have made significant contributions to the state's treasury, although their growth trajectories vary.

Graph 3.1 - Top five Minerals in Royalty Collection

(in Crores)

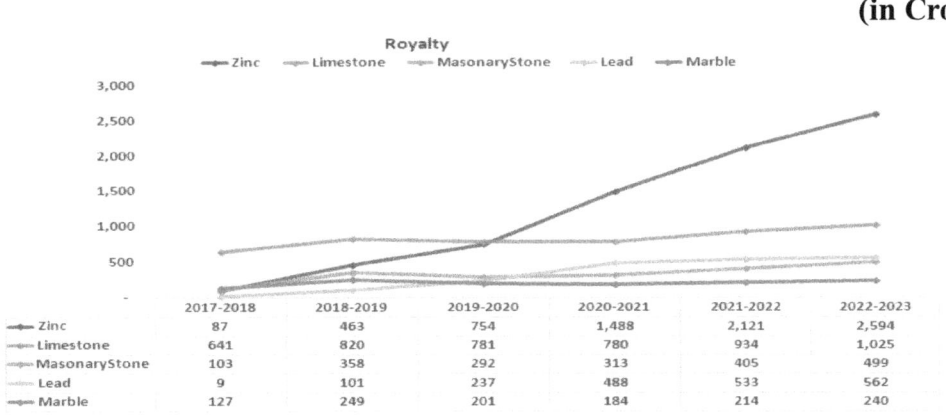

	2017-2018	2018-2019	2019-2020	2020-2021	2021-2022	2022-2023
Zinc	87	463	754	1,488	2,121	2,594
Limestone	641	820	781	780	934	1,025
MasonaryStone	103	358	292	313	405	499
Lead	9	101	237	488	533	562
Marble	127	249	201	184	214	240

- Zinc: Zinc emerges as the highest contributor to the state's royalty collection. Its contribution in the year 2022 - 23 amounted to Rs. 2,594 crores, compared to a mere Rs. 87 crores in 2017 - 18. Zinc has consistently demonstrated remarkable year - on - year growth, with increases of Rs. 463 crores, Rs. 754 crores, Rs. 1,488 crores, and Rs. 2,121 crores in subsequent years and finally, an impressive Rs.2,594 crores/ - in 2022 - 23. There is approximately 22% and 43% growth in Zinc royalty collection in the last two Financial Years.

- The second highest contributor to the state treasury is Limestone. The royalty collection figures stood at Rs.641/ - crores in the FY 2017 - 18, Rs. 820/ - crores in 2018 - 19, Rs.781/ - crores in 2019 - 20, Rs. 780/ - crores in 2020 - 21, Rs. 934/ - crores in 2021 - 22 and rs.1,025/ - crores in 2022 - 23. Thus, while there were fluctuations in some years, there has been a gradual and consistent growth in royalty collection by Limestone, except for the years 2019 - 20 and 2020 - 21.

- Lead stands third when it comes to contribution in terms of royalty to the state exchequer. It made a quantum leap from a mere Rs.9/ - crores in 2017 - 18 to Rs.562/ - crores in 2022 - 23. There is a continuous and extraordinary progression with contribution of Rs.9/ - crores in 2017 - 18, Rs.101/ - crores in 2018 - 19, Rs.237/ - crores in 2019 - 20, Rs.488/ - crores in 2020 - 21, Rs.533/ - crores in 2021 - 22 and Rs.562/ - crores in 2022 - 23.

- Masonry Stone, the fourth highest contributor, displayed an impressive growth trajectory. Except for the year 2019 - 20, this mineral witnessed continuous and remarkable growth in royalty collection. It contributed Rs.103/ - crores in 2017 - 18, Rs.358/ - crores in 2018 - 19, Rs.292/ - crores in 2019 - 20, Rs.313/ - crores in 2020 - 21, Rs.405/ - crores in 2021 - 22 and Rs.499/ - crores in 2022 - 23.

- Lastly, Marble, the mineral for which the state is known the world over, ranks fifth among the top contributors. Though it has contributed handsomely to the state revenues, the growth story has rather been uneven over the years. In the year 2017 - 18, Royalty collection in marble stood at Rs.127/ - crores, in 2018 - 19 it was Rs.249/ - crores, in 2019 - 20 it was Rs.201/ - crores, in 2020 - 21 it contributed Rs. 184/ - crores, in 2021 - 22 it brought 214/- crores to the exchequer account and in the year 2022 - 23 it added Rs.240/- crores to the state revenues. Thus, while it has made significant contributions to state revenues, the growth pattern fluctuated during the analyzed period.

3.2 Top five Minerals - Ravanna Generation

Masonry Stone and Limestone minerals are the most extracted minerals and have been extracted in huge quantities across years.

Graph 3.2 - Top five Minerals Ravanna Generation

(In Lakh)

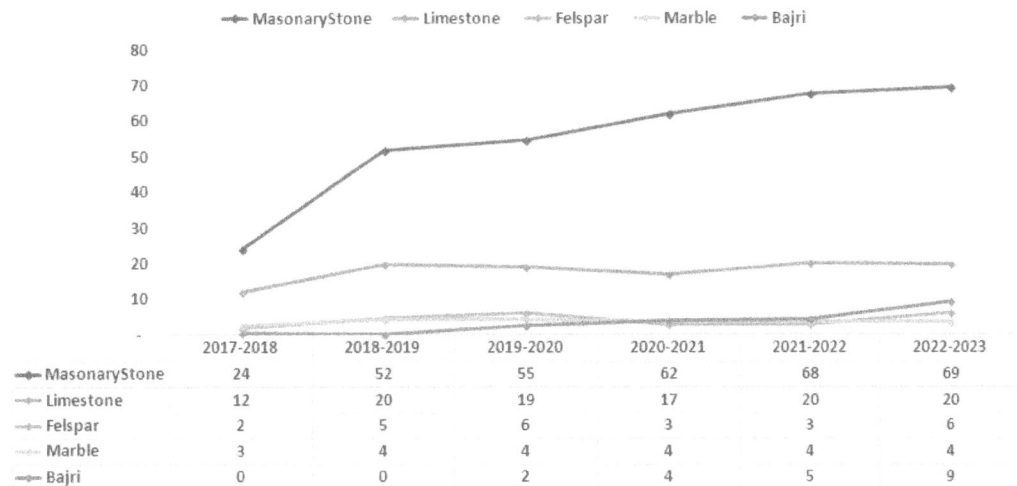

Graph 3.2 depicts the **Top 5 Minerals in terms of Ravanna generation (in Lakh)** from the Financial Year 2018 - 18 to FY 2022 - 23.

❖ It can be clearly observed from the graph given that **Masonary Stone** tops the list in the number of Ravanna generated during the year. There is a consistent growth with 24 lakh Ravanna generated in 2017 - 18, 52 Lakh in 2018 - 19, 55 Lakh in 2019 - 20, 62 Lakh in 2020 - 21, 68 Lakh in 2021 - 22 and 69 Lakh Ravanna generated in the year 2022 - 23.

❖ Next in line comes the **Limestone** with 12 Lakh Ravanna generated in 2017 - 18, 20 Lakh in 2018 - 19, 19 Lakh in 2019 - 20, 17 Lakh in 2020 - 21, 20 Lakh in 2021 - 22 and again 20 Lakh in 2022 - 23.

❖ Thereafter, it is the **Felspar** that secures the third position in the number of Ravanna generated during the year. 2 Lakh Ravannas were generated in the year 2017 - 18, 5 Lakh in 2018 - 19, 6 Lakh in 2019 - 20, 3 Lakh in 2020 - 21, again 3 Lakh in 2021 - 22 and 6 Lakh in 2022 - 23.

❖ Then comes the **Marble** with 3 Lakh Ravanna generations in 2017 - 18 and thereafter 4 lakh Ravanna generations continuously right through 2022 - 23.

❖ Finally comes the **Bajri**, with 2 lakh Ravannas generated in the year 2019 - 20, 4 Lakh in 2020 - 21, 5 Lakh in 2021 - 22 and 9 Lakh in 2022 - 23.

3.3 Top 5 Minerals in Quantity Metric Tons

Graph 3.3 Showcases a representation of the top five minerals excavated in metric tonnes (in Lakh). Among these minerals, **limestone** stands out as the most extensively excavated mineral in the state of Rajasthan.

Graph 3.3 - Top five Minerals in Quantity Metric Tonnes

(In Lakh)

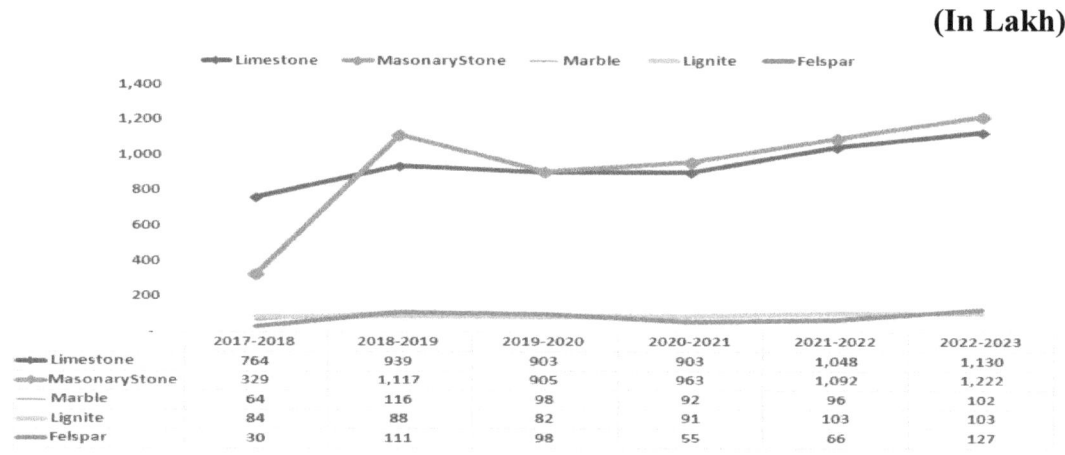

	2017-2018	2018-2019	2019-2020	2020-2021	2021-2022	2022-2023
Limestone	764	939	903	903	1,048	1,130
MasonaryStone	329	1,117	905	963	1,092	1,222
Marble	64	116	98	92	96	102
Lignite	84	88	82	91	103	103
Felspar	30	111	98	55	66	127

In the fiscal year 2017 - 18, an impressive 764 lakh tonnes of limestone was extracted from the region. This figure experienced a notable increase in subsequent years, reaching 939 lakh tonnes in 2018 - 19, 903 lakh tonnes in 2019 - 20, and maintaining the same quantity in 2020 - 21. The trend then took a remarkable upturn, with a substantial surge to 1048 lakh tonnes in 2021 - 22, followed by an even more substantial leap to an astounding 1130 lakh tonnes in the year 2022 - 23.

Next comes the **Masonry Stone** which ranks second in terms of excavation volume throughout the six - year period under review. Initially, in 2017 - 18, 329 Lakh Metric tons of Masonry Stone was extracted from the state. However, this figure experienced a remarkable surge to 1117 Lakh Metric tons in 2018 - 19. . In subsequent years, the quantity excavated remained high, with 905 Lakh Metric tons in 2019 - 20, 963 Lakh Metric tons in 2020 - 21, and 1092 Lakh Metric tons in 2021 - 22. Finally, the mineral reached a noteworthy peak of 1222 Lakh Metric tons in the fiscal year 2022 - 23.

Marble emerges as the third most excavated mineral albeit with a somewhat fluctuating growth pattern during the six - year period under study. With an excavation of 64 Lakh Metric tons in 2017 - 18, the extraction of marble witnessed a substantial increase, setting a record high of 116 Lakh Metric tons in 2018 - 19. Subsequently, the quantity excavated varied, with 98 Lakh Metric tons in 2019 - 20, 92 Lakh Metric tons in 2020 - 21, 96 Lakh Metric tons in 2021 - 22, and a slightly elevated figure of 102 Lakh Metric tons in the fiscal year 2022 - 23.

Lignite stands fourth on the list of the top five minerals. The excavation volumes for lignite were 84 Lakh Metric tons in 2017 - 18, 88 Lakh Metric tons in 2018 - 19, 82 Lakh Metric tons in 2019 - 20, 91 Lakh Metric tons in 2020 - 21, and 103 Lakh Metric tons in both 2021 - 22 and 2022 - 23.

Finally, occupying the fifth position is **Felspar**, which showcases a varying growth pattern over the years under analysis. The excavation quantities were recorded as 30 Lakh Metric tons in 2017 - 18, 111 Lakh Metric tons in 2018 - 19, 98 Lakh Metric tons in 2019 - 20, 55 Lakh Metric tons in 2020 - 21, 66 Lakh Metric tons in 2021 - 22, and an impressive 127 Lakh Metric tons in 2022 - 23 registering a growth of 200% over the previous year.

Top Minerals - Royalty Collection of Zinc and Lead

Graph 8 - Top Minerals Zinc and Lead Royalty Collection

(in Crores)

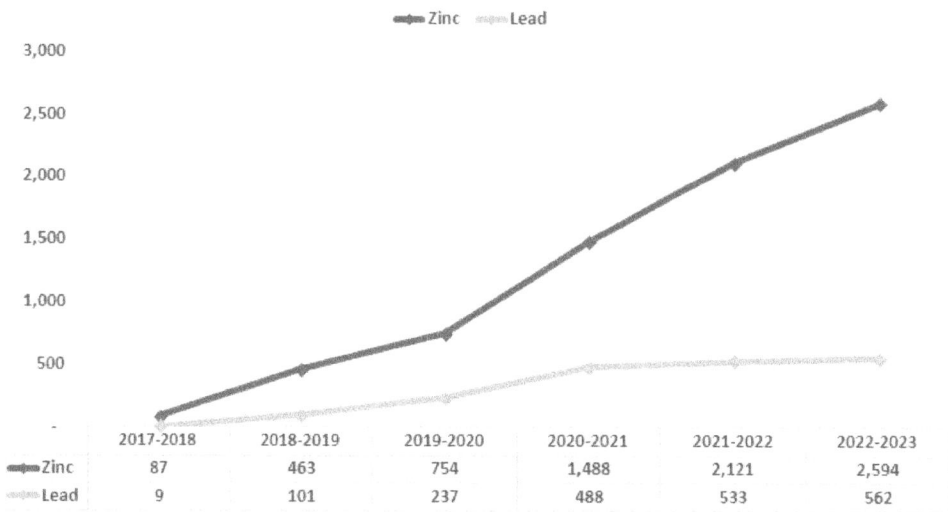

	2017-2018	2018-2019	2019-2020	2020-2021	2021-2022	2022-2023
Zinc	87	463	754	1,488	2,121	2,594
Lead	9	101	237	488	533	562

Key Insights –

1. There is approx. 22 % and 43% growth in Zinc royalty collection in FY 2022 - 23 & 2021 - 22
2. There is approx. 5 % and 9 % growth in Lead royalty collection in FY 2022 - 23 & 2021 - 22

Graph 8 presents a depiction of the significant growth in royalty collection for two prominent minerals, namely Zinc and Lead which have shown the most remarkable growth rate in terms of royalty collection. These minerals have exhibited impressive growth rates, as evidenced by the data presented.

Zinc: Over the span of six years, Zinc has experienced an astounding overall growth rate of 30 times. The progression of Zinc royalty collection from a mere 87 crores in the financial year 2017 - 18 to a staggering 2594 crores in the year 2022 - 23 clearly showcases the exponential growth trend. Notably, there was a substantial growth from 463 crores in 2018 - 19 to 754 crores in 2019 - 20, followed by a notable surge to 1488 crores in 2020 - 21. The growth trajectory continued with an impressive leap to 2121 crores in 2021 - 22, and finally culminated in an astonishing

2594 crores in 2022 - 23. Analyzing the data, it becomes evident that the growth rate in Zinc royalty collection during the financial years 2021 - 22 and 2022 - 23 stands at approximately 22% and 43% respectively.

Lead, another mineral of significance, has exhibited an exceptionally impressive growth rate, escalating 62 times over the course of six years. To illustrate this growth, consider the initial collection of a meager 9 crores as royalty in the financial year 2017 - 18, which grew substantially to 562 crores in the year 2022 - 23. The data reveals a consistent and substantial increase in Lead royalty collection over the years. Notably, there was a remarkable surge from 101 crores in 2018 - 19 to 237 crores in 2019 - 20, further followed by a significant escalation to 488 crores in 2020 - 21. The upward trajectory persisted, with a notable increase to 533 crores in 2021 - 22, and eventually reaching an impressive 562 crores in 2022 - 23. Analyzing the figures, it can be inferred that there was an approximate growth rate of 5% and 9% in Lead royalty collection during the financial years 2021 - 22 and 2022 - 23 respectively.

4. Analysis of top ten mining lease in Rajasthan in Terms of Royalty Collection

Table 2 - top 10 mining Lease

LESSEE_NAME_ENG	MINERAL	Royalty (Cr)	Ravanna	Quantity MT (Lakhs)
Hindustan Zinc Limited	Zinc	4,363	2,65,943	100
	Lead	1,258	42,672	16
Shree Cement Ltd.	Limestone (Cement Grade)	663	1,58,817	829
ULTRATECH CEMENT LTD	Limestone (Cement Grade)	269	2,521	336
Wonder Cement Ltd	Limestone (Cement Grade)	235	2,243	293
J K LaKshmi Cement Ltd	Limestone (Cement Grade)	209	2,729	261
Jindal Saw Limited	Iron Ore	154	4,416	31
Barmer Lignite Mining Company Limited Jaipur	Lignite	152	5,057	178
Binani Cement Ltd.	Rock Phosphate	137	89,384	30
R.S.M.M.Limited	Limestone (Cement Grade)	131	1,192	164

Note – As per last three financial Year E-Ravanna Data

Table 2 presents a comprehensive overview of the top 10 mineral leases based on their royalty collections in column 1. The table provides valuable insights into the

Ravanna generation over the last three years in column 2, while column 3 presents the quantity of minerals excavated by respective leases.

Hindustan Zinc Limited for Zinc: Topping the list is Hindustan Zinc Limited, demonstrating its dominance in the mineral industry, particularly in the Zinc sector. Hindustan Zinc Limited's remarkable contribution is evident through its payment of a substantial royalty amounting to Rs. 4,363 crores. This significant sum was disbursed against the excavation of a colossal 100 Lakh metric tonnes of Zinc. Furthermore, it generated a total of 2,65,943 Ravannas over the course of the last three financial years.

Hindustan Zinc Limited for Lead: Once again, Hindustan Zinc Limited secures the second position, this time for Lead mining. With a whopping payment of Rs. 1253 crores the company demonstrated its influence in the lead sector by excavating 16 Lakh metric tonnes of this mineral. The remarkable output is exemplified by the generation of 42,672 Ravannas by the company in the last 3 financial years.

Shree Cement Ltd for Limestone (Cement Grade): Claiming the third position is Shree Cement Ltd, emphasizing its significant contribution to the mining industry in the realm of Limestone (Cement Grade). The company paid a commendable royalty sum of Rs. 663 crores, against the excavation of a staggering 829 Lakh metric tonnes of Limestone. 1,58,817 Ravannas were generated by the company in the last 3 financial years.

Ultratech Cement Ltd for Limestone (Cement Grade): Securing the fourth position is Ultratech Cement Ltd. The company's royalty payment of Rs. 269 crores is a testament to the extraction of 336 Lakh metric tonnes of Limestone. Impressively, Ultratech Cement Ltd generated 2,521 Ravannas during the last three financial years, illustrating its sustained productivity.

Wonder Cement Limited for Limestone (Cement Grade): Following closely at the fifth position is Wonder Cement Limited, showcasing its commendable performance in Limestone (Cement Grade) extraction. The company paid a substantial royalty sum of Rs. 235 crores, correlating to the excavation of 293 Lakh metric tonnes of Limestone. Wonder Cement Limited generated a notable 2,243 Ravannas in the last 3 financial years.

J K Lakshmi Cement Ltd for Limestone (Cement Grade): J K Lakshmi Cement Ltd secures the sixth position for its notable involvement in Limestone (Cement Grade) mining. A remarkable royalty payment of Rs. 209 crores is attributed to the excavation of 261 Lakh metric tonnes of Cement Grade Limestone. Furthermore, the company's impressive output is highlighted by the generation of 2,729 Ravannas over the past three financial years.

Jindal Saw Limited for Iron Ore: Jindal Saw Limited claims the seventh position for its substantial contribution to Iron Ore mining. The company paid a total of Rs. 154 crores in royalty, reflecting the extraction of 31 Lakh metric tonnes of this mineral. Jindal Saw Limited generated an admirable 4,416 Ravannas in the last 3 financial years.

Barmer Lignite Mining Company Limited for Lignite: Barmer Lignite Mining Company Limited stands at the eighth position. The company's payment of Rs. 152 crores corresponds to the extraction of a substantial 178 Lakh metric tonnes of Lignite. Moreover, 5,057 Ravannas were generated by the company in the past three financial years.

Binani Cement Limited for Rock Phosphate: Binani Cement Limited secures the ninth position for its noteworthy contribution to Rock Phosphate mining. The company paid a significant royalty sum of Rs. 137 crores, signifying the excavation of 30 Lakh metric tonnes of Rock Phosphate. Remarkably, Binani Cement Limited generated an impressive total of 89,384 Ravannas during the last 3 financial years.

R.S.M.M. limited for Limestone (Cement Grade): Lastly, R.S.M.M. Limited concludes the top ten list with its commendable extraction of Limestone (Cement Grade). The company paid a royalty of Rs. 131 crores against the excavation of 164 Lakh metric tonnes of this mineral. Notably, R.S.M.M. Limited generated 1,192 Ravannas during the last three financial years, solidifying its place among the prominent mineral leases.

5. Analysis of top ten minerals in prospects of E-Ravanna

5.1 Royalty collection - top ten Minerals

Zinc and LimeStone are the highest royalty contributors in the Mining Department in the last 5 years as compared to other minerals such as Lead, Marble, Granite, Felspar, etc. extracted in the same time period within the state.

Graph 5.1 - Top Minerals Royalty Collected (Cr)

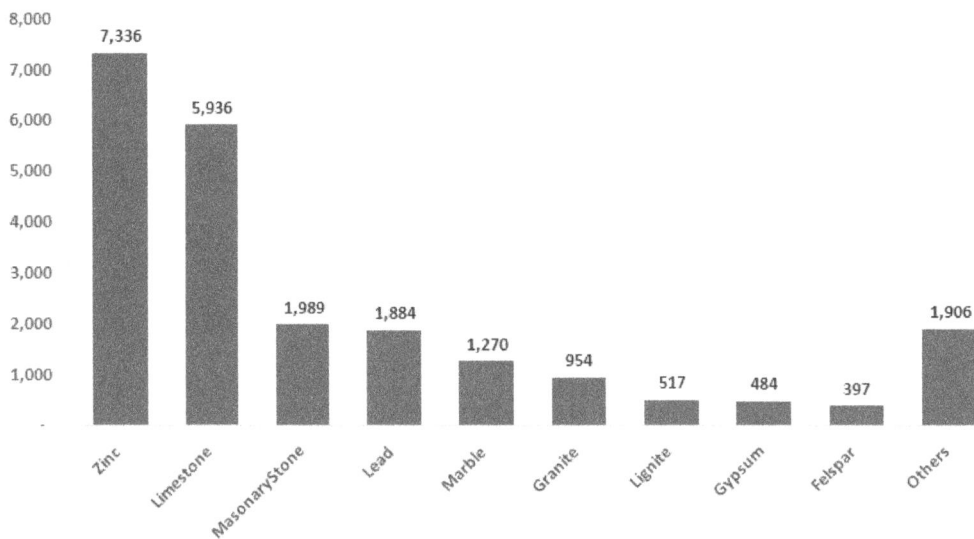

Graph 5.1 showcases the top minerals of the state in terms of royalty collection, offering a fascinating glimpse into the significant contributions made by various minerals to the state's exchequer

Zinc: Zinc emerges as the undisputed champion, occupying the highest pedestal. Over the course of the last five years, Zinc has contributed a magnificent sum of Rs. 7,336 crores in royalty, firmly establishing itself as a cornerstone of the state's mining sector.

Limestone: Following closely in second position, Limestone demonstrates its substantial value by adding another noteworthy Rs. 5,936 crores to the state's revenue over the same five - year period.

Masonry Stone: Securing the third position is Masonry Stone, which has proven its worth by furnishing a commendable Rs. 1,989 crores in royalty over the last five years. This mineral's contribution, although slightly lower than Zinc and Limestone, remains significant and should not be overlooked.

Lead: The fourth position is occupied by Lead, which has made a considerable impact by contributing Rs. 1,884 crores in royalty during the same five - year timeframe

Marble: Marble, residing in the fifth position, has made a notable contribution of Rs. 1,270 crores in royalty over the last five years.

Granite: Granite, claiming the sixth position, has proven its worth by contributing a respectable sum of Rs. 954 crores in royalty over the past five years. Although slightly lower in comparison to the minerals above it, Granite has demonstrated its significance and economic value.

Lignite: Positioned in the seventh spot, Lignite has made a noteworthy impact by generating Rs. 517 crores in royalty over the last five years.

Gypsum: In the eighth position, Gypsum has demonstrated its value by providing a sum of Rs. 484 crores in royalty over the past five years.

Felspar: Felspar, positioned at the ninth spot, has contributed Rs. 397 crores in royalty over the last five years. Although comparatively lower than the minerals preceding it, Felspar's financial contribution still adds to the overall revenue and highlights its presence within the state's mining industry.

Others: The combined contribution of all other minerals, collectively referred to as "Others," amounts to a substantial sum of Rs. 1,906 crores in royalty over the last five financial years. This figure signifies the cumulative impact of various minerals not individually listed among the top performers.

From the data presented in Graph 9, it is evident that Zinc and Limestone reign supreme as the highest royalty contributors within the mining department over the past five years. Their significant contributions far surpass those of other minerals such as Lead, Marble, Granite, Felspar, and others extracted within the state during the same period. The dominance of Zinc and Limestone underscores their economic importance, highlighting their substantial role in shaping the state's mining sector and their noteworthy contributions to the state's exchequer.

5.2 E-Ravanna generation - top ten Minerals

In terms of Ravanna generated in the past 5 years, Masonry Stone and Limestone have been the top contributors with approx. 54% E-Ravanna generated for Masonary Stone and approx. 19 % E-Ravanna generated for LimeStone

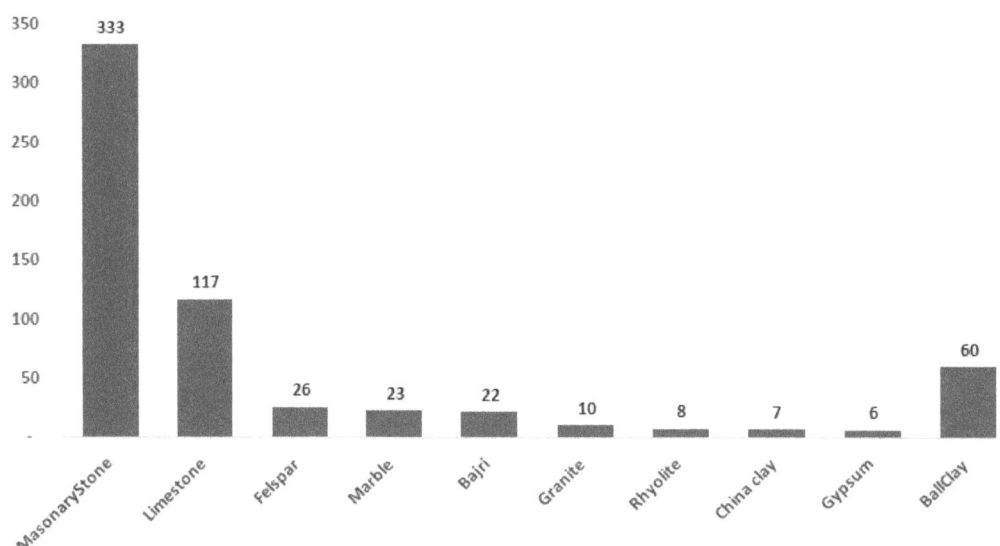

Graph 5.2 presents a compilation showcasing top ten minerals in terms of Ravanna generation over the course of the past five years. Each mineral's contribution to Ravanna generation is highlighted, illustrating their respective rankings within the list

Masonry Stone: Taking the leading position is the Masonry Stone, towering above all others with an astounding 333 lakh Ravanna generated during the preceding five years. Around 54% of all the Ravannas generated during the last five years were for Masonry Stone.

Limestone: Trailing at the second position is Limestone with an impressive tally of 117 lakh Ravannas generated during the preceding five years which constitutes approximately 19% of all Ravannas generated during that period.

Felspar: Felspar claims the third position with a generation of 26 lakh Ravannas over the past five years.

Marble: Occupying the fourth position is the Marble which accumulated a total of 23 Lakh Ravannas in the last five years.

Bajri: At the fifth position stands the Bajri, having generated a commendable 22 lakh Ravannas during the last five years.

Granite: The sixth position is claimed by Granite, which accumulated a total of 10 lakh Ravannas over the previous five years.

Rhyolite: Rhyolite stands at the seventh position. with a noteworthy contribution of 8 lakh Ravannas generated during the last five years. Despite a relatively lower quantity, Rhyolite's presence in the top ten reinforces its significance in the Ravanna generation process.

China Clay: China Clay takes the eighth position, having generated a total of 7 lakh Ravannas in the last five years.

Gypsum: Gypsum secures the ninth position, with a generation of 6 lakh Ravannas during the previous five years.

Ball Clay: Lastly, Ball Clay concludes the top ten ranking with 60000 Ravannas generated during the last five years. Although its quantity is notably lower than other minerals, its inclusion in the list highlights its contribution to Ravanna generation.

5.3 E-Ravanna generation - top ten Minerals

Limestone is the most extracted mineral in the state contributing approx. 40% in the total per lakh MT minerals extracted in the state in the last 5 years followed by MasonaryStone with approx. 33 % contribution in the overall mineral extraction.

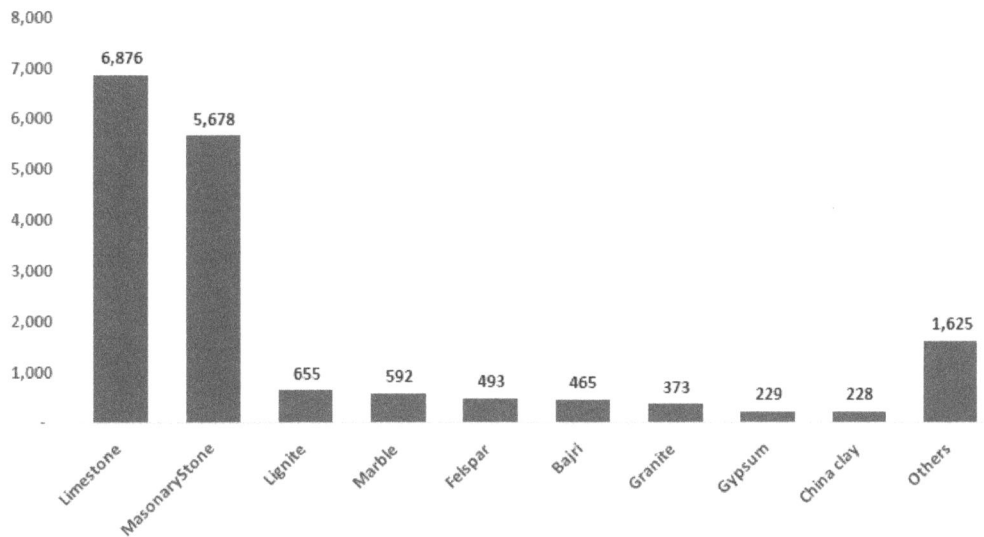

Graph 5.3 - Top Minerals Extracted Net Weight MT (Lakh)

Graph 5.3 depicts the Top Minerals extracted in the state of Rajasthan. The values given are presented in Lakh Metric Tonnes.

Limestone: At the zenith of the list is limestone reigning as the most abundantly extracted mineral in Rajasthan, with a staggering 6876 Lakh Metric Tonnes extracted during the aforementioned period. Limestone's prominence is further emphasized by its substantial contribution of approximately 40% towards the total quantity of minerals extracted per Lakh MT in the state

Masonry Stone: Taking the honorable second position is Masonry Stone, which showcases its impressive presence with an extraction volume of 5678 Lakh Metric Tonnes within the last five years. Notably, it accounts for nearly 33% of the total mineral extraction in the state,

Lignite: Securing the third position is Lignite, having been extracted to the tune of 655 Lakh Metric Tonnes during the last five years.

Marble: Marble claims the fourth position in the ranking, impressively accumulating 592 Lakh Metric Tonnes during the preceding five - year period.

Felspar: Occupying the fifth position, Felspar demonstrates its notable presence with 493 Lakh Metric Tonnes extracted from the earth over the last five years.

Bajri: Moving down the list, we come across Bajri in the sixth position, having accumulated 465 Lakh Metric Tonnes in the past five years.

Granite: In the seventh position, we find Granite, which showcases its noteworthy presence with an extraction volume of 373 Lakh Metric Tonnes within the previous five years.

Gypsum: Securing the eighth position, Gypsum impresses with an extraction volume of 229 Lakh Metric Tonnes over the preceding five years.

China Clay: Ninth position is claimed by China Clay with an extraction volume of 228 Lakh Metric Tonnes over the course of five years.

Others: Finally, the category labeled as "Others" combines the extraction volumes of various minerals, amounting to an impressive 1625 Lakh Metric Tonnes over the five - year period. Although individual mineral contributions are not detailed, the cumulative figure underscores the collective impact of these minerals on Rajasthan's mineral industry.

In conclusion, Graph 11 provides a comprehensive and visually appealing overview of the top minerals extracted in Rajasthan. The sheer magnitude of the extraction volumes underscores the state's rich mineral reserves and their critical role in driving economic growth and development.

6. District wise analysis of E-Ravanna

6.1 District wise Royalty collection - top ten districts

Bhilwara and Rajsamand district are the highest royalty collection contributors in the state followed by Udaipur, Chittorgarh & Pali after the introduction of the E-Ravanna system in the state.

Graph 6.1 showcases the Top Ten Districts in terms of cumulative Royalty Collection since introduction of E-Ravanna system in Rajasthan.

Graph 6.1 - Top District Wise Royalty Collection

(in Crores)

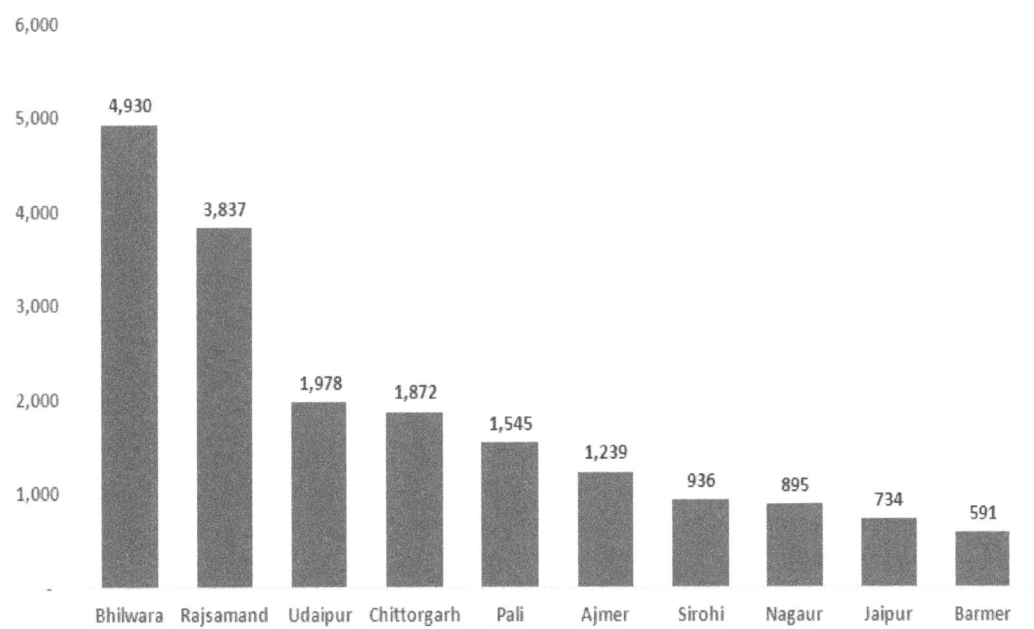

Leading the pack is the **Bhilwara** District, which made an outstanding contribution of Rs. 4930 crores as royalty to the state.

Following closely in second place is the **Rajsamand** District, which substantiated the state's revenues with a substantial addition of Rs. 3837 crores.

Securing the third position on the list is the **Udaipur** District, which contributed a commendable sum of Rs. 1978 crores to the state's treasury.

Occupying the fourth spot on the list is the **Chittorgarh** District, which made a praiseworthy and commendable contribution of Rs. 1872 crores to the state's coffers.

Notably, the fifth position is held by the **Pali** district, which delivered a substantial contribution of Rs. 1545 crores in royalty.

The sixth position is occupied by the **Ajmer** District, which demonstrated a notable commitment by contributing Rs. 1239 crores

Sirohi District secured the seventh position, contributing a commendable Rs. 936 crores.

Claiming the eighth spot on the list is the **Nagaur** District, which made a significant contribution of Rs. 895 crores.

The **Jaipur** District secures the ninth position, making a substantial contribution of Rs. 734 crores in royalty collection.

Last but certainly not the least, the **Barmer** District concludes the list of top contributors to the state's treasury.

Collectively, these top ten districts have made remarkable strides in royalty collection, demonstrating their significant and impressive contributions to the state exchequer

6.1.1 Top ten royalty collecting districts and top ten minerals in respect of districts

Zinc has been the highest contributor in royalty collected in the top 3 districts of Rajasthan with maximum royalty collection. Zinc and Limestone are majority contributors in overall royalty collection in 8 out of 10 top royalty collection districts in Rajasthan.

Graph 6.1.1 - Top District With Mineral Royalties Collection
(in Crores)

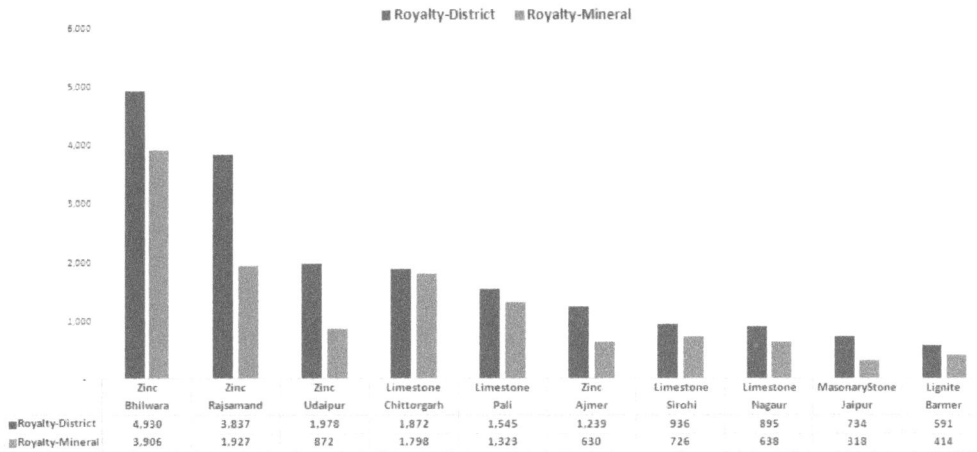

Graph 6.1.1 depicts the top ten districts of Rajasthan in terms of royalty collection along with top minerals in those respective districts which helped them achieve this feat.

Bhilwara reigns supreme with a total contribution of Rs. 4930 crores. Out of this **Zinc** alone has contributed 3906 crores, thus becoming the most significant mineral in terms of royalty realization.

Rajsamand comes second with a royalty collection of Rs. 3837 crores out of which once again **Zinc** alone has contributed Rs. 1927 crores. Alomost 50% of royalty in Rajsamand comes from a single mineral, Zinc.

Occupying the third position is the **Udaipur** district with a collection of Rs.1978 crores as royalty. Yet again, **Zinc** plays an exemplary role in helping Udaipur secure this position by contributing Rs.872 crores alone as royalty.

Chittorgarh claims the fourth position with a total contribution of Rs. 1872 crores as royalty. Here, more than 95% of the royalty comes from a single mineral that is **Limestone** which contributed a whopping Rs. 1798 crores single handedly.

Pali comes fifth in the coveted list with a contribution of Rs. 1545 crores. Here, **limestone** is the clear winner among minerals with a contribution of more than 85% at Rs. 1323 crores.

Next in line comes the **Ajmer** District at the sixth position with a contribution of Rs. 1239 crores to the state revenues. **Zinc**, again shines bright among other minerals in this district with a contribution of more than 50% at Rs.630 crores.

Claiming the seventh spot among all the districts is Sirohi with a contribution of Rs.936 crores. **Limestone**, with a contribution of more than 75% at Rs.726 crores is the heavyweight in this district.

At the ninth pedestal stands the capital **Jaipur** with a contribution of Rs. 734. **Masonry Stone** with a contribution of Rs.318 crores is the primary mineral excavated in this district.

Concluding the top ten list is the **Barmer** District of Rajasthan which added Rs. 591 crores to the state coffers and **Lignite** is the clear cut winner among minerals in this district with a contribution of Rs. 414 crores, constituting 70% of royalty contribution alone.

Thus, **Zinc** emerges as the undisputed leader of minerals with highest contribution in royalty in the top 3 districts of Rajasthan. **Zinc and Limestone** together are the highest contributors figuring as the top most minerals in 8 out of top 10 districts.

6.2 District wise E-Ravanna generation - top ten districts

Nagaur and Jaipur district recorded the highest Ravanna generation among all the districts in the state with almost 62 Lakh Ravanna generated from Jaipur district and almost 59 Lakh Ravanna generated from Nagaur district.

Graph 5.2 - Top District Wise Ravanna Generation (Nos. In Lakh)

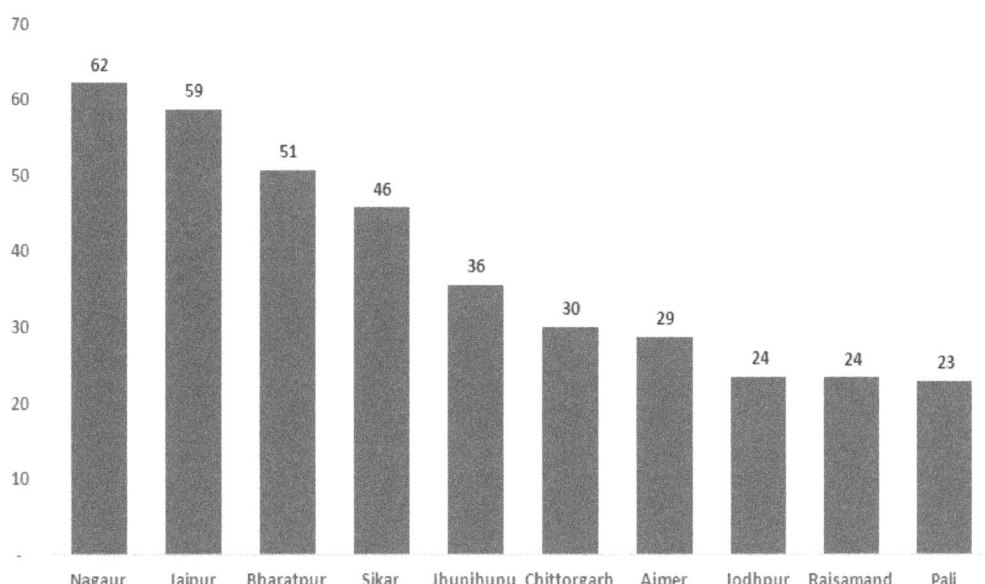

Graph 6.2 presents a comprehensive overview of the Top Ten districts in Ravanna generation

Nagaur – Among these districts, Nagaur stands as the foremost leader, with an astounding generation of 62 Lakh Ravannas, solidifying its position at the pinnacle.

Jaipur – Following closely behind, the Jaipur district occupies the **second** position, having generated an impressive 59 Lakh Ravannas.

Bharatpur – Not far behind, the Bharatpur district emerges at the **third** position with a commendable generation of 51 Lakh Ravannas.

Sikar – In the **fourth** position, we find the district of Sikar, which has contributed significantly to the Ravanna generation, amounting to 46 Lakh.

Jhunjhunu – Standing at the **fifth** position is the Jhunjhunu district with 36 Lakh Ravannas.

Chittorgarh – Chittorgarh attains the **sixth** position with a noteworthy contribution of 30 lakh Ravannas.

Ajmer – Taking its place at the **seventh** pedestal, the Ajmer District showcases a substantial generation of 29 Lakh Ravannas, solidifying its position among the top - ranking districts.

Jodhpur – Claiming the **eighth** position, Jodhpur also made a significant impact with a Ravanna generation of 24 Lakh.

Rajsamand - Rajsamand district captures the **ninth** position on this prestigious list, having generated an appreciable amount of 24 lakh Ravannas.

Pali – Lastly, concluding the esteemed top ten list, the Pali District impresses with its contribution of 23 lakh Ravannas, thus making its mark in the realm of Ravanna generation.

6.2.1 Top ten royalty collecting districts and top ten minerals in respect of districts

In Nagaur district, 35 Lakh (56% of total) E-Ravanna generated were for Limestone. In Jaipur district 53 Lakh of E-Ravanna generated were for Masonry Stone contributing 90% in the total number of E-Ravanna generated in the district.

Graph 6.2.1 - Top District With Mineral E-Ravanna Generation (Lakh)

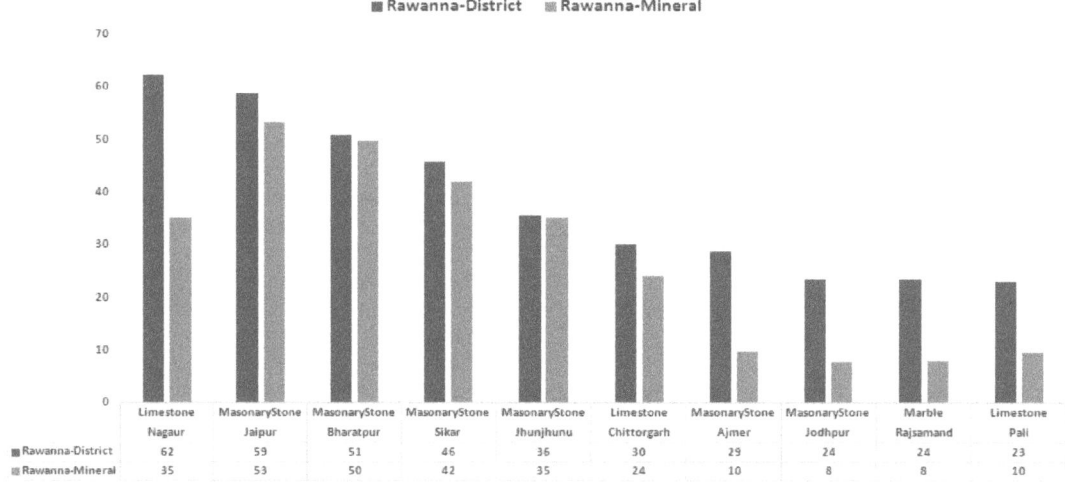

Graph 6.2.1 depicts the top ten districts of Rajasthan in terms of Ravanna generation along with top minerals in those respective districts which helped them achieve this feat.

Nagaur reigns supreme with a generation of 62 Lakh Ravannas. Out of this **Limestone** alone has contributed 35 lakh Ravannas, thus becoming the most significant mineral in terms of Ravanna generation.

Jaipur comes **second** with a Ravanna generation of 59 Lakh out of which 53 lakh Ravannas have been generated for **Masonry stone** alone. Thus almost 90% of all Ravannas generated were for a single mineral, Masonry Stone.

Occupying the **third** position is the **Bharatpur** district with 51 Lakh Ravanna generation. Once again **Masonry Stone** beats all other minerals with a whopping 98% of all Ravannas in the district.

Sikar claims the **fourth** position with a total generation of 46 lakh Ravannas. Here, more than 91% of all Ravannas generated were for a single mineral, **Masonry Stone.**

Jhunjhunu comes **fifth** in the coveted list with a contribution of 36 lakh Ravannas. Here, once again **Masonry Stone** is the clear winner among minerals with a contribution of more than 97% at 35 Lakh Ravannas.

Next in line comes the **Chittorgarh** District at the **sixth** position with 30 lakh Ravanna generation. **Limestone** shines bright among other minerals in this district with a generation of 24 lakh Ravannas generated for this mineral which is 80% of all Ravannas.

Claiming the **seventh** spot among all the districts is the **Ajmer district** with a generation of 29 lakh Ravannas. **Masonry Stone**, with a contribution of 10 lakh Ravannas is the heavyweight in this district.

At the **eighth** pedestal stands the **Jodhpur** district with a generation of 24 lakh Ravannas and yet again, **Masonry Stone** is the major mineral with 8 lakh Ravannas out of the total 24 Lakh .

Ninth place in the list is claimed by **Rajsamand** District by generating 24 lakh Ravannas with **Marble** as the primary mineral in the district for which 8 Lakh Ravannas were generated.

Concluding the top ten list is the **Pali** District of Rajasthan which generated 23 lakh Ravannas and **Limestone** is the clear cut winner among minerals in this district with a generation of 10 lakh Ravannas for this mineral.

Thus, Masonry stone is the mineral for which the maximum number of Ravannas are generated in the state. Next comes the Limestone in terms of Ravanna generation in the state.

6.3 District wise E-Ravanna generation - top ten districts

Chittorgarh and Pali District are the highest quantity contributors in Mineral Extraction in the state followed by Jaipur, Sirohi & Nagaur.

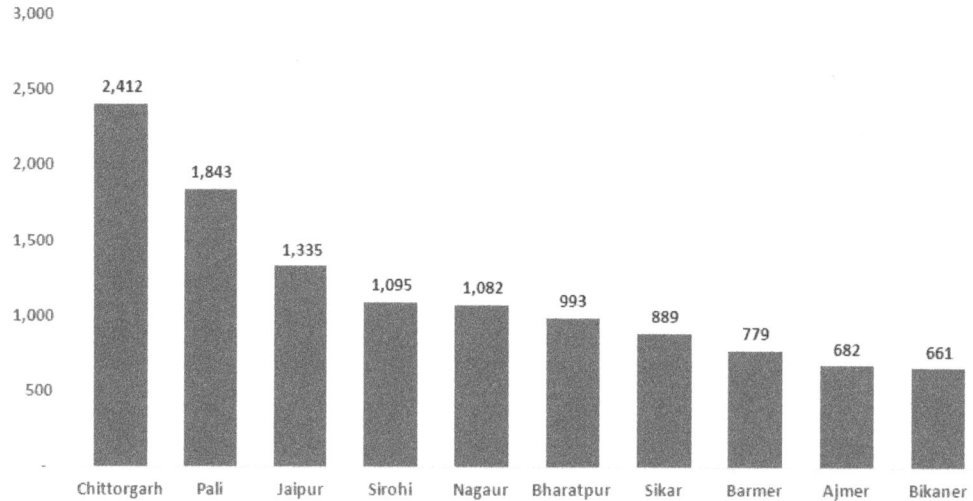

Graph 6.3 - Top District Wise Quantity MT (Lakh)

Graph 6.3 showcases a compelling visual depiction of the Top Ten Districts in terms of Mineral extraction. The significant scale of mining in these districts underscores the rich deposits of earth minerals they have been blessed with.

Chittorgarh: At the zenith of the list is Chittorgarh reigning as the district with maximum extraction of mineral in the state with 2412 Lakh Metric tonne of excavation.

Pali: Taking the honorable **second** position is Pali district with an extraction of 1843 Lakh Metric tonnes of mineral.

Jaipur: Securing the **third** position is Jaipur district having extracted minerals to the tune of 1335 Lakh Metric Tonnes.

Sirohi: Sirohi claims the **fourth** position in the ranking, impressively extracting 1095 Lakh Metric Tonnes.

Nagaur: Occupying the **fifth** position, Nagaur demonstrates its notable presence with 1082 Lakh Metric Tonnes extracted from the earth.

Bharatpur: Moving down the list, we come across Bharatpur in the **sixth** position, having excavated 993 Lakh Metric Tonnes.

Sikar: In the **seventh** position, we find Sikar, which showcases its noteworthy presence with an extraction volume of 889 Lakh Metric Tonnes.

Barmer: Securing the **eighth** position, Barmer impresses with an extraction volume of 779 Lakh Metric Tonnes.

Ajmer: **Ninth** position is claimed by Ajmer with an extraction volume of 682 Lakh Metric Tonnes.

Bikaner: Close behind at the **tenth** position is the Bikaner District which excavated 661 Lakh Metric Tonnes of minerals.

Although individual mineral contributions are not detailed in this graph, the cumulative figures highlight the collective impact of these districts on Rajasthan's mining industry and the state's rich mineral reserves.

6.3.1 Top ten royalty collecting districts and top ten minerals in respect of districts

Graph 6.3.1 - Top District With Mineral Quantity MT (In Lakh)

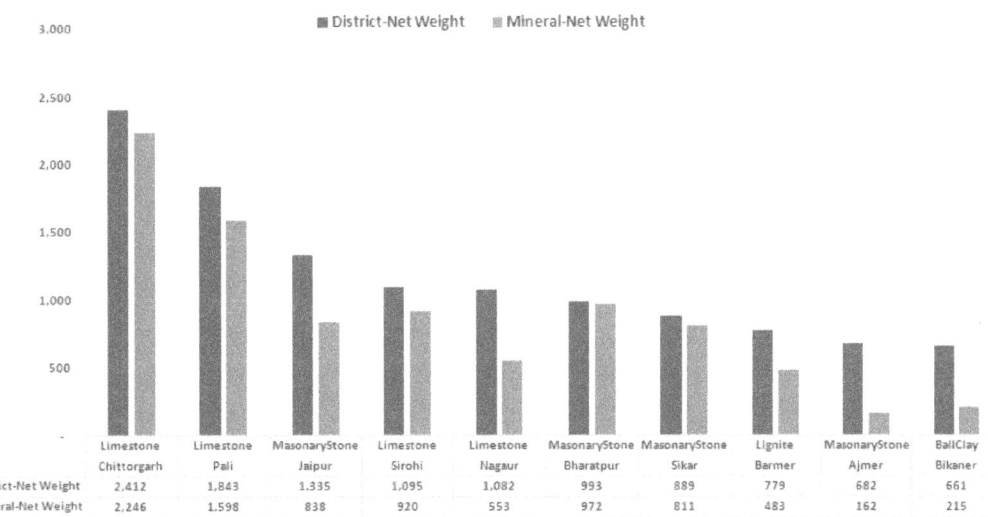

Graph 6.3.1 presents the Top Ten districts with Maximum Extraction of minerals along with the top mineral excavated in these districts.

Chittorgarh reigns supreme with an extraction of 2412 Lakh Metric Tonnes of mineral. Out of this Limestone alone has contributed 2246 Lakh Metric tonnes, thus becoming the most significant mineral having 93% share.

Pali comes second with Excavation of 1843 Lakh Metric tonnes of mineral out of which 1598 Lakh Metric Tonnes is contributed by Limestone alone. Thus almost 86% of all minerals extracted from mother earth are Limestone in this district.

Occupying the third position is the Jaipur district having extracted 1335 Lakh Metric Tonnes of mineral with 838 Lakh Metric Tonnes of Masonry Stone.

Sirohi claims the fourth position with a total excavation of 1095 Lakh Metric Tonnes of minerals. Here, approximately 84%% of all minerals extracted is Limestone at 920 Lakh Metric Tonnes.

Nagaur comes fifth in the coveted list with a contribution of 1082 Lakh Metric Tonnes of minerals. Here, once again Limestone is the clear winner among minerals with a contribution of 553 Lakh Metric Tonnes.

Next in line comes the Bharatpur District at the sixth position with 993 Lakh Metric Tonnes of mineral extraction. Masonry Stone shines bright among other minerals in this district with an excavation of 972 Lakh Metric Tonnes which is almost 98% of all minerals extracted.

Claiming the seventh spot among all the districts is the Sikar district with an extraction of 889 Lakh Metric Tonnes. Masonry Stone, with a contribution of 811 Lakh Metric Tonnes is the heavyweight in this district.

At the eighth pedestal stands the Barmer district with an excavation of 779 Lakh Metric Tonnes and Lignite is the major mineral with 483 Lakh Metric tonnes of extraction.

Ninth place in the list is claimed by Ajmer District by extracting 682 Lakh Metric Tonnes of mineral with yet again Masonry Stone as the primary mineral in the district with 162 Lakh Metric Tonnes .

Concluding the top ten list is the Bikaner District of Rajasthan which extracted 661 Lakh Metric Tonnes and Ball Clay is the clear cut winner among minerals in this district with an extraction of 215 Lakh Metric Tonnes.

Thus, Limestone and Masonry stone are the most extracted minerals in these top ten districts of Rajasthan.

COTTON CLOTH BAGS INDUSTRY IN RAJASTHAN: A STEP TOWARDS ENVIRONMENTAL SUSTAINABILITY AND ECONOMIC GROWTH

Introduction

In recent years, the world has witnessed a growing concern about pollution and the importance of protecting the environment. Environmental issues such as global warming, soil pollution, air pollution, and water pollution have become matters of concern nowadays. People are now more concerned about the impact of their daily choices and opting for alternatives choices.

As part of the global movement towards sustainability, the "Make in India" campaign has been instrumental in encouraging Indian businessmen to manufacture products within the country. This initiative has seen significant success, particularly in promoting eco - friendly alternatives. One such successful endeavor is the production of Cotton cloth Bags, a sustainable solution that addresses the pressing issue of plastic pollution.

The plastic waste, especially single - use plastic bags, has a very bad impact on the environment. To control this problem, many countries have imposed bans on plastic bags, necessitating the adoption of greener alternatives. Among the options available, reusable bags, made from various materials, have gained popularity. Reusable bags are designed to be more durable, ensuring a longer lifespan compared to single - use plastic bags. While reusable bags are preferred for their potential environmental benefits, they must be used repeatedly.

Paper bags have been an alternative choice for carrying items, but they also pose environmental challenges. The production of paper bags requires cutting down trees, which has devastating consequences for the environment. Additionally, paper bags have limited reusability, making them less sustainable in the long run.

The use of cotton carry bags represents a significant step towards protecting the environment and reducing plastic pollution. India, in particular, has witnessed a rise in the adoption of cotton carry bags, especially with the nationwide ban on plastic.

Cotton carry bags offer several advantages over their plastic and paper counterparts. They are not only aesthetically pleasing and vibrant but also available in various shapes and sizes to suit individual preferences. Children colorful carry bags, while others may opt for designer bags. Additionally, cotton bags can be customized according to customer needs. They come in various types, including shopping bags, clothing bags, wine bags, and more, making them versatile and suitable for multiple purposes.

One of the key advantages of cotton carry bags is their reusability and durability. These bags can be washed and reused multiple times, reducing the generation of waste and contributing to a cleaner environment. Though cotton production does have its resource - intensive aspects, with proper reuse, the overall environmental impact can be significantly reduced.

Various types of cotton carry bags, such as Cotton Hand Bags, Cotton Shoulder Bags, Cotton Designer Bags, Cotton Gift Bags, and Cotton Tote Bags, are now popularly used worldwide.

However, in India, the adoption of cotton carry bags faces certain challenges, particularly regarding pricing and availability. Middle - class consumers, in particular, may be hesitant to buy cotton bags due to their relatively higher price compared to other options. Nevertheless, with the increasing momentum of the plastic - free city concept, more companies have started manufacturing cotton carry bags, offering a wider range of choices to customers.

Non - Governmental Organizations (NGOs) in India have also played a vital role in promoting cotton carry bags. For instance, the NGO "Swatch" in Nagpur is manufacturing and distributing cotton carry bags to vendors and retailers, who, in turn, encourage customers to opt for eco - friendly alternatives. By working closely with shopkeepers, NGOs can facilitate large - scale changes and drive consumer awareness about sustainable choices.

In Bangalore, private companies have also stepped up their production of cotton carry bags. These bags come in various qualities, with prices ranging from Rs. 12 to Rs. 20 or more, depending on the fiber's quality used in their construction.

The rise of cotton carry bags as an eco - friendly alternative marks a significant step towards environmental sustainability. As the world battles against plastic pollution and strives to protect the environment, the adoption of reusable and durable cotton bags offers a promising solution. Encouraging the use of cotton carry bags, promoting awareness, and making them more accessible to consumers are crucial steps in fostering a greener and more sustainable future for generations to come.

Designer Shoulder Bag   Normal Shoulder Bag   Normal Hand Bags   Designer Hand Bags

1. Progress and prospects and practice of Cotton Bag industry

1.1 Global scenario for Cloth Bag

The detrimental impact of plastic bags on the environment has spurred many countries worldwide to take action against their use. As a result, several Asian Pacific and European nations have implemented bans on plastic bags, leading to a surge in demand for cloth bags as an eco - friendly alternative. This article delves into the escalating popularity of cloth bags, the forces driving their market growth, and the transformative effect of government legislation on the packaging industry.

Cloth bags have witnessed a remarkable surge in demand as countries increasingly seek sustainable alternatives to plastic bags. Grocery stores, supermarkets, and online retailers are actively promoting the use of cloth bags, thereby driving the market's expansion. Unlike their single - use plastic counterparts, cloth bags are reusable, durable, and environment - friendly, making them a popular choice among environmentally conscious consumers.

Governments in Austria and Estonia have taken bold steps to address the plastic bag issue. Austria initiated a complete ban on non - biodegradable plastic bags from January 1, 2010, while Estonia amended its Packaging Act in 2017 to restrict plastic bag use starting from 2019. Such stringent legislation has played a pivotal role in bolstering the demand for cloth bags in these regions. European countries, in general, have seen a substantial increase in the adoption of cloth bags due to progressive government initiatives.

In the Asia - Pacific region, increasing consumer prices for plastic - based goods, including bags, straws, cups, and food containers, have prompted consumers to shift towards sustainable alternatives like cloth bags. China and India, as emerging economies, are expected to witness significant growth in the cloth bag industry. With a rising awareness of environmental issues, consumers are actively embracing eco - friendly options, thereby extending the market reach of cloth bags in the region.

Manufacturers of cloth bags are exploring opportunities to expand their business operations in countries across South Africa and North Africa. These regions present promising prospects for the cloth bag market, as consumers become more environmentally conscious and seek sustainable solutions. Furthermore, Mexico's cloth bag market is predicted to experience substantial growth due to the increasing demand from the country's environmentally aware consumers.

Brand owners, manufacturers, and food service companies are now leveraging cloth bags for branding and marketing purposes. Cotton and other fabric bags provide an excellent canvas for displaying logos and promotional messages, making them an attractive option for businesses. This trend is expected to further fuel the demand for cloth bags in the coming years.

The global shift towards sustainable practices and the ban on plastic bags in various countries have contributed to the remarkable growth of the cloth bag industry. As consumers and businesses increasingly embrace eco - friendly alternatives, cloth bags have emerged as a popular choice for packaging and carrying goods. With the ongoing commitment of governments and businesses to reduce plastic waste, the demand for cloth bags is expected to continue rising steadily, promoting a greener and more sustainable future for the planet.

1.2 Indian scenario of Cloth bag

In the past, shops in India used cloth bags mainly for marketing purposes. However, due to the ban on plastic bags, it has become essential for everyone to switch to cloth bags as they are more environmentally friendly. By manufacturing these bags within India, the cost can be reduced since there would be no need to pay for transportation.

As a result of the government's ban on plastic bags, the demand for cloth bags has increased significantly. To meet this demand, cloth bag manufacturers in India are increasing their production capacity. Cloth bags have become the best alternative to plastic bags, thanks to their eco - friendly nature and cost - effectiveness. They have become an important product in the Indian market.

Starting a cloth bag business has created many opportunities in the market. On one hand, we are contributing to the welfare of our society by using eco - friendly bags, and on the other hand, we are creating new job opportunities. The future for cloth bags in the Indian market looks promising.

1.3 Target Group for Cloth Bag

The target group for cloth bags includes various businesses and retailers, including:

i. Supermarkets

ii. Wholesalers

iii. Shopping Malls

iv. Sweet Shops

v. General Stores

1.4 Leading Cloth Bag Manufacturers in India

Some of the prominent cloth bag manufacturers in India are:

i. Param Jute Products - Kolkata, West Bengal

ii. Ronak Industries - Jaipur, Rajasthan

iii. Arawinda Polybag - Virudhunagar, Tamil Nadu

iv. Sekawati Impex - Jaipur, Rajasthan

2. Market trend of Hand bags and shopping bags of cotton in Rajasthan

2.1 Total value of cotton bags transported through E-Way bills in Rajasthan

Based on E-Way bill data analysis for last three financial years data for Hand bags and shopping bags of cotton

Graph 1 - Total value of cotton bags transported through E-Way bills in Rajasthan

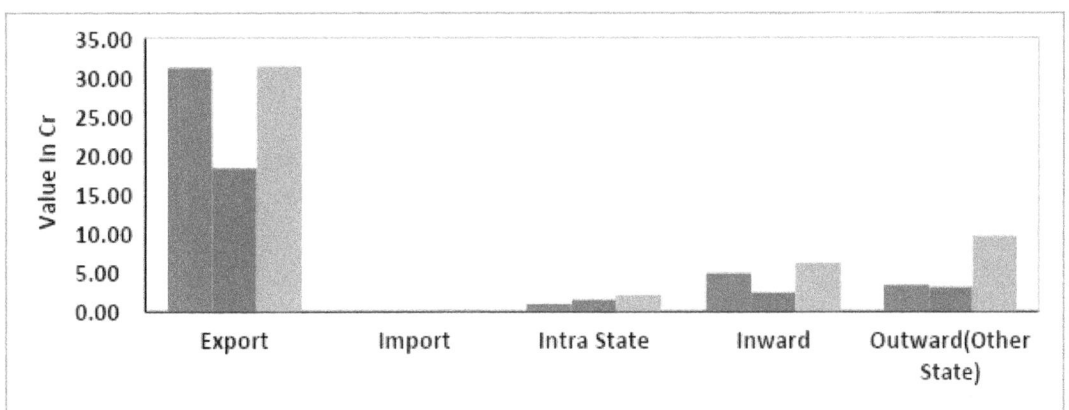

To analyze the trend of the total value of cotton bags transported through E-Way bills in Rajasthan. The Export category shows an increase in value from 31.18 Crore to 31.36 Crore over the three years, with a dip in the financial year 2020 - 2021. The Import category has no values for the first two years, but there is a small value of 0.18 Crore in the financial year 2021 - 2022. The Intra State category shows a gradual increase in value over the three years. The Inward category had a significant improvement in value from 4.86 Crore to 6.16 Crore in the financial year 2021 - 2022 which shows impressive growth. The Outward category shows a tremendous growth in 3.37 Crore to 9.66 Crore in the last year.

2.2 Top State where Cotton bag are supplied from Rajasthan

As per E-Way bill system Top State where Cotton bag are supplied from Rajasthan are Haryana, Maharashtra, Delhi, West Bengal and Uttar Pradesh

The Graph clearly shows that Rajasthan supplies a significant portion of cotton bags to five top states: Haryana, Maharashtra, Delhi, West Bengal, and Uttar Pradesh. Rajasthan supplies one third cotton bags to Haryana out of total outward supply of cotton bags in FY 2021 - 2022 and around one fourth to Maharastra and around 12.5 percent each to Delhi, West Bengal and Uttar Pradesh.

Graph 2 - Top State where Cotton bag are supplied from Rajasthan

(in Crores)

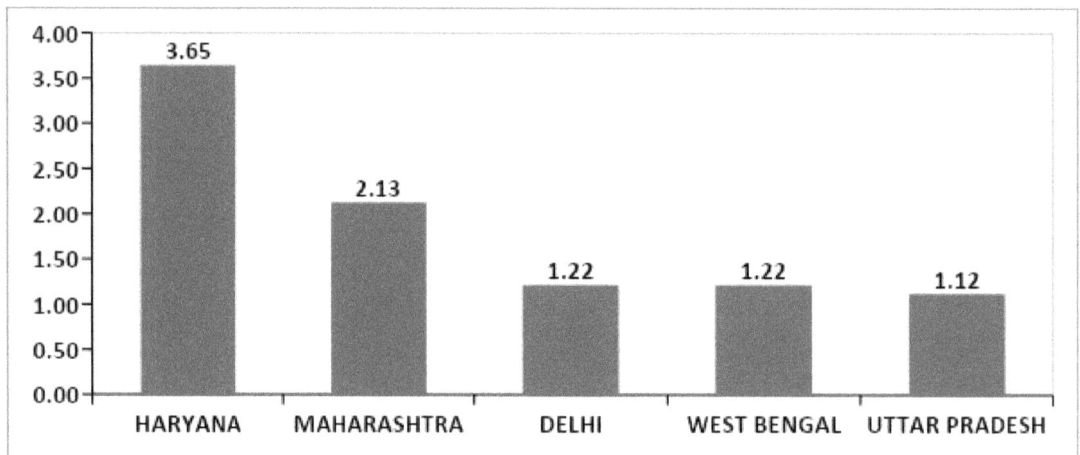

Based on these percentages, it is clear that the majority of the outward supply of cotton bags from Rajasthan is concentrated in these five states. The combined supply to Haryana, Maharashtra, Delhi, West Bengal, and Uttar Pradesh accounts for more than 95% of the total outward supply of cotton bags from Rajasthan in the fiscal year 2021 - 2022.

2.3 Top Places which import/Outward Supply cloths bags based on E-Way bill study

Graph 3 - Top Places which Supply cloths bags based on E-Way bill (FY 2021 - 2022)

(in Crores)

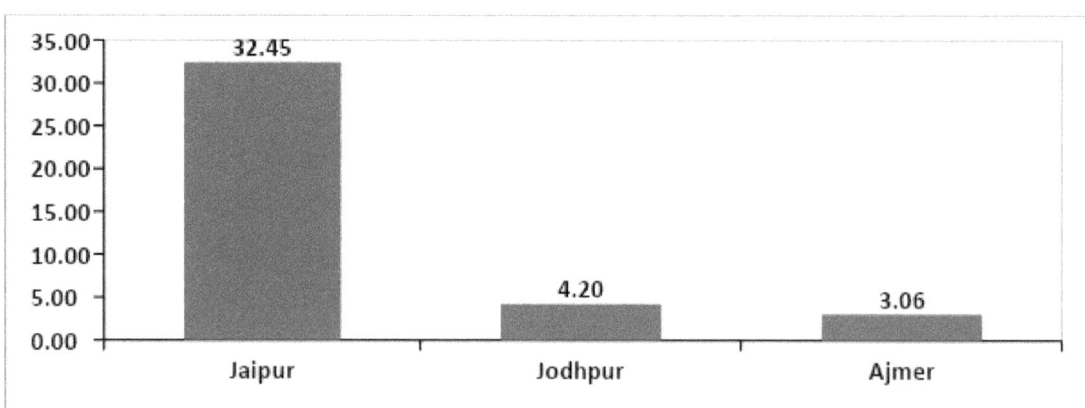

Above graph shows that Jaipur, Jodhpur and Ajmer contribute 80 per cent of the total supply of cotton bags from Rajasthan.

3 SWOT Analysis of the Cotton Bag Industry in Rajasthan

A SWOT analysis of the cotton bag industry reveals its strengths, weaknesses, opportunities, and threats.

Strengths:

- Eco - friendly and high - quality products
- In line with current fashion trends
- Utilization of modern technology
- Durable and soft fabric
- Availability of designer bags

Weaknesses:

- Heavy and bulky for shipping
- Not moisture - resistant unless chemically treated
- Limited advertising efforts

Opportunities:

- Increasing awareness of plastic hazards
- Rising demand for eco - friendly products
- Favorable government policies
- Growing online market

Threats:

- Competition from substitute products
- Intense competition in the market
- Jute bags preferred by high - end customers

3. Why Use Cotton Bags Over Other Alternatives

Choosing cotton bags over other bag options offers several environmental and practical advantages:

i. Low Environmental Impact: Only a small percentage of plastic bags are recycled worldwide, and the production of paper bags involves the felling of numerous trees. In contrast, cotton bags are reusable, reducing waste and pollution significantly.

ii. Long Lifespan: Reusable cotton bags can be used hundreds of times, making them more sustainable compared to single - use plastic and paper bags.

iii. Eco - Friendly: Cotton bags are biodegradable and do not contribute to air pollution.

iv. Freshness Preservation: Cotton bags are ideal for carrying fruits, vegetables, and seeds, keeping them fresh for extended periods.

v. Waste Reduction: Using cotton bags saves up to 500 plastic bags per year, contributing to a reduction in domestic waste.

5. Technological Necessities

To further strengthen the cotton bag industry and its environmental impact, certain technological advancements are essential:

i. Domestic Manufacturing of High - Performance Fibers: Encouraging the production of high - performance fibers like aramids, UHMWPE, carbon, and Nylon 66 can cater to the anticipated surge in demand for technical textiles.

ii. Adoption of Sustainable Technologies: Promoting modern technologies such as 3D nonwovens, multiaxial braiding, and 3D weaving through the Technology Upgradation Fund Scheme can lead to sustainable growth.

iii. Development of Smart Textiles and Electronic Textiles: Collaborative efforts between textile, electronics, and information technology sectors can facilitate the development of smart and electronic textile products.

6. Necessity of Research, Education, and Skill Development

To nurture the growth of the cotton bag industry, emphasis on research, education, and skill development is vital:

i. Strengthen Educational Institutes: Focus on enhancing technical textile education infrastructure in select textile engineering/technology institutes across the country.

ii. Establish Department/Centre of Technical Textiles: Create specialized centers dedicated to technical textiles research and knowledge dissemination.

iii. Faculty Development: Support faculty development in emerging areas of technical textiles.

iv. New Courses: Introduce specialized courses in technical textiles at undergraduate and postgraduate levels.

Necessity of Textile Research Associations and Centres of Excellence

To accelerate innovation and collaboration, the role of Textile Research Associations (TRAs) and Centres of Excellence (COEs) is crucial:

i. Attract and Retain Talent: Strengthen TRAs by attracting and retaining high - quality talent through competitive compensation.

ii. Augment Research Infrastructure: Regularly upgrade R&D facilities in TRAs based on global developments in technical textiles.

iii. Foster Collaboration: Encourage collaboration between Indian COEs and overseas counterparts to enhance research outcomes and interdisciplinary applications.

7. Conclusion

The Cotton Cloth Bags Industry in Rajasthan holds immense potential for sustainable growth, environmental protection, and economic development. As the demand for eco - friendly alternatives to plastic

References –

1. https://tkwsibf.edu.in/wp - content/uploads/2020/07/cloth - bag - manufacturing.pdf
2. https://okcredit.in/blog/cloth - bags - manufacturers - in - india/

GRANITE INDUSTRY IN RAJASTHAN - PROGRESS AND PROSPECTS

Introduction

The word "Granite" comes from the Latin word "Granum," which means "grain" because of its grainy texture. Granite is a type of rock that is light - colored and consists mainly of feldspars, plagioclase, quartz (about 35%), and smaller amounts of mafic minerals (approximately 45%), such as biotite, hornblende, pyroxene, iron oxides, and more. In India, Granite holds a significant position in dimensional stone exports, accounting for about 95% of the total share.

The export of high - value items like tiles, polished slabs, and monument stones has been growing at an impressive rate of over 50% each year. When we look at the distribution of total resources across different states, Karnataka and Rajasthan have the highest share of about 20% each, followed by Jharkhand (19%), Gujarat (18%), Andhra Pradesh (5%), and Madhya Pradesh & Odisha (4% each). Together, these states account for 90% of the total resources.

In terms of quality, about 7% of the total resources are classified as Black granite, while 92% fall under Colored granite. There is also a small percentage (about 1%) of resources that are unclassified in terms of grade.

1. Geographical distribution granite in Rajasthan

Rajasthan is known for stones like Marble, Sandstone, Limestone, Slate etc. Recently granite has also been added to this list. Granite has gained popularity due to its hardness, durability, ability to achieve a mirror - like polish, and captivating colors. As a result, the use of granite as a dimensional and decorative stone has increased worldwide, leading to a thriving export market for Indian Granite.

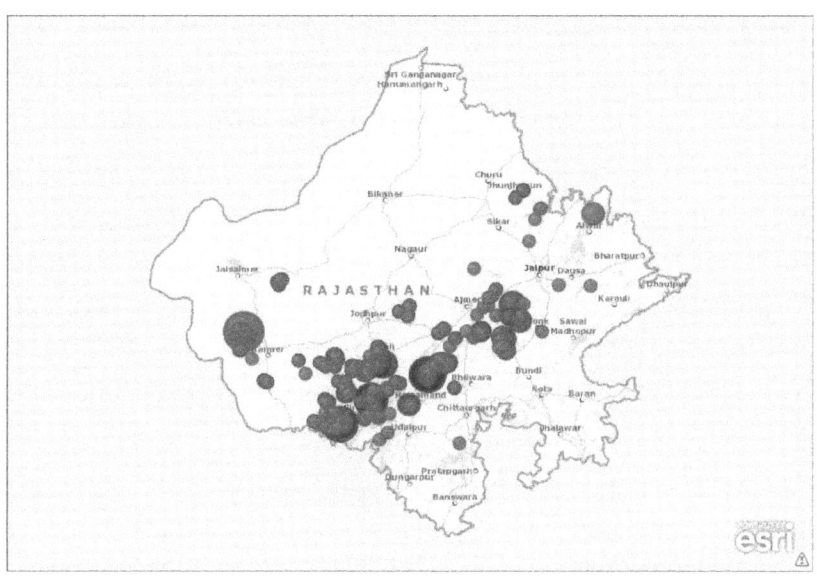

Rajasthan is blessed with extensive reserves of various granite varieties, found in 23 districts of the state. More than 200 locations with granite deposits have been identified so far. Some of the major districts contributing to granite production in Rajasthan include Jalore, Sirohi, Bhilwara, Ajmer, Barmer, Jaipur, Udaipur, Jhunjhunu, Tonk, and Jodhpur.

2. **Granite excavation based on E-Ravanna data**

The table presents data on Granite Extraction based on E-Ravanna over a period of six fiscal years:

Table 1 - Granite Extraction based on E-Ravanna data		
FY	Net Weight (MT)	Royalty(Rs)
2017 - 2018	18,25,705	43,72,32,658
2018 - 2019	52,44,954	1,22,53,26,408
2019 - 2020	58,53,839	1,37,12,20,724
2020 - 2021	66,50,774	1,53,58,15,474
2021 - 2022	82,35,330	2,23,41,99,124
2022 - 2023	89,34,986	2,58,22,25,509

The table shows the amount of granite extracted (measured in Metric Tons) and the corresponding royalty revenue generated (measured in Indian Rupees) during each fiscal year.

The data highlights a notable increase in both the net weight of granite extracted and the royalty revenue collected over the years. This indicates a significant growth in granite mining activities and its demand in various industries and construction projects.

Between 2017 - 2018 and 2022 - 2023, the net weight of granite extraction has surged from 18,25,705 MT to 89,34,986 MT, displaying a substantial rise in production. Similarly, the royalty revenue generated has seen substantial growth, increasing from Rs.43,72,32,658 in 2017 - 2018 to Rs. 2,58,22,25,509 in 2022 - 2023, reflecting the increasing value and economic importance of granite extraction in Rajasthan.

The data suggests a positive trend in the granite industry, driven by rising demand, increased mining activities, and enhanced revenue generation for the government through royalty payments.

3. District - wise granite mining extraction Net Weight in (MT) - Top ten districts

The table provided represents the excavation of granite by various districts over five consecutive years. The data is presented in tabular form with each row corresponding to a specific district, and each column representing a different financial year. This data could be used to analyze trends in granite excavation over the years for each district, identify growth patterns, and make comparisons between different districts' excavation activities.

Table 2 - Excavation of granite by top ten districts over five consecutive years
Net Weight in (MT)

District	2018 - 2019	2019 - 2020	2020 - 2021	2021 - 2022	2022 - 2023
RAJSAMAND	6,86,976	8,66,801	12,64,406	17,30,483	17,83,006
BHILWARA	10,31,987	10,40,743	11,91,445	13,00,894	11,12,452
PALI	8,85,886	9,81,504	9,37,308	10,67,846	11,81,926
SIROHI	9,41,929	8,84,491	8,17,141	9,21,671	10,30,997
AJMER	4,29,491	6,22,280	7,27,070	7,86,542	7,52,045
JALORE	6,17,184	6,50,405	4,06,193	5,28,006	6,38,327
TONK	68,742	91,735	3,10,741	5,78,350	7,10,692
BARMER	3,34,136	3,35,609	3,27,173	2,97,690	3,34,398
JAIPUR	40,359	77,984	93,691	1,60,122	1,95,096
JAISALMER	1,49,709	1,13,566	74,590	1,17,963	99,134

The table provides information on the granite excavation in metric tonnes for each district over the given years. For instance, in the district of Rajsamand, the excavation quantities have increased from 6,86,976 metric tonnes in 2018 - 2019 to 17,83,006 metric tonnes in 2022 - 2023. Similarly, the other districts also show varying trends in granite excavation over the five - year period.

Overall, most districts showed an increasing trend in granite production, with a few experiencing minor fluctuations. Jaipur and Tonk stood out with significant growth in production over the years. However, Bhilwara and Jaisalmer experienced some decline in production in certain years.

4. District - wise royalty collection of granite - top ten Districts

The district - wise royalty collection data shows varying trends, with some districts experiencing consistent growth, while others display fluctuations in revenue generation. The overall picture suggests that several districts have seen positive development in royalty collections, contributing to the economic growth of the region. However, some districts may require further analysis to understand the reasons behind the fluctuations in revenue over the years.

The table provides information on the district - wise royalty collection for five consecutive years.

(in Crores)

District	2018 - 2019	2019 - 2020	2020 - 2021	2021 - 2022	2022 - 2023
RAJSAMAND	16	20	30	47	52
BHILWARA	24	24	28	36	32
PALI	21	23	22	29	34
SIROHI	22	21	19	25	30
AJMER	10	15	17	21	22
JALORE	14	15	10	14	18
TONK	2	2	7	16	21
BARMER	8	8	8	8	10
JAIPUR	1	2	2	4	6
JAISALMER	3	3	2	3	3

The table provided displays the district - wise royalty collection in crore rupees for five consecutive years. The table provides understanding of the trends and patterns in royalty collections for each district.

Rajsamand shows a consistent increase in royalty collection over the years, starting from 16 crore rupees in 2018 - 2019 and reaching 52 crore rupees in 2022 - 2023. This indicates a positive growth trend for the district.

Bhilwara royalty collection remained relatively stable from 2018 - 2019 to 2020 - 2021, and then decreased slightly in the subsequent years. This suggests that the district's royalty revenue saw a minor fluctuation but overall maintained a steady pattern.

Pali royalty collection witnessed a gradual increase over the years, starting from 21 crore rupees in 2018 - 2019 and reaching 34 crore rupees in 2022 - 2023. The district's revenue growth indicates positive development in terms of royalty generation.

Sirohi experienced fluctuations in royalty collection during the five years. While there was a decrease in 2020 - 2021, the revenue picked up again in the following years, ending at 30 crore rupees in 2022 - 2023.

Ajmer royalty revenue showed a consistent growth trend over the five - year period, starting at 10 crore rupees and reaching 22 crore rupees in 2022 - 2023. This reflects positive development in royalty collections.

Jalore saw a dip in royalty collection in 2020 - 2021, but it recovered in the subsequent years, ending at 18 crore rupees in 2022 - 2023.

Tonk experienced a significant increase in royalty collection, with the revenue growing from 2 crore rupees in 2018 - 2019 to 21 crore rupees in 2022 - 2023. This indicates substantial growth for the district.

Barmer royalty collection remained relatively stable over the years, showing a consistent revenue of around 8 - 10 crore rupees.

Jaipur royalty revenue started from a low value of 1 crore rupee in 2018 - 2019, but it showed gradual growth, reaching 6 crore rupees in 2022 - 2023.

Jaisalmer royalty collection remained constant at around 3 crore rupees throughout the five - year period.

5. Types of Granite in Rajasthan

Rajasthan, a state in India, is renowned for its abundant natural stone resources. Various types of dimensional stones are produced in the region, serving construction, architectural, and decorative purposes. Here are the common types of stone found in Rajasthan:

Sandstone: Rajasthan is famous for its high - quality sandstone available in various colors such as red, beige, pink, and yellow. This versatile stone is widely used for construction, cladding, and landscaping. The state holds the largest deposits of sandstone in India, with estimated reserves of around 1,500 million tonnes, accounting for approximately 90% of India's total sandstone reserves.

Marble: Rajasthan boasts some of the world's finest marble, including the renowned Makrana marble, known for its whiteness, purity, and durability. Marble from the state is utilized for flooring, wall cladding, and sculptures. Rajasthan's marble reserves are estimated to be around 1,100 million tonnes, making up about 93% of India's total marble reserves.

Granite: Rajasthan is a significant producer of granite, a robust and durable stone widely used for kitchen countertops, flooring, and wall cladding. The state holds reserves of around 800 million tonnes of granite, which constitutes approximately 60% of India's total granite reserves.

Slate: Rajasthan produces a variety of slate stones in colors like black, green, and gray. These slate stones find application in roofing, flooring, and wall cladding.

Overall, Rajasthan's abundant natural stone resources, including sandstone, marble, granite, and slate, contribute significantly to the construction and architectural industries, not only in India but also globally.

It is important to note that these are estimated reserves, and the actual reserves may vary depending on various factors such as the quality of the stone, the depth of the reserves, and the level of exploration and mining activities in the region.

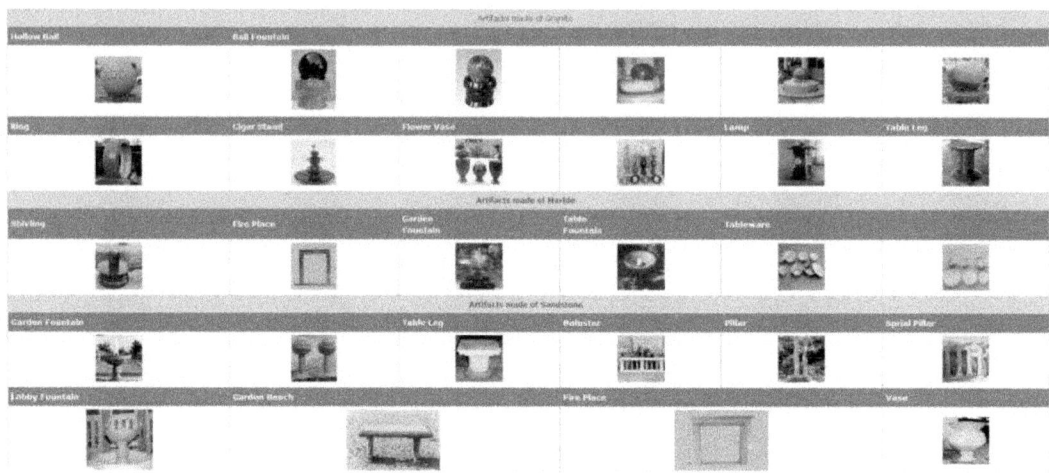

The production of these stones is carried out through a combination of mechanized and manual techniques, depending on the type of stone and its application. The stones are extracted from quarries using machinery and tools such as drilling machines, diamond wire saws, and excavators. Once the stones are extracted, they are cut, polished, and finished by skilled craftsmen to produce high - quality dimensional stones that are ready for use in construction and decoration.

Rajasthan is well - known for its vast reserves of granite. Rajasthan accounts for a significant portion of India's granite production, and the state has many granite quarries that are actively mined. Some of the popular granite varieties found in Rajasthan include Imperial Red, Jhansi Red, Lakha Red, Merry Gold, and Desert Brown. These granite varieties are widely used for both domestic and commercial purposes, including flooring, wall cladding, countertops, and monuments.

i. Imperial Red Granite: This is a popular red - colored granite with black and white flecks that is quarried in the Jalore district of Rajasthan.

ii. Jhansi Red Granite: This is a deep red - colored granite with black and white speckles that is quarried in the Jhansi district of Rajasthan.

iii. Lakha Red Granite: This is a bright red granite with black and white speckles that is quarried in the Sikar district of Rajasthan.

iv. Merry Gold Granite: This is a yellow - colored granite with black and white speckles that is quarried in the Jalore district of Rajasthan.

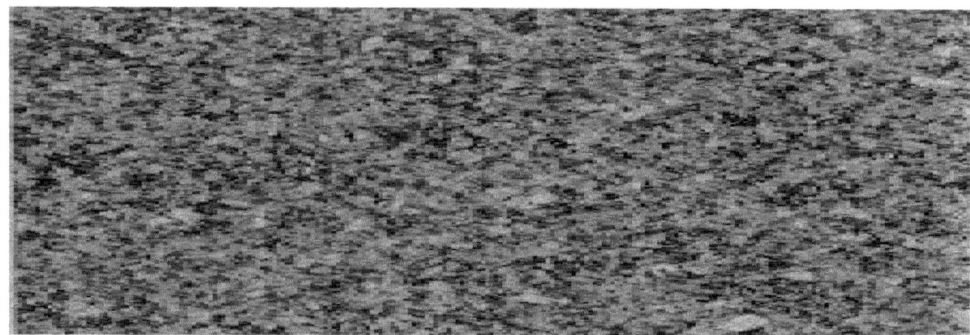

v. Desert Brown Granite: This is a brown - colored granite with black and white speckles that is quarried in the Jalore district of Rajasthan.

vi. Black Galaxy Granite: This is a black - colored granite with golden speckles that is quarried in the Chittoor district of Andhra Pradesh but processed and exported from Rajasthan.

6. Usages of Granite –

Granite is a versatile material that is used in many industries due to its durability, strength, and aesthetic appeal.

Granite is a remarkable natural stone with a wide range of applications across various industries, owing to its durability and versatility. Let's explore some common uses of granite:

Construction: Granite is a preferred building material for construction projects, including buildings, bridges, monuments, and roads. Its strength and durability make it an excellent choice for structures that require long - lasting performance.

Countertops: In homes and commercial spaces, granite is a popular choice for kitchen and bathroom countertops. Its heat resistance, durability, and beautiful appearance add elegance to the space.

Flooring: Granite is commonly used as a flooring material in homes, hotels, and commercial buildings. Its natural beauty and toughness make it perfect for areas with high foot traffic, ensuring long - lasting and attractive floors.

Landscaping: Granite finds its place in landscaping projects for creating pathways, walls, and decorative features. Its presence adds a touch of elegance and functionality to outdoor spaces. Granite is also used as a natural stone for decorative elements in gardens and parks.

Memorials: Due to its ability to withstand the elements and retain its appearance over time, granite is a preferred choice for creating memorials and monuments. It serves as a lasting tribute to loved ones and historical figures.

Art and Decoration: Granite's unique colors and textures make it a favored material for sculptures, decorative items, and art projects. Its aesthetic appeal allows artists to create intricate and eye - catching pieces.

In summary, granite's durability, strength, and aesthetic appeal make it an invaluable resource across multiple industries. From construction and countertops to landscaping and art, granite's versatility ensures it remains a popular choice for a wide array of applications.

7. Sculpture (Memorials, Modern Art & Decoration) using latest technology–

Rajasthan holds a rich heritage of stone sculpture and carving, and in recent times, modern technologies have been seamlessly integrated to enhance these traditional techniques.

1. CNC (Computer Numerical Control) Machines: One of the cutting - edge technologies used is CNC machines. These machines utilize computer programs to precisely carve stone based on predetermined designs. The advantage is that intricate and complex designs can be achieved with a high level of accuracy and efficiency. CNC technology allows artists to bring their visions to life with incredible detail and precision.

2. 3D Printing: Another modern technology revolutionizing stone carving is 3D printing. Artists can now create designs on a computer and then print them layer by layer using stone material. This opens up new possibilities for crafting intricate and detailed sculptures that were once challenging or even impossible with traditional methods. 3D printing has sparked creativity and enabled sculptors to explore uncharted territories in their art.

In Rajasthan, numerous stone carving and sculpture workshops have embraced these modern technologies alongside traditional techniques. This harmonious blend has not only preserved the timeless art form but also provided artists with exciting new avenues for creative expression.

The blend of modern technology and traditional craftsmanship has brought about a new beginning in stone carving and sculpture. It has enabled artists to preserve their cultural heritage while taking on the advancements of the digital era. Today, stone sculptures stand as exquisite pieces of art, be it intricate memorials, contemporary masterpieces, or decorative marvels, all enriched by the synergy of old and new techniques. The infusion of modern technologies into stone carving has breathed new life into this ancient art form in Rajasthan. The result is a vibrant and relevant expression of creativity that honors the past while taking on the possibilities of the future.

Type of Stone Sculpture

In modern - day India, stone sculpture manufacturing continues to be an important art form, with a range of traditional and contemporary styles.

i. Hand - carved stone sculpture: Many stone sculptures in India are still made by hand, using traditional techniques and tools. These sculptures are typically carved from a single block of stone, such as marble, granite, or sandstone, and can range in size from small statues to large monuments.

ii. Machine - carved stone sculpture: With the advent of modern machinery, some stone sculptures in India are now created using automated carving techniques. These machines use computer - controlled tools to carve complex shapes and designs into stone blocks.

iii. 3D printing of stone sculpture: In recent years, 3D printing technology has also been used to create stone sculptures in India. This technique allows for highly detailed and intricate designs to be printed in stone, using a range of materials such as sandstone, marble, and granite.

iv. Contemporary stone sculpture: While many stone sculptures in India are still made in traditional styles, there is also a growing movement of contemporary stone sculptors who are pushing the boundaries of the art form. These artists use a range of styles and techniques to create unique and innovative stone sculptures that explore modern themes and ideas.

Machine Curved   Hand Curved   3D Printing

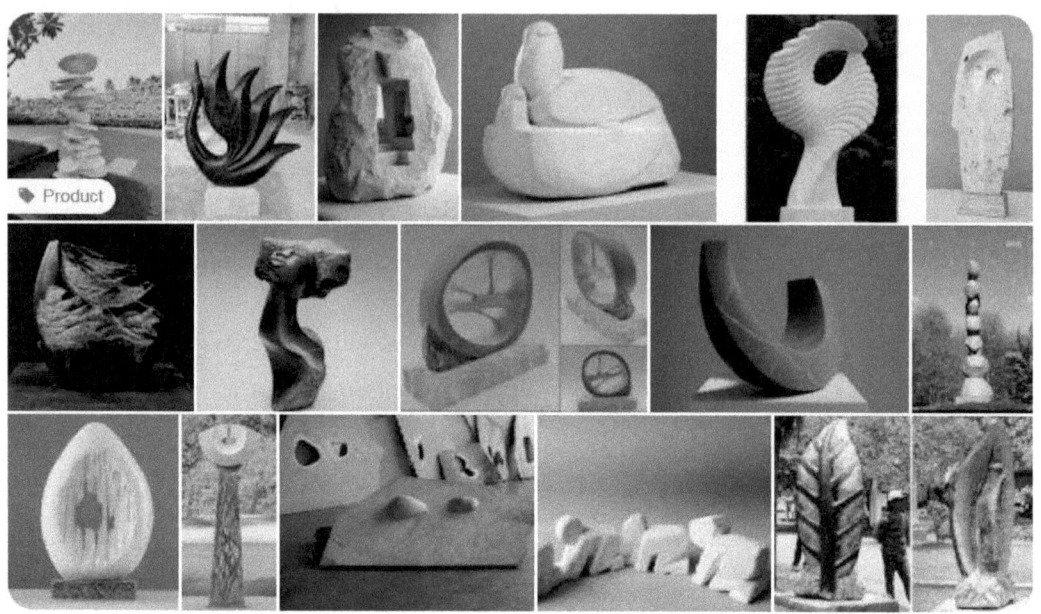

Contemporary Stone Sculpture

Overall, stone sculpture manufacturing in modern - day India is a vibrant and diverse industry, with a range of traditional and innovative techniques being used to create beautiful and inspiring works of art.

Some finest latest examples of sculpture are Statue of Subhas Chandra Bose, Vishwas Swaroopam (Statue of Belief) etc

8. Government of Rajasthan Initiatives

The government of Rajasthan has taken several initiatives in recent years to promote the growth of the granite industry in the state. Some of the latest initiatives are:

1. Granite Policy 2020: The Rajasthan government has launched a new granite policy in 2020 that aims to promote the sustainable development of the granite industry in the state. The policy includes measures to encourage investments, promote exports, and ensure environmental sustainability.

Key features of RIPS scheme 2022 Under MSMEs - All incentives for MSMEs will be capped annually at INR 5 Crore

> Investment Subsidy of 75% of State tax due and deposited for a period of seven years from the date of commencement of commercial production. Additionally, Interest subsidy for 5 years will be provided as per the following matrix

Loan Amount*	Interest Subsidy per year
1 - 5 Crores	6%
5 - 10 Crores	4%
1 - 15 Crores	3%

- Exemption from payment of 100% of Electricity Duty for seven years;
- Exemption from payment of 100% of Land Tax for seven years;
- Exemption from payment of 100% of Market Fee (Mandi Fee) for seven years;
- Exemption from payment of 100% of Stamp Duty
- Reimbursement of 50% of employers' contribution towards EPF and ESI, for seven year

Green Incentives

a) Water Conservation and Waste Management Subsidy in the form of Reimbursement

   i. 50% of cost incurred on water audit by any Government empanelled or Government approved agency subject to maximum of rupees two lakh;

   ii. 50% of amount paid to the suppliers for the plant, excluding civil work, for establishing zero liquid discharge based effluent treatment plant;

   iii. Waste Management – 50% of amount paid to the suppliers for the plant, excluding civil work, for establishing ZLD based ETP, adopting green building measures & establishing industrial reduce, reuse, recycle plant up to 1 crore

Other Incentives

- Quality Certification Incentive - One - time reimbursement of 50% of cost incurred in obtaining quality certification for manufacturing or processes or certification related to export, issued by any Government agency or any agency authorized by Government of India or Government of Rajasthan, subject to maximum of INR twenty - five lakh

- IP Creation Incentive - Subsidy up to 75% of the cost of acquiring patents up to INR 5 lacs to be provided. For obtaining geographical identification & trademark registration, the State will match the financial assistance provided by Government of India

- Fund Raising Incentive - One - time financial assistance on raising funds (capital) through SME platform, to the extent of 50% of the investment made in process of raising funds (capital), subject to a maximum of five lakh

Startup Booster Incentives –

- Asset Creation Incentives - Investment Subsidy of 75% of State tax due and deposited for a period of seven years from the date of commencement of commercial production.

- Seed Support - In sectors identified as "Sunrise Sectors", one - time financial assistance of 10% of external capital raised to be provided up to INR 30 Lakh

- 100% exemption of electricity duty, mandi fee & land taxes for 7 years

- 100% Stamp Duty benefit will be given in stages as notified by the State

- 100% conversion charges benefits given in stages as notified by the State

2. Simplified Procedures: The Rajasthan government has simplified the procedures for the grant of mining leases and other approvals required for granite mining and processing. This has helped to reduce the time and cost involved in setting up new granite mining and processing units in the state.

3. Infrastructure Development: The government of Rajasthan is investing in infrastructure development to support the growth of the granite industry. The state government has taken several steps to improve road connectivity, power supply, and other infrastructure facilities in the granite mining areas.

4. Skill Development: The Rajasthan government has launched various skill development programs to train and upskill the workforce engaged in the granite industry. The government is working with training institutes and

industry associations to provide training programs in areas such as mining, processing, and polishing.

5. Promotion of Export: The Rajasthan government is promoting the export of granite to increase the demand for the state's granite products in international markets. The government is participating in trade fairs and exhibitions to showcase the state's granite products and attract foreign buyers.

Stone Mart 2022 is a biennial international trade fair and exhibition focused on the stone industry, held in Jaipur, Rajasthan, India. Stone Mart 2022, is held on February 3 - 6, 2022, at the Jaipur Exhibition and Convention Center (JECC).

Stone Mart 2022 provided a platform for stone industry professionals from all over the world to showcase their latest products, technologies, and services. It is also offered an opportunity for buyers and sellers to connect and network with each other. The exhibition feature a wide range of natural stones, including marble, granite, sandstone, limestone, slate, and quartzite, as well as products and services related to the stone industry such as machinery, tools, accessories, and chemicals. The exhibition is expected to attract exhibitors and visitors from various countries, including India, Italy, Turkey, China, Egypt, Spain, and many more. Stone Mart 2022 is an excellent platform for stone industry professionals to explore new business opportunities, discover new trends and innovations, and expand their business networks.

Overall, the Rajasthan government is taking proactive steps to promote the growth of the granite industry in the state and create a favorable business environment for investors and entrepreneurs.

9. Study of top granite products based on last four years E-Way bill analysis

During study of E-Way bills focusing on Granite based products, it was identified that there were some products that are supplied from Rajasthan, meaning thereby these products are produced in Rajasthan. Top Two products identified are as follows:

Worked monumental or building stone (except slate) and articles thereof

value in Lakh

FY	Export	Import	Intra State	Inward	Outward
2018 - 2019	70,402	6,028	1,00,218	63,821	1,97,349
2019 - 2020	89,566	9,812	1,41,240	81,728	2,19,469
2020 - 2021	1,24,556	5,100	1,85,937	87,607	2,40,750
2021 - 2022	1,43,449	7,934	2,28,975	1,11,233	3,36,236

The table pertains to "Worked monumental or building stone (except slate) and articles thereof," and it shows the value of exports, imports, intra - state, inward, and outward transactions in Lakh for four financial years.

The value of exports for worked monumental or building stone has shown a consistent increase over the years, starting from 70,402 Lakh in 2018 - 2019 and reaching 1,43,449 Lakh in 2021 - 2022. This indicates a positive growth trend in export demand for these stone products.

The import value remains relatively stable over the years, with a slight increase from 6,028 Lakh in 2018 - 2019 to 7,934 Lakh in 2021 - 2022. This suggests a consistent demand for certain stone products that are not sufficiently met by domestic production.

The value of intra - state transactions for worked stone has steadily increased over the years. Starting from 1,00,218 Lakh in 2018 - 2019, it reached 2,28,975 Lakh in 2021 - 2022. This indicates a growing demand for these products within the state itself.

The value of inward transactions has experienced steady growth over the years, from 63,821 Lakh in 2018 - 2019 to 1,11,233 Lakh in 2021 - 2022. This suggests an increasing inflow of these stone products into the region.

Outward transactions have also shown consistent growth, rising from 1,97,349 Lakh in 2018 - 2019 to 3,36,236 Lakh in 2021 - 2022. This indicates an expanding outflow of these stone products from the region.

The data reflects a positive trend in the trade of worked monumental or building stone in the region, with consistent growth in exports, intra - state, inward, and outward transactions. The stable imports indicate a balance between domestic production and import requirements. This analysis highlights the significant economic contribution of the stone industry and its growing demand both within the state and in the global market.

1. Granite, porphyry, basalt, sandstone and other monumental or building stone, whether or not roughly trimmed or merely cut, by sawing or otherwise, into blocks or slabs of a square or rectangular shape

value in Lakh

FY	Export	Import	Intra State	Inward	Outward
2018 - 2019	64,848	152	99,859	40,582	1,05,730
2019 - 2020	56,061	346	1,09,673	34,271	90,345
2020 - 2021	47,102	827	1,59,818	25,347	91,128
2021 - 2022	42,670	1,190	1,58,572	27,218	96,593

The table represents the HSN code 2516, which includes "Granite, porphyry, basalt, sandstone, and other monumental or building stone, whether or not roughly trimmed or merely cut, by sawing or otherwise, into blocks or slabs of a square or rectangular shape." It displays the value of exports, imports, intra - state, inward, and outward transactions in Lakh for four financial years. The "Grand Total" row shows the cumulative values for the entire period.

The export value for granite and other monumental stone has shown a fluctuating trend over the years. It started at 64,848 Lakh in 2018 - 2019, decreased to 42,670 Lakh in 2021 - 2022, but still, the cumulative exports for the four years amounted to a substantial 2,10,681 Lakh .

The import value for the specified stone category has remained relatively low and consistent over the years, ranging from 152 Lakh in 2018 - 2019 to 1,190 Lakh in 2021 - 2022.

The value of intra - state transactions for granite and other monumental stones has increased consistently over the years, from 99,859 Lakh in 2018 - 2019 to 1,58,572 Lakh in 2021 - 2022, contributing significantly to the overall trade.

The value of inward transactions has shown a consistent growth trend, reaching 27,218 Lakh in 2021 - 2022. This indicates an increasing inflow of granite and other monumental stones into the region.

The outward transactions have also increased consistently over the years, with a value of 96,593 Lakh in 2021 - 2022, indicating a growing outflow of these stone products from the region.

The data indicates a dynamic and thriving trade for granite, porphyry, basalt, sandstone, and other monumental or building stone in the region. The growth in intra - state and outward transactions reflects an increasing demand for these stone products, both within the region and in the global market. The cumulative values affirm the industry's significance in contributing to the overall economy and showcasing the enduring appeal of these natural stones in construction and other applications.

Granite Export

value in Lakh

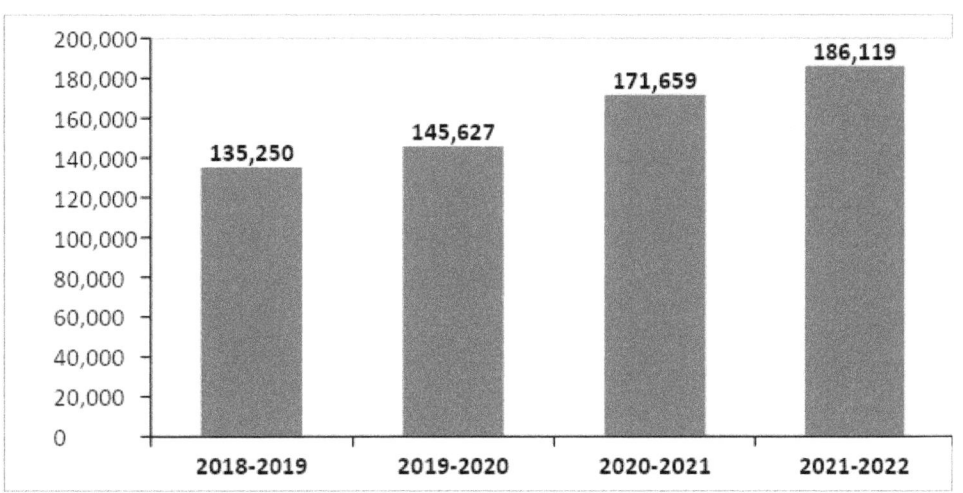

1. Granite exports: According to data from the Ministry of Commerce and Industry, Karnataka is the largest exporter of granite in India, accounting for 38% of total granite exports in 2020 - 21. Rajasthan, on the other hand, accounted for 9% of total granite exports in the same period.
2. Value of exports: The value of granite exports from Karnataka was much higher than that of Rajasthan in 2020 - 21. Karnataka exported granite worth $1.16 billion, while Rajasthan exported granite worth $217 million.
3. Major export destinations: The major export destinations for granite from Karnataka include the United States, the United Kingdom, and Germany. For Rajasthan, the major export destinations are the United States, the United Kingdom, and China.
4. Variety of granite: Karnataka produces a wider variety of granite than Rajasthan, including black, pink, gray, and white varieties. Rajasthan primarily produces pink and red varieties of granite.

10. Exploring New Avenues in Marble and Granite Industry:

A - Class Marble has embraced the rising global demand for luxurious marble and stone by venturing into innovative applications. While marble was traditionally used for flooring, walls, and bathrooms, designers are now exploring unique avenues such as furniture, panels, and facades. A - Class continually reinvents marble to align with contemporary design trends, making it a symbol of luxury for prominent architects and interior designers. It finds its place in various typologies, including luxury homes, farmhouses, hotels, showrooms, corporate offices, clubs, and malls.

In contrast, the granite industry in Rajasthan has historically focused on quarrying, processing raw blocks, and crafting artifacts. However, to diversify and expand its business, the granite industry can explore several potential new verticals:

Granite Tiles and Slabs: Producing polished granite tiles and slabs can be a lucrative venture. These products find extensive applications in construction and interior design, catering to both domestic and international markets.

Granite Monuments and Memorials: Specializing in granite monuments and memorials can be a rewarding niche. These products have significant demand in the funeral services industry, and Rajasthan's cultural heritage provides a unique advantage in this field.

Granite Countertops: Venturing into granite countertops for kitchens and bathrooms can be a high - value opportunity. The demand for these products in the home renovation and remodeling sector can ensure stable revenue.

Granite Sculptures: Exploring the production of granite sculptures and statues is a potential niche market. The demand for such products in the art and decor industry, coupled with Rajasthan's stone carving tradition, can create a competitive edge.

Granite Landscaping Products: Manufacturing granite landscaping products like paving stones, curbstones, and garden stones can provide sustainable revenue. These products are sought after in the landscaping and outdoor decor industry.

The granite industry in Rajasthan has various promising verticals to explore and expand its business. Leveraging its cultural heritage, skilled workforce, and access to high - quality raw materials, the industry can become a leader in these new avenues. By embracing innovation and meeting contemporary demands, the marble and granite industries can continue to flourish and contribute to the ever - evolving world of design and construction.

Key Challenges in the Granite Industry in Rajasthan

Lack of Modern Technology: The industry's heavy reliance on traditional methods of extraction and processing hinders its competitiveness compared to countries with advanced modern techniques. Adopting modern technology can improve efficiency and productivity.

Labour Issues: The industry's dependence on manual labor poses challenges due to low wages, unsafe working conditions, and a shortage of skilled workers. Addressing these issues is essential for maintaining a skilled and motivated workforce.

Environmental Concerns: Granite extraction can have adverse effects on the environment, leading to land degradation and water pollution. The industry must adopt sustainable practices and responsible mining to minimize its ecological footprint.

Infrastructure Challenges: Inadequate transportation and logistics infrastructure can result in delays and increased costs for product transportation. Improving infrastructure facilities can enhance the industry's ability to reach markets more efficiently.

Competition from Other Regions: While Rajasthan is a major producer of granite, it faces stiff competition from other regions within India and globally, particularly from countries like China and Brazil. To stay competitive, the industry needs to differentiate its products based on quality, uniqueness, and competitive pricing.

Overcoming these challenges will be critical for the granite industry in Rajasthan to maintain its position as a leading producer and exporter of granite. Embracing modern technology, ensuring fair labor practices, adopting sustainable mining practices, improving infrastructure, and enhancing product differentiation can pave the way for a thriving and sustainable future for the industry.

11. Key Policy Comparison between the Government of Rajasthan and Other States for Granite Industry

Additional Package of Incentives and Concession for Export: Rajasthan offers a comprehensive incentive package to boost exports for new MSME export enterprises. It includes 100% electricity tax exemption for eligible businesses and a performance subsidy of 1% of FOB value (up to INR 10,000 Lakh) for MSMEs that double their exports in subsequent years. Similar incentives are provided for bank charges, certification charges, and ECGC charges. It is essential to compare these incentives with those offered by other states to attract and retain businesses in Rajasthan.

Export Promotion Measures: Rajasthan focuses on creating export infrastructure and logistics to facilitate trade. Participation in international trade fairs, awareness campaigns for export promotion, and global market intelligence are emphasized to enhance the export capabilities of businesses in the state. It is crucial to evaluate how these measures align with or differ from export promotion initiatives in other states.

Sarthak Scheme: The proposed 'Sarthak' scheme aims to support the granite industry through an online technology platform and the establishment of a Centre of Excellence (CoE). The platform will provide services such as improved market access, access to credit, dissemination of quality control standards, and technology adoption. The CoE will offer technology acceleration programs, funding assistance, and next - generation manufacturing technical support. Comparing the 'Sarthak' scheme with similar schemes implemented in other states can provide insights into its effectiveness and uniqueness.

District Industrial Cluster Development Program: Rajasthan's focus on product - specific industrial cluster development aims to increase production capacities by creating dedicated manufacturing clusters. Comparing this program with similar initiatives in other states can help determine its impact on the granite industry's competitiveness and growth.

12. Suggested Initiatives and Plans for Granite Industry in Rajasthan

Establishment of Industries: Identifying opportunities for new granite - based industries, encouraging the adoption of modern technologies in stone carving and sculpture, and developing dedicated corridors with required facilities can boost the industry's growth.

Cluster - based Approach: Implementing cluster development programs to enhance productivity and competitiveness, providing quality infrastructure through government and private partnerships, and supporting technology up - gradation for small - scale industries can improve the overall performance of the granite industry.

Granite Cluster Improvement: Initiatives for cluster modernization and restructuring, support for common facility centers and skill up - gradation centers, along with certificate programs on CNC machines and NC parts, can enhance the industry's capabilities.

Research Institute: Establishing a dedicated research institute for modernization and industry development can accelerate technological advancements.

Waste Utilization: Focusing on the gainful utilization of marble and granite waste can promote sustainable practices and reduce environmental impacts.

Export Incentives: Offering additional export incentives to MSMEs can stimulate higher growth rates and competitiveness.

Integrated e - Portal: Creating an integrated e - portal connecting multiple services for MSMEs can streamline processes and improve efficiency.

District Dedicated Clusters: Developing district - dedicated clusters based on specific products can foster specialized growth and competitiveness.

Effective Strategies: Developing competitive and effective strategies, including product - market approaches for target markets, will facilitate strategic trade development and expansion.

By implementing these initiatives and comparing policies with other states, the granite industry in Rajasthan can enhance its competitiveness, sustain growth, and contribute significantly to the state's economic development.

Suggested Initiatives and Plan for Granite Industry –

1. Establishment of industries
    i. Identify scope for new granite - based industries on account of products made likes – Morden arts sculptures, Contemporary sculptures etc
    ii. Increases the uses of modern technologies with traditional methods in stone carving and sculpture to new avenues of artistic expression
    iii. Develop dedicated corridor basis on road connectivity and other required facilities. Jalore's stone business slips, threat on 4 thousand crore industry due to absence of highway
    iv. Single Window Clearance for target industries
    v. Easy and accessible financing schemes for new enterprises with dedicated bank branches

2. Cluster based approach for Granite industries
    i. Cluster development for enhancing productivity and competitiveness as well as capacity building of micro and small enterprise
    ii. Enhance competitiveness of domestic industry by providing quality infrastructure through Government and Private Partnership approach for select clusters with potential to become globally competitive
    iii. Technology up gradation of small - scale industry by providing upfront capital

3. Initiatives for Granite cluster improvement
    i. Initiatives for cluster modernization and restructuring
    ii. Support to setup common facility centers
    iii. Support for setting up skill upgradation centers

iv. Provided Certificate Program on CNC Machines and NC Part to

4. A dedicated research institute is essential for modernization as well as development of the industry

5. Utilization of marble and granite waste – Gainful utilization of stone wate and slurry

6. More Export incentives to MSMEs for more growth rate

7. Creating Integrated e - portal to connecting multiple services for MSMEs

8. Creating district dedicated clusters based on products specific

9. Approach to build competitive and effective strategies –

Product - Market approach being applied to estimate growth rates for exports of each of the product groups. The existing and potential markets for each of the product groups to be identified and estimated import scenarios.

For each of the product groups, separate strategies to be built for existing and new markets. The approach used is to clearly identify in which of the markets the State is required to aggressively harvest the advantages and market linkages and where pioneering efforts are needed to develop the trade.

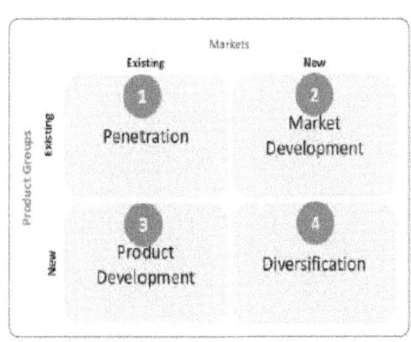 

Product - Market grid approach to build growth strategiesIllustration of stack up of exports in a product group

These strategies are supported by effective action plans to address aggressively by building on existing strengths and mitigating weaknesses in the State's infrastructure and trade promotion. Soft and hard interventions should also be planned to keep the State equipped to tap emerging opportunities and effectively face forecasted threats.

References –

https://mines.rajasthan.gov.in/dmgcms/show_archived?menuName=IQjxowdlvrCe;455611;yn1RNErlGVhSJmjz/9r

https://www.samyakexports.com/modern_art/

https://www.thehindu.com/entertainment/art/chiselling-a-new-era/article66110484.ece

https://goachronicle.com/jalores-marble-business-slips-threat-on-4-thousand-crore-industry-due-to-absence-of-highway/

TOP FIVE MAJOR AND MINOR MINERALS IN RAJASTHAN - AN OUTLINE

Brief outline of mines and minerals in Rajasthan

Rajasthan is the leading state in India in respect of availability and variety of minerals. The State has around 81 varieties of minerals, out of which in 57 minerals mining is being done. The area under mining leases/licenses is approximately 1,846 sq km which is only 0.54% of total land cover of the State. The State contributed about 12% to the total value of mineral production in the country. Mining is a major source of employment in the rural and tribal areas of the State, also a major source of revenue to the State exchequer. The mineral based industries are growing vertically and horizontally in the state and play an important role in the socio - economic aspect of the state.

The State is a leading producer of ball clay, calcite, clay, copper ore/conc., feldspar, fireclay, limestone, ochre, phosphorite/rock phosphate and steatite. The State is also an important producer of marble, granite, sandstone & Kota stone of various shades. The State possesses substantial share of the total resources of potash (94%), lead & zinc ore (89%), wollastonite (88%), silver ore (88%), gypsum (82%), ochre (81%), bentonite (75%), fuller's earth (74%), diatomite (72%), feldspar (66%), marble (63%), asbestos (61%), copper ore (54%), calcite (50%), talc/steatite/soapstone (49%), ball clay (38%), rock phosphate (31%), fluorite (29%), and tungsten (27%).

Majority of mining activities of the state are controlled by the State Department of Mines & Geology. Mines and minerals are regulated by MMDR Act, 1957 and MCR 2016 for major minerals and Rajasthan State Minor Mineral Concession Rules, 2017 for minor minerals.

1. Top five Revenue earning Major Mineral in Rajasthan

From the below table, it can observe the trends for the major minerals in Rajasthan in terms of their production per hectare, sale value per ton, and revenue per ton:

Top five Revenue earning Major Mineral in Rajasthan

S. No.	Mineral	Leases (No.)	Area (in Hec.)	Production per Hec.	Production (Lac' Tons)	Sale value per Tons	Sale Value (Rs in Crore)	Revenue (Rs. In Crore.)	Revenue per Ton
1	Lead and Zinc	7	7089.27	429.38	30.44	18872404.73	5744.76	2540.08	8344546.65
2	Limestone	45	21385.35	4051.23	866.37	794178.01	6880.52	716.6	82712.93
3	Silver (By product)	0	0	0	0.0056	55862857142.86	3128.32	239.49	4276607142.86
4	Iron ore	15	2297.06	2075.70	47.68	4645260.07	2214.86	103.92	217953.02
5	Lignite	7	14633.74	700.64	102.53	1954598.65	2004.05	103.65	101092.36
6	Copper Ore	3	706.75	4086.31	28.88	250069.25	72.22	54.88	190027.70

Financial year 2021 - 2022

Lead and Zinc:

The trend for Lead and Zinc shows that they have a relatively moderate production per hectare compared to other minerals on the list. However, the sale value per ton and revenue per ton are significantly higher than other minerals. This suggests that despite lower production levels, the demand and market value for Lead and Zinc are significant, resulting in higher revenues despite the lower production per hectare.

Limestone:

Limestone has the highest production per hectare among all the minerals listed indicating that it is one of the major minerals extracted in significant quantities in Rajasthan. However, its sale value per ton and revenue per ton are comparatively lower. This could be due to its widespread availability and relatively lower demand in comparison to other minerals.

Silver (By product):

Silver is a by-product of zinc and lead mining, the sale value and revenue per ton for Silver are extraordinarily high, indicating that it is a valuable byproduct in Rajasthan's mining activities.

Iron ore:

Iron ore shows a moderate production per hectare and a relatively high sale value per ton, which results in a reasonable revenue per ton. It is an essential mineral with a steady demand in the industrial sector.

Lignite:

Lignite has the lowest production per hectare and a moderate sale value per ton, but its revenue per ton is still reasonable. Lignite is a type of coal, and despite its lower production levels, it still contributes to revenue generation.

Copper Ore:

Copper Ore has a high production per hectare, and while its sale value per ton is not as high as some other minerals, its revenue per ton is still relatively good. Copper is an essential metal used in various industries.

In summary, the trends observed in the table show that Lead and Zinc are highly profitable minerals with high sale values and revenues despite relatively lower production per hectare. Limestone has the highest production but lower sale value and revenue per ton. Silver has exceptionally high sale value and revenue, Iron ore and Copper Ore show moderate to high production and reasonable revenue per ton. Lignite has the lowest production but still manages to generate decent revenue per ton.

2. Top five Revenue earning Minor Mineral in Rajasthan

From the given table, it can observe the trends for the major minerals in Rajasthan in terms of their production per hectare, sale value per ton, and revenue per ton:

Top five Revenue earning Minor Mineral in Rajasthan

S. No.	Mineral	Leases (No.)	Area (in Hectors)	Production per Hec.	Production (Lac' Tons)	Sale value per Tons	Sale Value (Crore' Rs.)	Revenue (Crore' Rs.)	Revenue per Ton
1	Masonry Stone	5848	6553.1	17835.20	1168.76	193659.54	2263.408	515.145	44076.35
2	Granite	1679	3610.4	2436.29	87.96	1947425.18	1712.955	306.594	348560.72
3	Marble	1596	2823.6	3767.56	106.381	1738203.90	1849.112	245.948	231196.30
4	Sandstone	1024	4953.2	2543.84	126.002	872480.18	1099.346	208.7	165631.78
5	Limestone (Burning)	440	10172	1279.32	130.138	353980.11	460.6614	158	121409.90

Masonry Stone:

Masonry stone has a relatively high production per hectare, which suggests that it is one of the significant minor minerals extracted in Rajasthan. The sale value per ton is moderate, resulting in reasonable revenue per ton. This indicates that masonry stone is being utilized and sold at a stable price. It contributes significantly to revenue generation

Granite:

Granite shows a lower production per hectare compared to masonry stone, but the sale value per ton is considerably higher. This leads to a substantial revenue per ton, indicating that granite is a valuable minor mineral resource in Rajasthan. Indicate that granite contributes significantly to revenue of the state.

Granite exhibits a moderate production per hectare, suggesting that it is not as abundant as some other minor minerals. However, the sale value per ton and revenue per ton are relatively high,

Marble:

Marble has a higher production per hectare than granite but lower than masonry stone. The sale value per ton is significant, contributing to good revenue per ton.

This suggests that marble mining is economically beneficial and plays an essential role in Rajasthan's mineral industry.

Sandstone:

Sandstone exhibits a moderate production per hectare and a moderate sale value per ton, leading to a reasonable revenue per ton. Sandstone is relatively abundant in the region and is widely used in construction, which may explain its stable market value.

Limestone (Burning):

Limestone (Burning) has the lowest production per hectare among the listed minerals. However, its sale value per ton is relatively high, resulting in a reasonably good revenue per ton. This suggests that despite lower production levels, limestone (burning) is economically valuable and in demand.

In summary, the trends for the Minor Minerals in Rajasthan indicate that each mineral has a unique position in the market based on its production per hectare, sale value per ton, and revenue per ton. Granite stands out with the highest sale value and revenue per ton, while masonry stone and marble have high production levels and contribute significantly to the revenue. Sandstone and limestone (burning) have moderate production levels but still maintain a stable market value and generate decent revenue per ton.

3. Top five Major Mineral Districts - Revenue

From the given table, it can observe the trends for the top five districts of major minerals in Rajasthan in terms of their production per hectare, sale value per ton, and revenue per ton:

Top five Major Mineral Districts - Revenue

S. No.	District	Leases	Area(in Hectors)	Production per Hec.	Production(Lac' Tons)	Revenue(Crore Rs.)	Revenue Per Ton
1	Bhilwara	11	3364.62	169194916.5	5692766	1349.321	23.70
2	Rajsamand	4	1730.19	52083672.31	901146.49	990.261	109.89
3	Udaipur	7	6304.11	38012518.82	2396351	467.045	19.49
4	Chittorgarh	11	5824.51	572736189.8	33359076.65	285.442	0.86
5	Pali	9	2590	738167335.9	19118534	159.885	0.84

Bhilwara:

Bhilwara stands out as the district with the highest production per hectare, indicating that it is a significant mining area for major minerals in Rajasthan. The revenue generated from Bhilwara is substantial (1349.321 Crore Rs.), and the revenue per ton is relatively higher (23.70 INR) compared to the other districts in the top five. This suggests that the mineral extraction in Bhilwara is economically lucrative.

Rajsamand:

Rajsamand follows Bhilwara in terms of production per hectare and revenue generated. While its production is significantly lower than Bhilwara, the revenue per ton is quite high (109.89 INR), indicating that the minerals extracted in Rajsamand have a high value in the market.

Udaipur:

Udaipur ranks third in terms of production per hectare and revenue. While its production is lower than Bhilwara and Rajsamand, the revenue per ton is relatively moderate (19.49 INR), indicating that the minerals from Udaipur contribute reasonably to the overall revenue from major minerals in Rajasthan.

Chittorgarh:

Chittorgarh has the highest production per hectare among the top five districts, but its revenue per ton is significantly lower (0.86 INR). This suggests that while Chittorgarh produces a large quantity of major minerals, the sale value per ton is relatively low, resulting in a relatively lower revenue contribution.

Pali:

Pali has the highest production per hectare among all the districts listed, but like Chittorgarh, its revenue per ton is quite low (0.84 INR). This means that despite the significant production, the value of minerals extracted in Pali is relatively lower compared to the other top districts.

Overall Trend:

The trends for the top five Major Mineral Districts in Rajasthan indicate that Bhilwara and Rajsamand are the major contributors to revenue, with high revenue per ton. Udaipur follows closely with a moderate revenue per ton. Chittorgarh and

Pali have the highest production per hectare, but their revenue per ton is comparatively low, resulting in a relatively lower revenue contribution compared to the top three districts.

It's essential to consider various factors that can influence these trends, such as the types of minerals mined, their demand in the market, transportation costs, and processing expenses. Nonetheless, this analysis provides an overview of the relative importance of each district in terms of revenue generation from major minerals in Rajasthan.

4. Top five Minor Mineral Districts (in terms of No. of leases)

From the given table, it can observe the trends for the top five districts of major minerals in Rajasthan in terms of their production per hectare, sale value per ton, and revenue per ton.

Top five Minor Mineral Districts - No. of leases

S. No.	District	Leases	Area (in Hectors)	Production per Hec.	Production (Lac' Tons)	Revenue(Crore' Rs.)	Revenue Per Ton
1	Rajsamand	1967	6999.01	129691213.5	9077101	258.927	2.85
2	Bhilwara	1258	10526.82	211337202.6	22247086.91	182.78	0.82
3	Ajmer	1123	3840.94	180099166.5	6917500.925	139.596	2.02
4	Nagour	1045	10691.49	173204557.3	18518147.92	220.391	1.19
5	Jaipur	888	3442	399192853	13740218	96.769	0.70

Rajsamand:

Rajsamand has the highest number of leases among the top five districts, indicating that it is a significant area for minor mineral extraction in Rajasthan. The production per hectare is substantial (129,691,213.5 tons), and the revenue per ton is relatively high (2.85 INR), suggesting that the minerals extracted in Rajsamand are valuable and contribute significantly to revenue.

Bhilwara:

Bhilwara ranks second in terms of the number of leases. It has a higher area compared to Rajsamand, but the production per hectare is also higher (211,337,202.6 tons). However, the revenue per ton is relatively lower (0.82 INR), indicating that the value of minerals in Bhilwara is lower compared to Rajsamand.

Ajmer:

Ajmer holds the third position in terms of the number of leases. Its production per hectare is significant (180,099,166.5 tons), and the revenue per ton is relatively moderate (2.02 INR), suggesting that the minerals in Ajmer have a decent market value.

Nagaur:

Nagaur ranks fourth in the number of leases. It has a higher area compared to the previous districts, and its production per hectare is also substantial (173,204,557.3 tons). The revenue per ton is relatively moderate (1.19 INR), indicating that the value of minerals from Nagaur is moderate.

Jaipur:

Jaipur holds the fifth position in terms of the number of leases. It has a relatively lower area compared to the other top districts, but its production per hectare is the highest (399,192,853 tons). However, the revenue per ton is relatively low (0.70 INR), suggesting that the minerals in Jaipur have a lower market value.

Overall Trend:

The trends for the top five Minor Mineral Districts in Rajasthan (in terms of the number of leases) show that Rajsamand has the highest production per hectare and relatively high revenue per ton, making it a significant contributor to revenue. Bhilwara and Nagaur have substantial production per hectare but relatively lower revenue per ton. Ajmer has moderate production and revenue per ton. Jaipur has the highest production per hectare but the lowest revenue per ton among the top five districts, indicating that despite high production, its minerals have a lower market value.

STATISTICAL ANALYSIS OF ROAD ACCIDENTS IN RAJASTHAN

SNAPSHOT OF KEY ROAD SAFETY INDICATORS - 2021

Number of Road Accidents:	20,951 road accidents	**No. of Registered Vehicles (2021)**	13057269 Vehicles
Number of Fatal Accidents:	9,055 fatal accidents	**Road Accident Rate**	10.4 Accidents per 10,000 Vehicles
Number of Fatalities:	10,043 fatalities	**Road Accident Fatality Rate**	4.9 Fatalities per 10,000 Vehicles
Number of Total Injuries:	19,344 injuries	**Road Accident Risk**	26.4 Accidents per Lakh Population
Road Accident fatality rate :	4.9 per 10,000 Vehicles	**Road Accident Fatality Risk**	12.7 Fatalities per Lakh Population

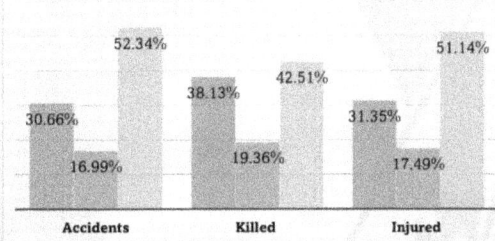

Road-wise Accidents, deaths and Injuries (2021)
*Data from PWD, Rajasthan as on 31.03.2019

Accidents: National Highways 30.66%, State Highways 16.99%, Other Roads 52.34%
Killed: National Highways 38.13%, State Highways 19.36%, Other Roads 42.51%
Injured: National Highways 31.35%, State Highways 17.49%, Other Roads 51.14%

Road Accident Fatalities Distribution by Gender

MALE: 8,920 (88.8%) Fatalities

FEMALE: 1,123 (11.2%) Fatalities

Road Accident Fatalities Distribution by Road User Categories

 12.9% Pedestrians
 10.2% Trucks/Lorries
 40.9% Two-wheelers
 20.8% Cars, Jeeps, Taxis

Road Accident Fatalities Distribution by Age Groups

>18 yrs.	18-25 yrs.	25-35 yrs.	35-45 yrs.	45-60 yrs.	<60 yrs.
3.8%	27.0%	31.1%	22.8%	12.4%	2.4%

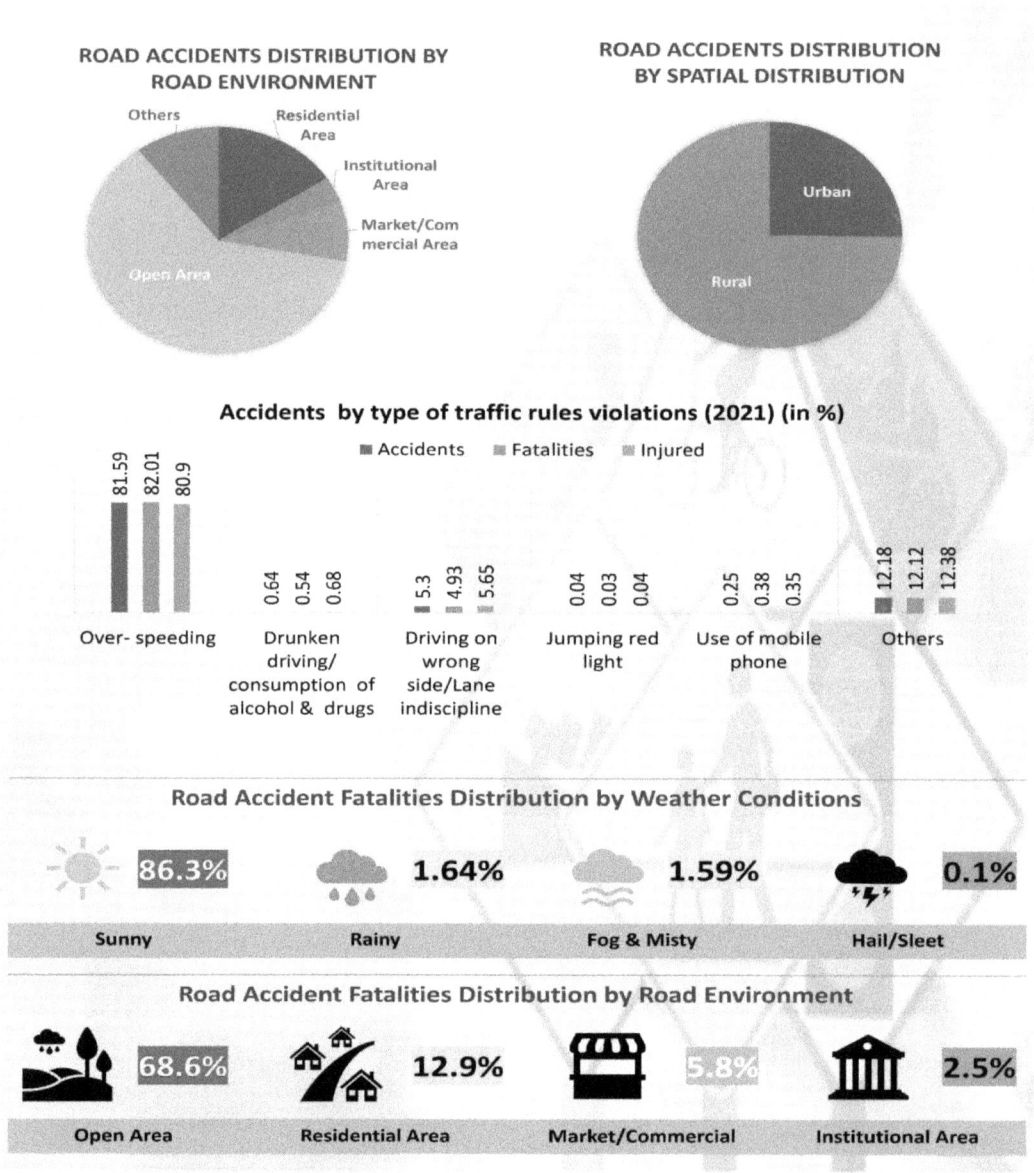

Road accidents have become an area of concern for the State due to its increasing numbers in the past decade with the fatality rate continuously rising and was recorded at 47.9 in the year 2021. The same year 20,951 accidents, 10,043 fatalities and 19,344 injuries were recorded in the State of Rajasthan. Considering these numbers, it became necessary to analyze, predict and curb the impact of these road accidents on the State and its citizens.

1. Coefficient of Determination: R - squared (R^2) is a number between 0 and 1 that measures how well a statistical model predicts an outcome. You can interpret the R^2 as the proportion of variation in the dependent variable that is predicted by the statistical model. We will leverage the capability of this coefficient to predict the variation in number of road accidents, fatalities and injuries based on the data available with us of the State and identify trends and relations among these parameters.

2. Formula for Coefficient of Determination:

Formula: R^2 =1 - [VSS/TSS]

Where, R^2 = Coefficient of Determination

VSS = Sum of Squares of Values

TSS = Total Sum of Squares

The range of R^2 stays between 0 to 1. The value of R^2 determines the chances of future values to follow the same trend as observed from the trend of past values. Closer the value of R^2 is to 1, higher the chances of the same trend being followed in the future.

Coefficient of determination: R^2	Interpretation
0	The model **does not** predict the outcome.
Between 0 and 1	The model **partially** predicts the outcome.
1	The model **perfectly** predicts the outcome.

An R - squared above 0.7 would generally be seen as showing a high level of correlation. Magnitude between 0.4 and 0.7 indicate variables which can be considered moderately correlated. Whereas a measure below 0.4 would show a low correlation. This is not a hard rule, however, and will depend on the specific analysis.

0 to 0.4 Low correlations

0.4 to 0.7 Moderate correlated

0.7 to 1 Strong correlated

R^2 of 0.5 indicated that 50% of the variability in the outcome data cannot be explained by the model.

3. Based on the data available with us from the State report of Rajasthan Status Report on Road Safety - 2021 we were able to identify R^2 trend for the following parameters:

   (i) Year wise share (in percentage) of Fatal Accidents in Total Accidents in Rajasthan

   (ii) Trend in the number of Road Accidents during 2009 to 2021

   (iii) Trend of Fatal Accidents during 2009 - 2021

   (iv) Trend of Persons Killed in Accidents during 2009 - 2021

   (v) Trend of Persons Injured in Accidents during 2009 - 2021

   (vi) Road Accident Risk during year 2011 – 2021 in Rajasthan

   (vii) Trend in number of Persons Killed in Accidents per lakh Population in Rajasthan (Fatality Risk)

   (viii) Trend of number of accidents per 10,000 Vehicles in Rajasthan (Road Accident Rate)

   (ix) Trend in number of Persons killed per 10,000 Vehicles in Rajasthan (Road Accident Fatality Rate)

   (x) Road Accident Density during year 2011 to year 2019

   (xi) Road Accident Fatality Density during year 2011 to year 2019 in Rajasthan

   (xii) Trend of Number of Fatal Accidents by category of roads in Rajasthan (2016 - 2021)

   (xiii) Accidents by Road Categories during Year 2014 to Year 2021

   (xiv) Fatalities by Road Categories in Rajasthan from Year 2014 to Year 2021

   (xv) Injuries by Road Categories In Rajasthan during Year 2014 to Year 2021

4. Detailed Charts reflecting trends with R^2 value:

1) Year wise share (in percentage) of Fatal Accidents in Total Accidents in Rajasthan

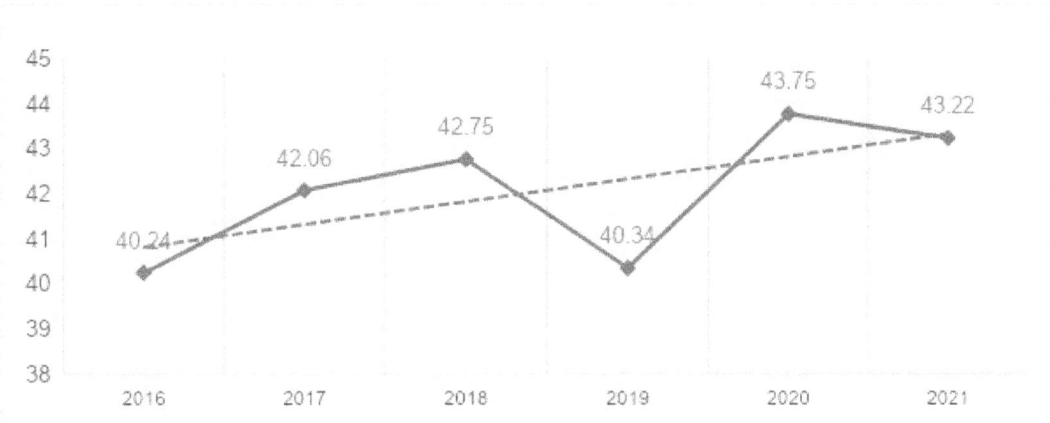

2) Forecasted trend fatal accidents (in percentage) in Rajasthan during year 2016 - 2030

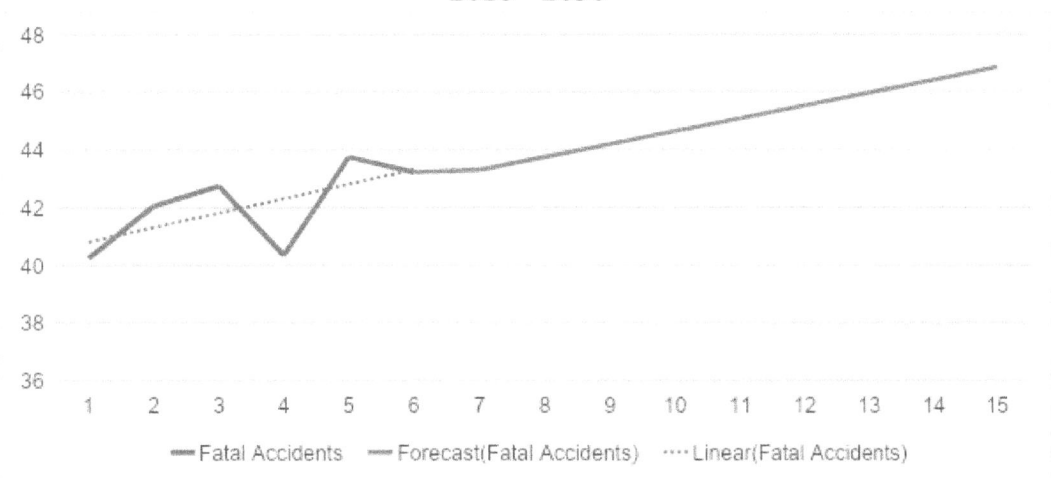

In the above chart (1), fatal accidents from 2016 to 2021 have been depicted. In 2016 the share of fatal accidents in total accidents was 40.24 which has gone up to 43.22 in the year 2021. This indicates a continuous rise in the number of fatal accidents over the years. The reasons for the same can be attributed to construction of more highways with high speed limits, rise in manufacturing and purchase of vehicles and growth in population. However, R^2 value for the same is computed to be 0.4023 which gives moderate confidence on the same trend being followed in the future and percentage share of fatal accidents is projected to be 46.86 percent in the state in 2030. (R^2 value near to 1 gives better confidence of association)

3) Trend in the number of Road Accidents during 2009 to 2021

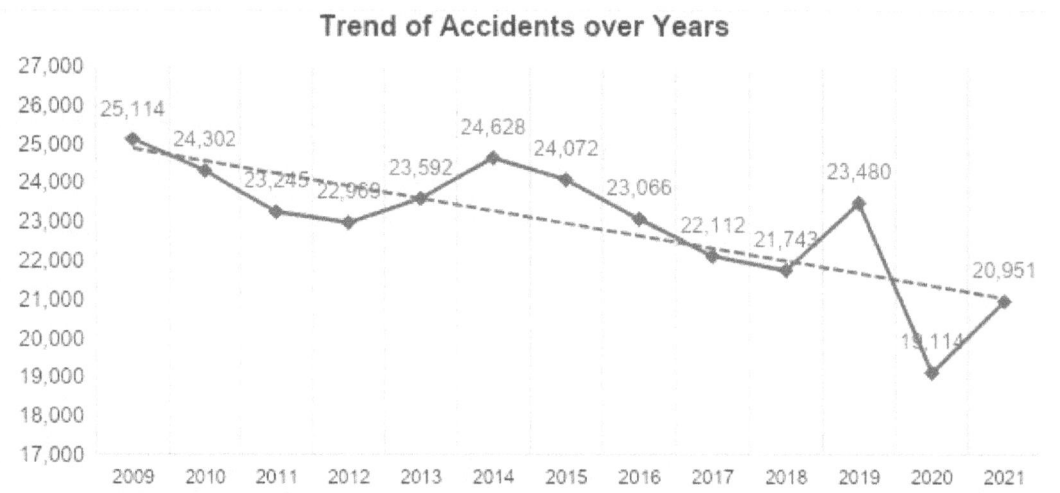

4) Forecasted trend of road accidents in Rajasthan during years 2009 to 2030

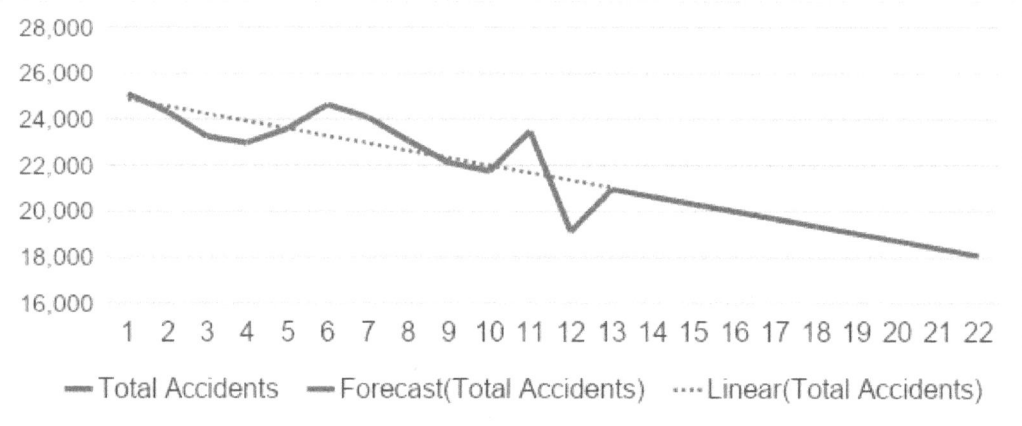

Despite some fluctuations, road accidents depict a general decreasing trend over the years. The number of accidents has decreased from the year 2009 to year 2012 and for the year 2014 to year 2018. In the year 2019, the number of accidents increased and thereafter due to Covid - 19 pandemic it went from 23,480 in the year 2019 to 19,114 in the year 2020. If total accidents in the year 2019 (23,480 accidents) is compared with accidents in the year 2021 (20,951 accidents), it is evident that the total number of accidents have decreased by 13.75%. Few reasons for the decline are increase in traffic rule enforcements, better road infrastructure and public awareness in the past years. The R^2 value of 0.5767 favors the possibility of a similar decrease in the number of accidents in the future as well and shows moderate correlation in the trend of road accidents. Based on the R^2 value it is projected that the state will witness around 18,074 accidents in the year 2030.

5) Trend of Fatal Accidents during 2009 - 2021

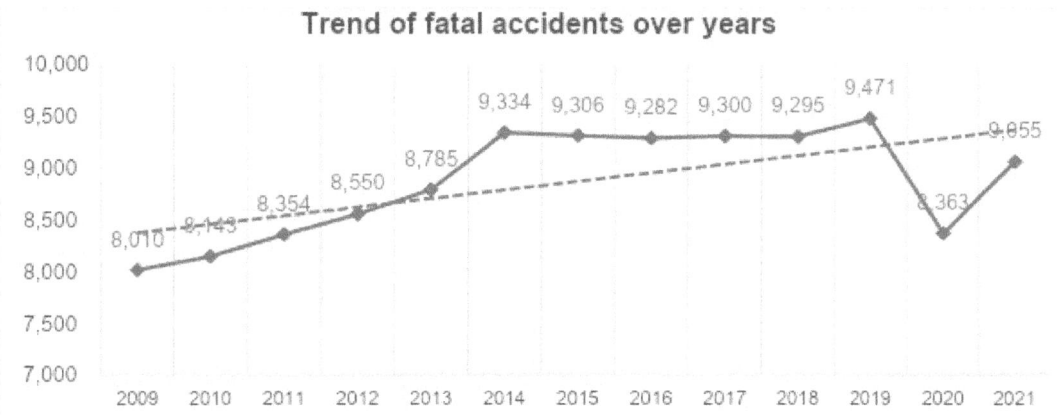

During the study of fatal accidents, it was found that during the years 2009 to 2021, the normal trend of fatal accidents has been on an increasing side. The rise can be accounted for from reasons such as high motorization rate, increased population, advanced roads, and lack of traffic hygiene being followed by the citizens. However, the 0.3845 value of coefficient of determination indicates low correlation which means less probability of similar trend to continue further. It is predicted based on the model below that there will be around 9,799 fatal accidents in the state in the year 2030 which is a rise from the 9,055 fatal accidents recorded in the state in the year 2021.

6) Forecasted Trend of Fatal Accidents in Rajasthan during years 2009 to 2030

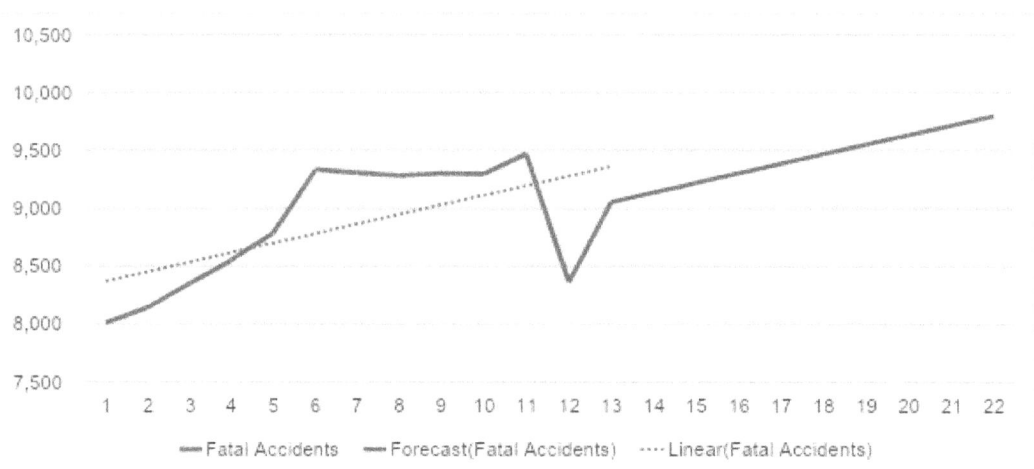

7) Trend of Persons Killed in Accidents during 2009 - 2021

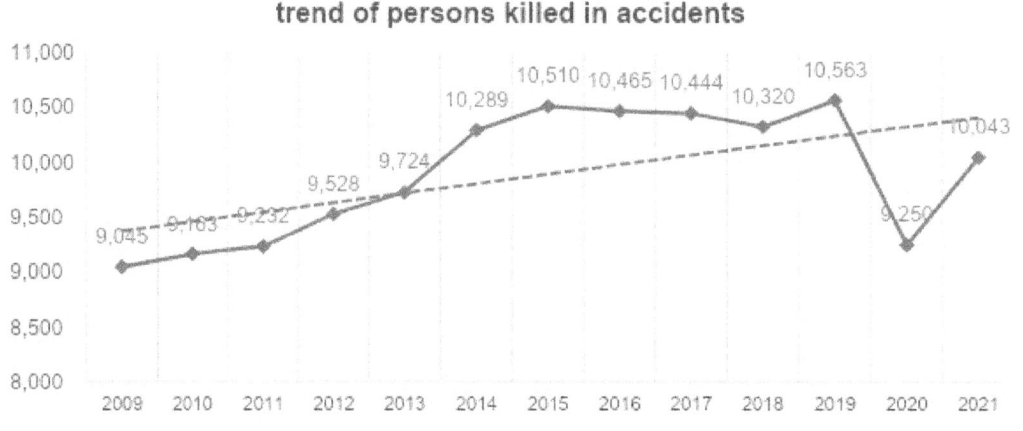

8) Forecasted trend of persons killed in Rajasthan during years 2009 to 2030

Analyzing total persons killed in road accidents, it is observed that during 2009 to 2021, there is an increasing trend in the number of persons killed over the years. This rise in number of fatalities is due to slow emergency response in golden hour, lack of help from citizens due to unawareness of government schemes, over-speeding and rash driving of vehicles, lack of maintenance of roads and traffic, weather conditions, etc. When determining future trends, it was observed that R^2 value of 0.3331 points to less correlation which means there is a lesser possibility of the numbers of deaths increasing in the future. However, if the above trend continues the R^2 value of number of persons killed in Rajasthan in 2030 is forecasted to be 10,821 persons.

9) Trend of Persons Injured in Accidents during 2009 - 2021

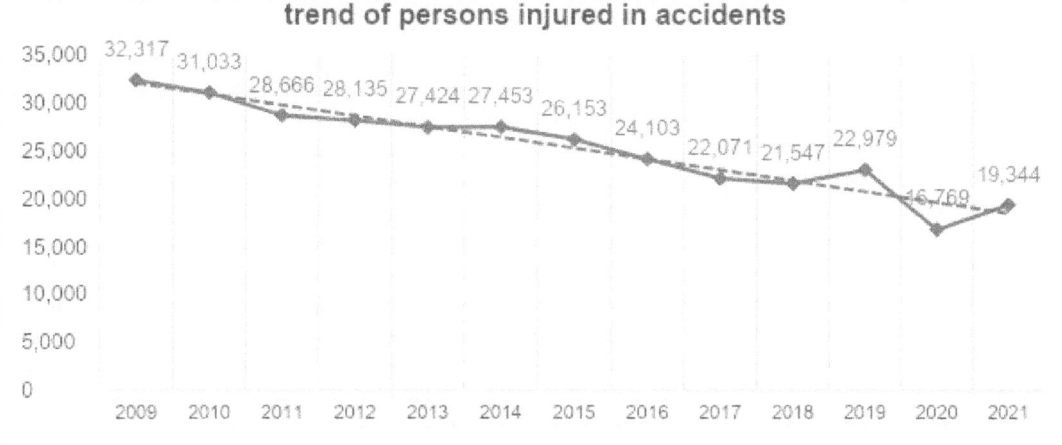

10) Forecasted trend of persons injured in Rajasthan during years 2009 to 2030

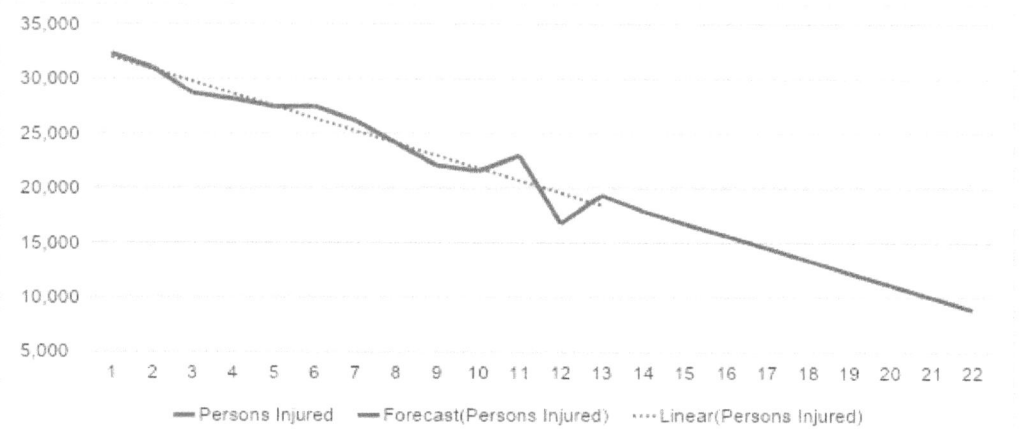

As far as the trend of the number of persons injured during the same period is concerned it has a decreasing trend. Reasons for decrease in persons injured is due to SOS facilities available on highways, set up of Trauma Centres, traffic rules awareness among residents of cities, etc. Also, the high value of $R^2=0.927$ reflects strong correlation and possibility of similar trend to continue in the future which means the number of road accident injuries are likely to keep on decreasing in the upcoming years. It is predicted that the number of persons injured in the state would be decreased to 8,851 persons in the year 2030 which would be more than 50 percent less than the injuries recorded in the state in 2021.

11) Trend of Road Accidents, fatal accidents, persons killed, and persons injured during years 2009 - 2021 in Rajasthan

Year	2009	2010	2011	2012	2013	2014	2015	2016	2017	2018	2019	2020	2021
Total Accidents	25,114	24,302	23,245	22,969	23,592	24,628	24,072	23,066	22,112	21,743	23,480	19,114	20,951
Fatal Accidents	8,010	8,143	8,354	8,550	8,785	9,334	9,306	9,282	9,300	9,295	9,471	8,363	9,055
Persons Killed	9,045	9,163	9,232	9,528	9,724	10,289	10,510	10,465	10,444	10,320	10,563	9,250	10,043
Persons Injured	32,317	31,033	28,666	28,135	27,424	27,453	26,153	24,103	22,071	21,547	22,979	16,769	19,344

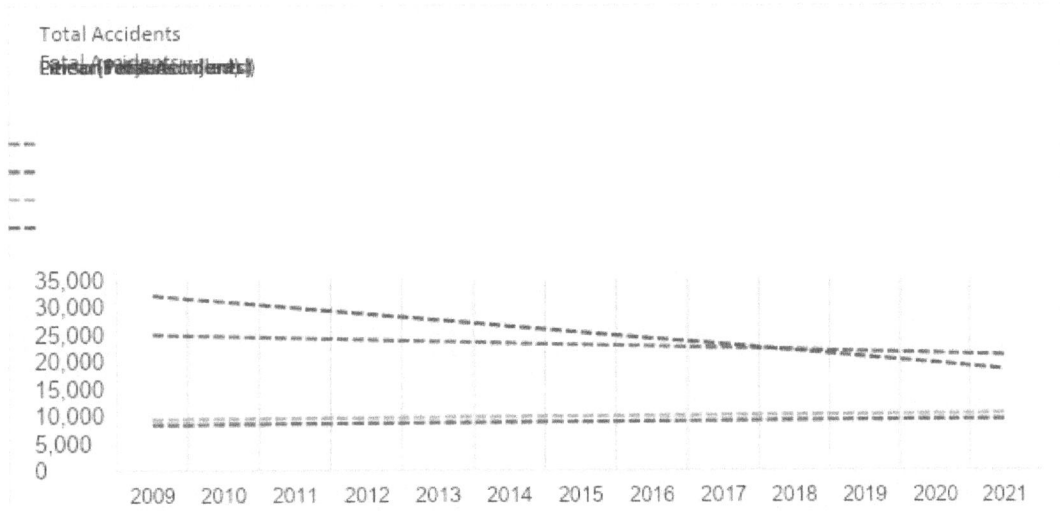

12) Road Accident Risk during year 2011 – 2021 in Rajasthan

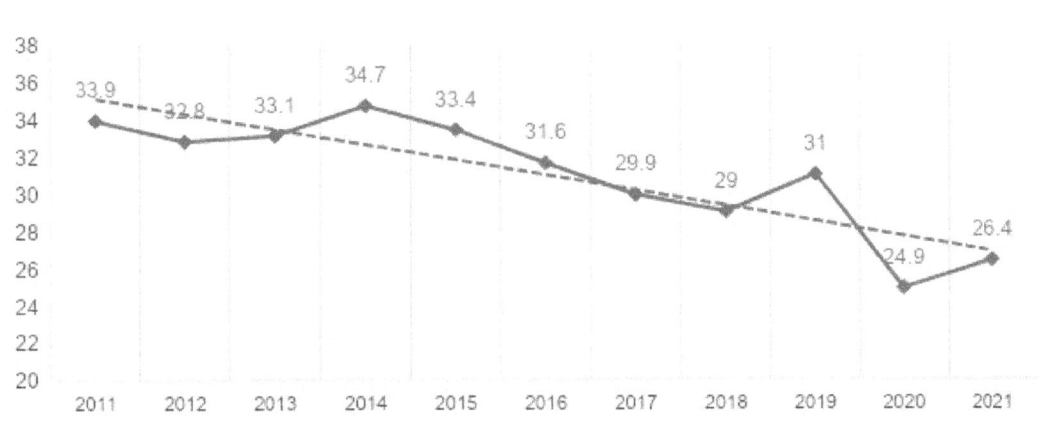

13) Forecasted Trend in Road Accident Risk during years 2011 - 2030 in Rajasthan

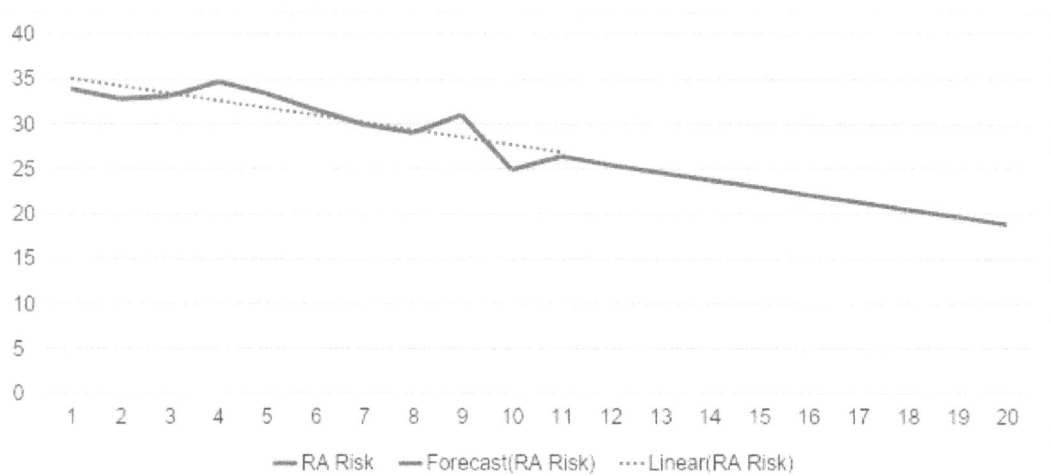

Road Accident Risk is a measure to observe the number of road accidents in the State in a year relative to the population for the year. It is expressed in terms of road accidents per lakh population, and which provides appropriate measures of incidence of accidents in the State. Number of accidents per lakh of population in Rajasthan do not reflect any uniform trend it has increased from 29 in 2018 to 31 in 2019 then it dropped to 24.9 in 2020. The causes of road accidents include human error or driver's fault, traffic rules violations, driving without valid driver license, non - use of safety devices, road environment, weather conditions, overloading, etc. However, Road Accident Risk in general shows a decreasing trend during years 2011 to 2021 having marginal fluctuations and 0.7454 value or R^2 Indicates high correlation and thus similar trend to continue in the future. Road accident risk is predicted to be 18.8 for the state in 2030.

14) Trend in number of Persons Killed in Accidents per lakh Population in Rajasthan (Fatality Risk)

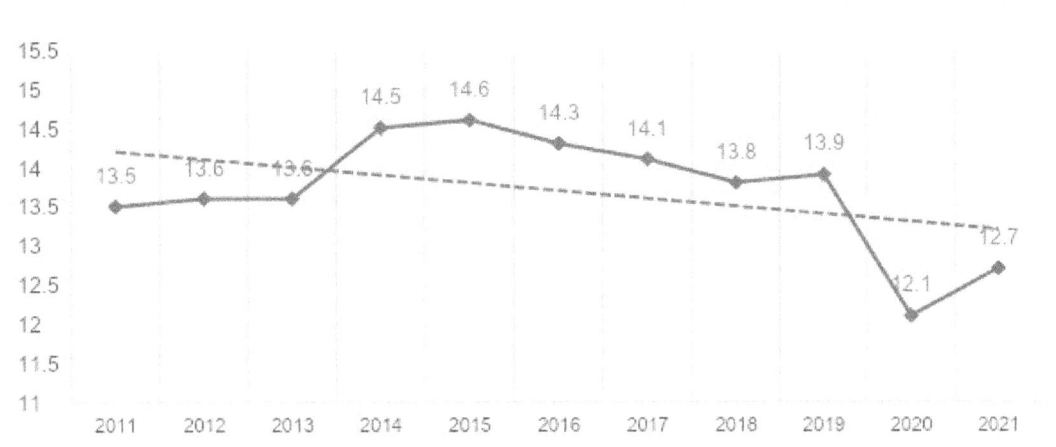

15) Forecasted Trend in Road Accident Fatality Risk from 2011 to 2030 in Rajasthan

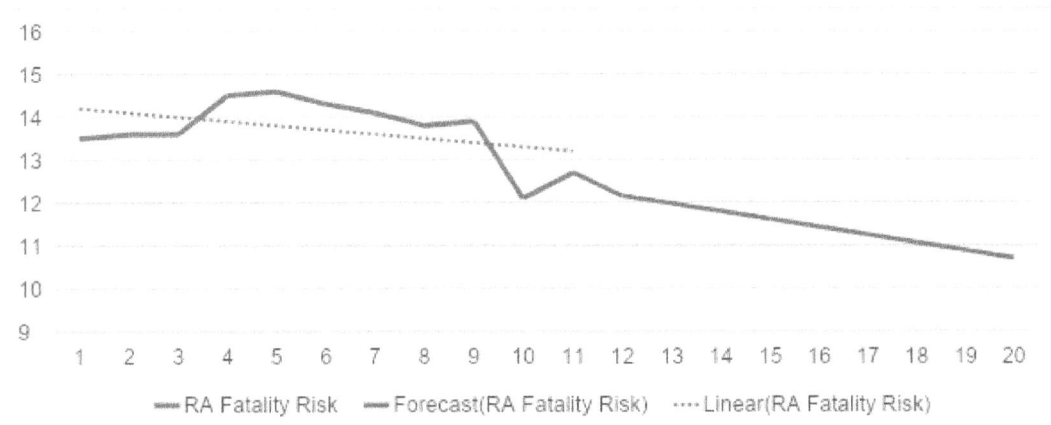

Road Accident Fatality Risk is measured by the number of accident fatality (persons killed) in a year per 1,00,000 population. Accident fatality risk exhibits a decreasing trend during the year 2011 to 2021 with some marginal fluctuations. However, low R2 value brings less confidence in determining the possibility of a similar decreasing trend to continue in the future. Since R^2 value is having low correlation, it is not confirmed that Road accident fatality risk will continue to decrease in the future. It is predicted to be 10.7 in the state in the year 2030 which is a 15.74 percent decrease from the road accident fatality risk of 12.7 in the state in 2021.

16) Road Accident Risk and Road Accident Fatality Risk during years 2011 - 2021 in Rajasthan

Years	2011	2012	2013	2014	2015	2016	2017	2018	2019	2020	2021
Road Accident Risk	33.9	32.8	33.1	34.7	33.4	31.6	29.9	29	31	24.9	26.4
Road accident Fatality Risk	13.5	13.6	13.6	14.5	14.6	14.3	14.1	13.8	13.9	12.1	12.7

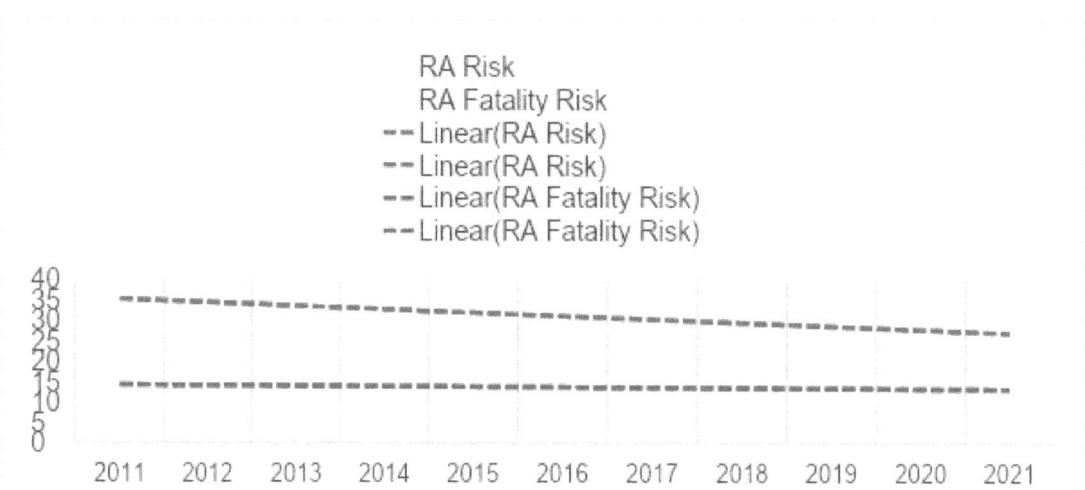

17) Trend of number of accidents per 10,000 Vehicles in Rajasthan (Road Accident Rate)

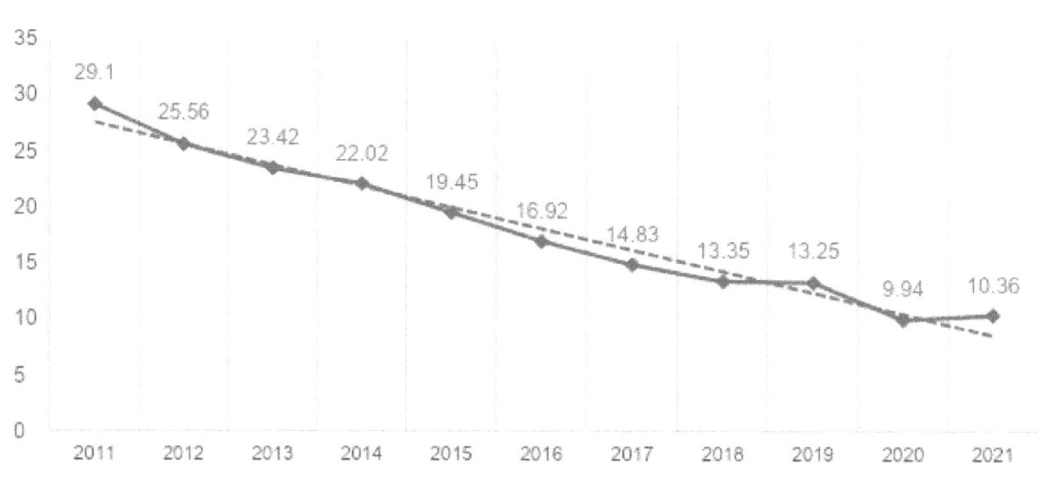

18) Forecasted Trend in Road Accident Rate during years 2011 - 2030 in Rajasthan

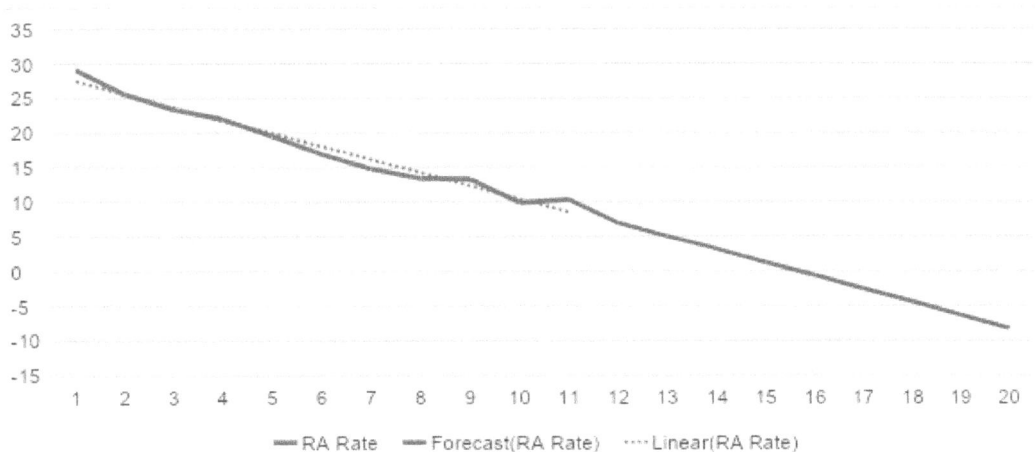

Road Accident Rate is measured by the number of road accidents per 10,000 vehicles, denoting the rate of road accidents relative to vehicular population. The long-run trend of road accidents per 10,000 registered vehicles reveals a high rate of motorization in Rajasthan, as the ratio declines consistently over the years. Surge in motorization and a rising population are two major factors contributing to the trend of road accident rate in the State. The above chart also depicts the overall downward trend in road accident rate in the State and indicates the same trend to follow in the upcoming years. The high value of R^2 reflects high correlation and predicts the road accident rate to be -8.3 in the state in the year 2030. Although this figure is not possible and is impractical it still justifies the downward trend expected in the State in upcoming years.

19) Trend in number of Persons killed per 10,000 Vehicles in Rajasthan (Road Accident Fatality Rate)

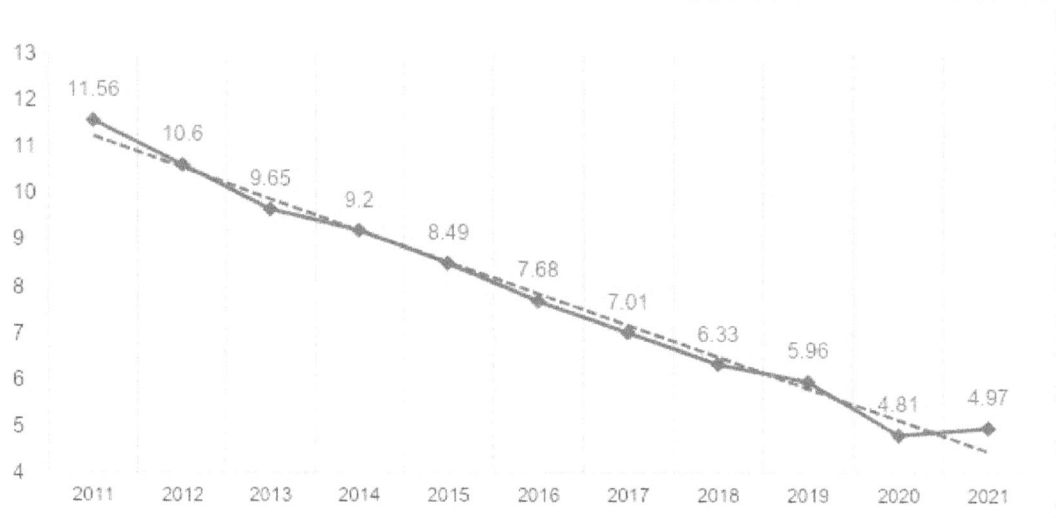

20) Forecasted trend in Road Accident Fatality Rate during years 2011 - 2030 in State

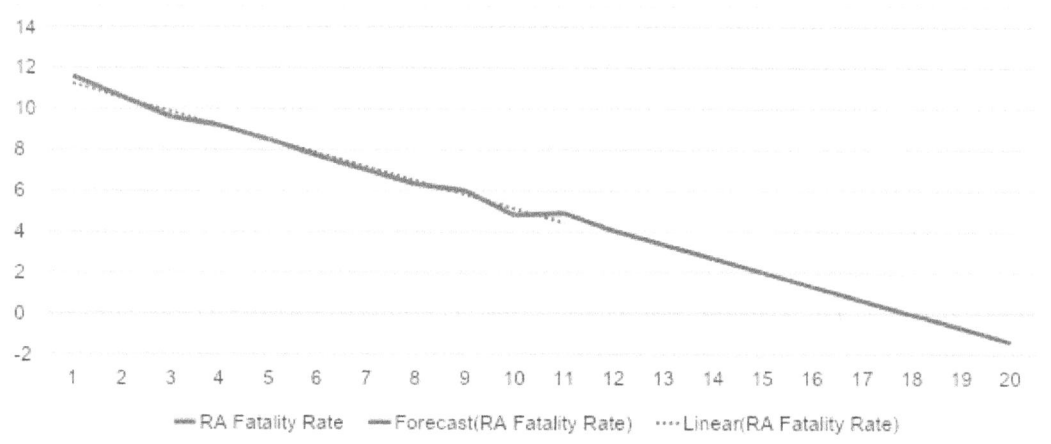

Road Accident Fatality Rate is another indicator which compares the number of fatalities (persons killed) with the number of vehicles in the state. It is expressed in terms of road accident fatality per 10,000 vehicles. Road Accident Fatality Rates have shown a declining trend in the long term as well as in the short term. Also, the high R^2 value of 0.9876 stipulates that the road accident fatality rate will continue to decline in the future thus resulting in less fatalities per 10,000 vehicles. The R^2

value reflects high correlation, and it is believed that the RA Fatality rate will be less than 0 from 2028 onwards in the upcoming years.

21) Road Accident rate and Road Accident Fatality rate in years 2011 - 2021 in State

Years	2011	2012	2013	2014	2015	2016	2017	2018	2019	2020	2021
Road Accident Rate	29.1	25.6	23.4	22	19.5	16.9	14.8	13.4	13.3	9.9	10.4
Road Accident Fatality Rate	11.6	10.6	9.6	9.2	8.5	7.7	7	6.3	6	4.8	4.9

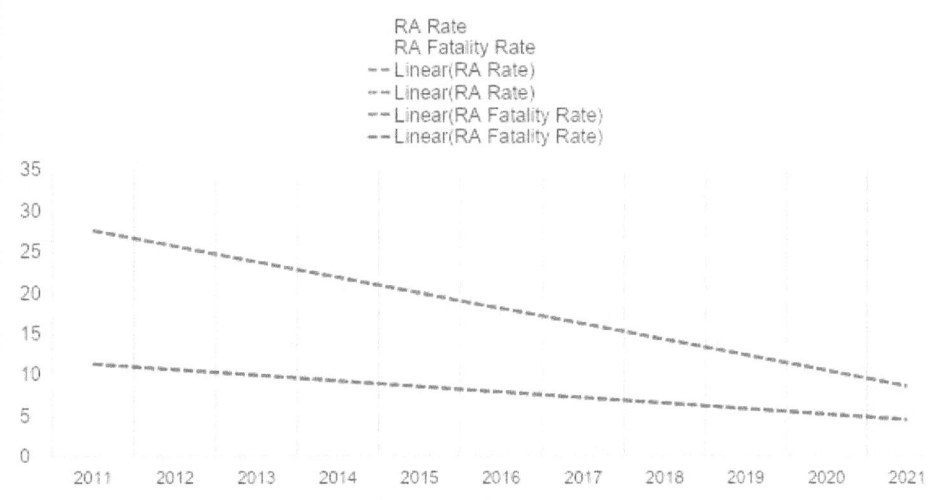

22) Road Accident Density during year 2011 to year 2019

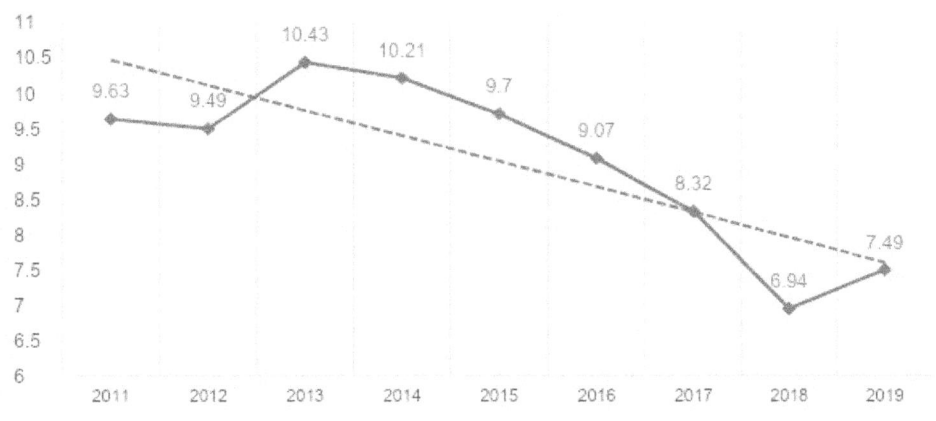

23) Forecasted trend in Road Accident Density during years 2011 - 2030 in Rajasthan

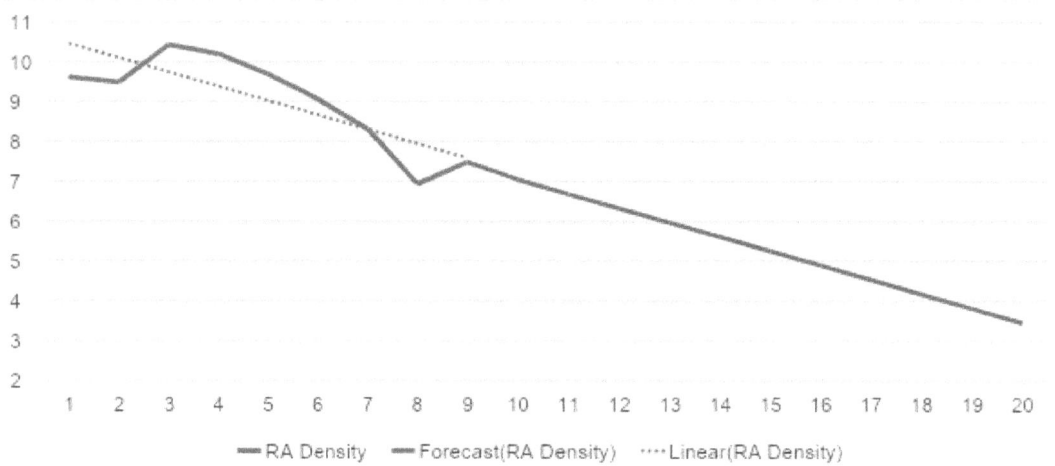

Road Accident Density is measurement in terms of the number of accidents per 100 Km. of road. During 2011 to 2019, Road Accident Density has reflected a decreasing trend. Expansion in road networks, usage of trending technologies in highway development, safer road environment and extensive enforcement of traffic rules and regulations are some of the reasons for the decline in Road Accident Density. However, R^2 value of 0.6674 reflects moderate correlation and thus confirms in determining the possibility of a similar decreasing trend to continue in the future. It is expected that the road accident density will decrease to 3.46 in the State in 2030 which is almost 54% less than the current figure of 7.49 in the State in the year 2019.

24) Road Accident Fatality Density during year 2011 to year 2019 in Rajasthan

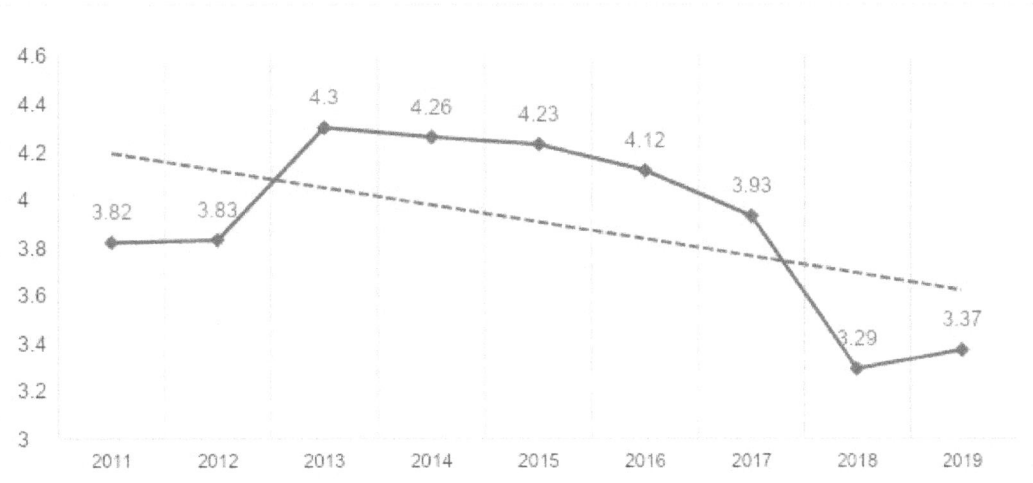

25) Forecasted trend in Road Accident Fatality Density during years 2011 - 2030 in Rajasthan

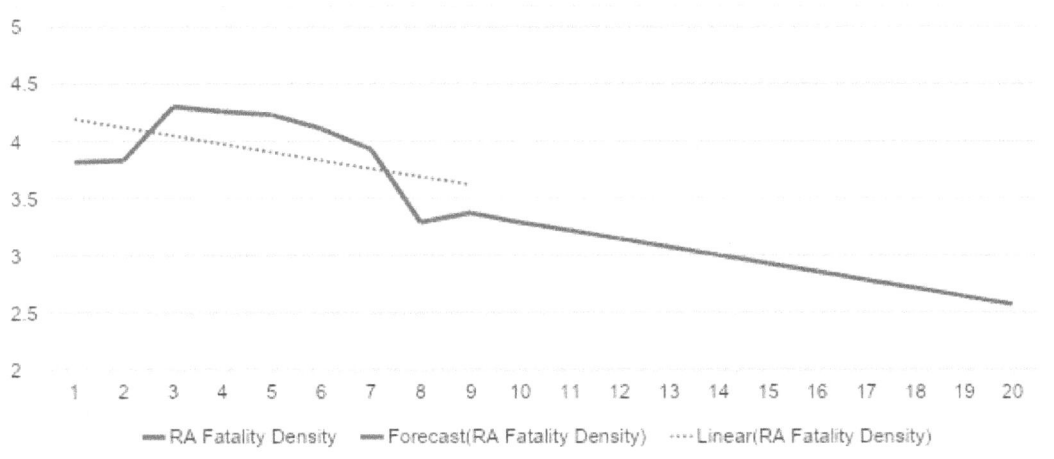

Road Accident Fatality Density is measurement of the number of persons killed per 100 km. of road in Rajasthan. Upon analysis, it is identified that it is on a declining trend during years 2011 - 2019 having some fluctuations. A large road network is inversely proportional to RA Fatality Density. But the low value of R^2 which is 0.2795 brings low correlation and thus less possibility of a similar trend to continue in the upcoming years. If the trend continues to go downwards then the road accident fatality density is expected to be 2.57 in the State in 2030.

26) Road Accident Density and Road Accident Fatality Density during years 2011 - 2019 in Rajasthan

Years	2011	2012	2013	2014	2015	2016	2017	2018	2019
Road Accident Density	9.63	9.49	10.43	10.21	9.7	9.07	8.32	6.94	7.49
Road Accident Fatality Density	3.82	3.83	4.3	4.26	4.23	4.11	3.93	3.29	3.37

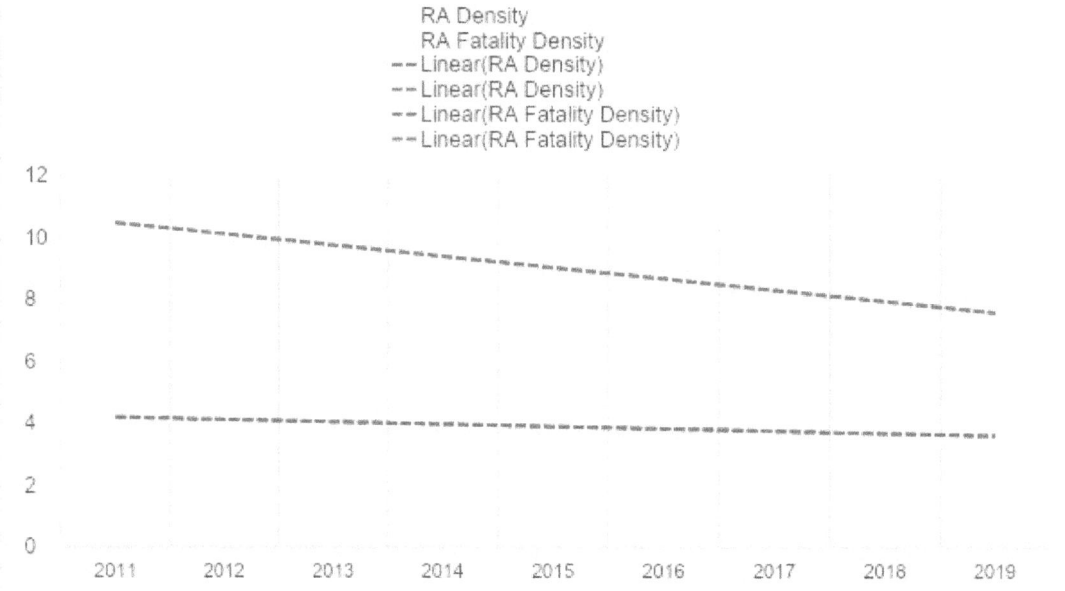

27) Trend of Number of Fatal Accidents by category of roads in Rajasthan (2016 - 2021)

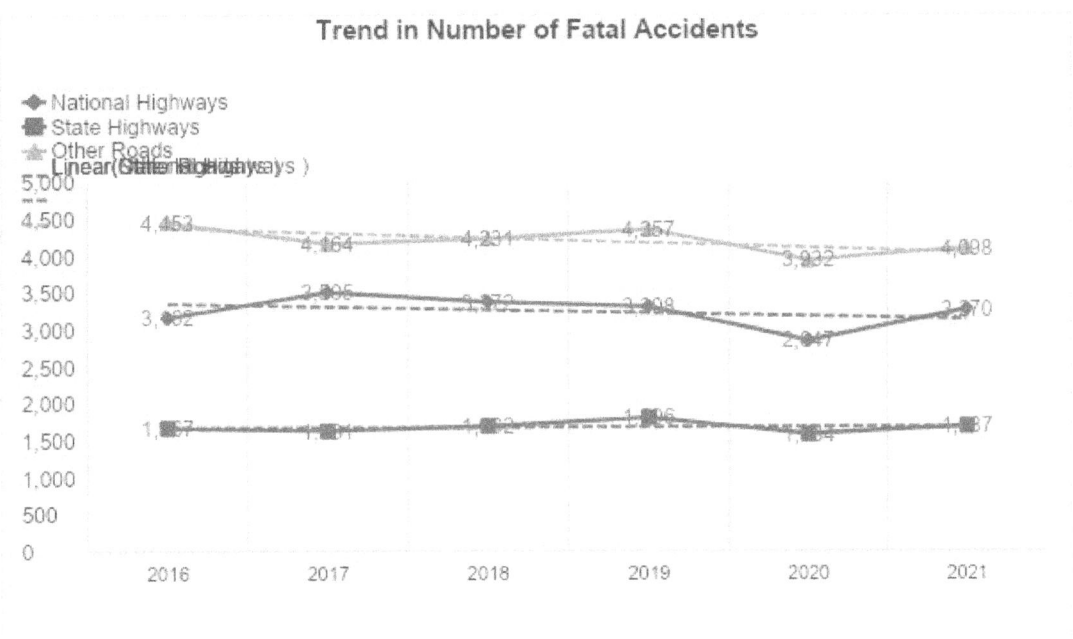

It can be understood from the above chart that there is a general decreasing trend of fatal accidents on Roads. National Highways and Other Roads have a higher magnitude of decrease year on year than the State Highways. In the year 2020, there is a tangible decrease in fatal accidents across all categories of roads (NH, SH, Others) particularly due to Covid - 19 effect. The CAGR of fatal accidents on NH, SH and Other Roads is 35.38%, 34.95% and 33.52% respectively. It shows that fatal accidents on NH are growing at a faster pace than the other roads. Road category wise trend in number of fatal accidents have stabilized with marginal fluctuations during 2016 to 2020, thereafter, registered an increase in 2021.

28) Accidents by Road Categories during Year 2014 to Year 2021

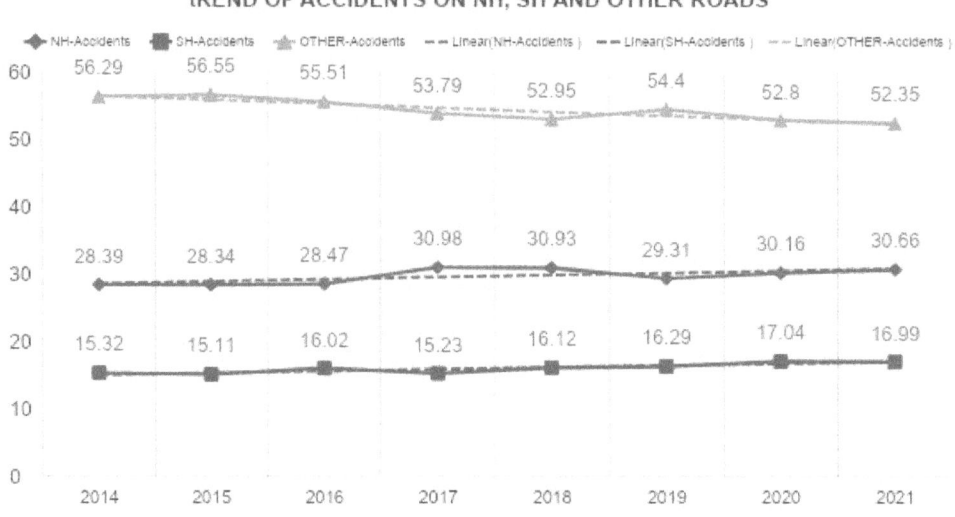

It can be concluded from the above chart that Accidents on National and State Highways in general have an increasing trend over years whereas accidents on other types of roads have in general observed a decreasing trend. The CAGR of accidents on NH, SH and Other Roads is 28.82%, 28.82% and 27.62% respectively. It shows that accidents on NH and SH are growing at the same pace and accidents on Other roads are growing at a marginally lesser pace than those on NH and SH.

29) Fatalities by Road Categories in Rajasthan from Year 2014 to Year 2021

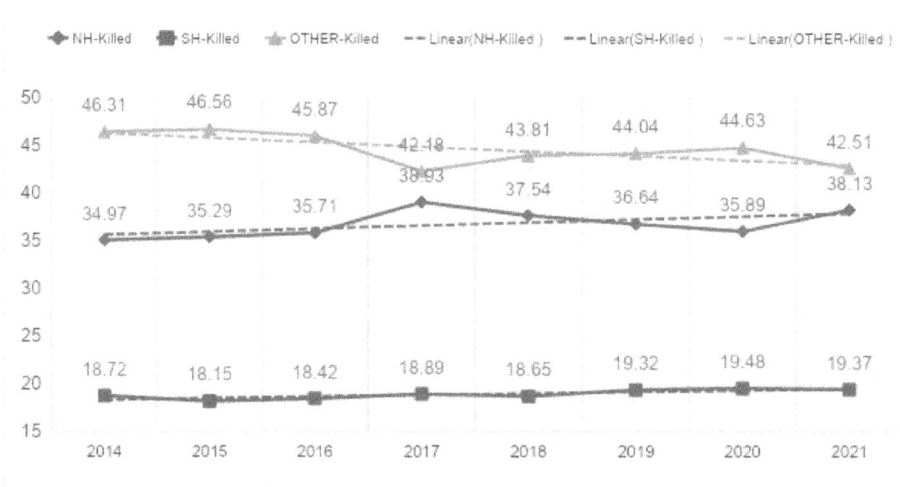

From the above chart, it is noticeable that fatality (persons killed in accidents) has in general an increasing trend on National Highways. It was highest in the year 2017 and it again reached almost the same level in the year 2021. Fatality on Other types of roads has in general a decreasing trend and it reached its lowest in the year 2017. It marginally increased during the year 2020 but came down next year i.e., in the year 2021. On the State highways, fatalities have remained constant over the years with marginal fluctuations. It is also noticeable that post 2019, fatalities on SH have been increasing as compared to pre 2019 years. The CAGR of fatalities on NH, SH and Other Roads are 30.36%, 29.73% and 28.95% respectively. It shows that the fatality on NH is growing fastest followed by SH and Other roads.

30) Injuries by Road Categories in Rajasthan during Year 2014 to Year 2021

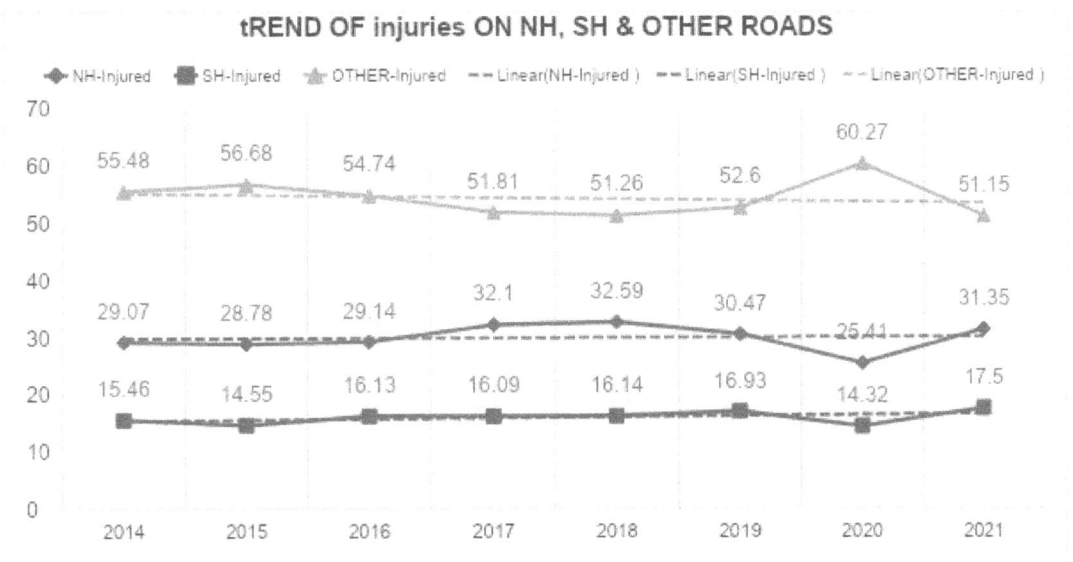

From the different trend lines in the above chart, it can be clearly observed that the percentage of injuries on NH, SH and Other Roads to total injuries have largely remained constant over the years with marginal fluctuations. It is also observed that during 2015 to 2018, there is an increase in accident injuries on NH but decrease on Other Roads. In 2020, percent of injuries on NH and SH decreased but it increased on Other Roads in the same year. It can also be understood that accident injuries on State Highways have been lower than on NH and Other roads during the period 2014 to 2021.

Important Road Safety Provisions and Penalties are as under:

A. Strengthening Enforcement and Road Safety

    (a) Stricter penalties to improve deterrence effect

    (b) Minimum Penalty of ₹500/- as against present amount of ₹100 for minor offenses

    (c) New Section for Juvenile offenders included for the first time with strict penalties

    (d) Drunken driving - Penalty increased to ₹10,000/- from present level of ₹2,000/- and mandatory suspension of license

    (e) Impounding and suspension of License in case of over speeding, dangerous driving, drunk and driving, use of unsafe vehicles, not wearing helmets, use of mobiles, etc.

    (f) Recognizing the use of IT enabled enforcement equipment.

    (g) Recognition of driver refreshing training course as a remedial measure in case of suspension of license.

    (h) Mandatory automated testing for fitness certification.

    (i) Constitution of National Road Safety Board to render advice on Road Safety and Traffic Management.

B. Speedy Assistance to Accident Victims

    (a) Protection of Good Samaritans who help accident victims

    (b) Heavy Penalties on those not giving way to Ambulances

    (c) Cashless treatment during golden hour

    (d) Faster and hassle - free provisions for compensation of ₹2.5 Lakh for grievous hurt and ₹5 Lakh for death.

    (e) Enhanced compensation of ₹2 Lakh in case of death and fifty thousand for grievous hurt for victims of hit and run accidents.

    (f) Simplification of procedures for 3rd Party Insurance and hired Driver brought under the insurance cover.

C. Simplification and citizen facilitation

    (a) Permitting issue of driving license anywhere in the State

    (b) Facilitating grant of online learning license.

    (c) Registration of new vehicles at the dealer's end including grant of registration number before the delivery of the vehicle is given.

    (d) Renewal of transport license after five years as against present provision of three years.

    (e) Documentation permissible in electronic form.

    (f) Provision for recycling of vehicles

    (g) Adapted vehicles for Divyang

D. Strengthening Public Transport

    (a) Aggregators recognized as a legal entity

    (b) Promote Rural Transport

    (c) Promote Public Transport

    (d) Promote last mile connectivity

    (e) National and State Level Transportation plans

    (f) States can formulate Schemes for promotion of public transport waiving the conditions in the Act.

E. Automation and Computerization

    (a) Promoting use of electronic forms and documents.

    (b) Migration from State registers of driving license and vehicle registration to National level database.

F. Empowerment of States

    (a) Compound offenses at amounts equal to the penalty or higher amounts

    (b) Impose a multiplier up to 10 to any penalty

    (c) Exempt the requirement of Stage Carriage in interest of rural transport

(d) Exempt the requirements for promoting the last mile connectivity

(e) Can authorize any other person to exercise the powers

(f) Regulating pedestrians' movements and non - motorized traffic

Preventive measures to mitigation Road accident

The road accidents are multi - causal which requires multi - pronged measures to mitigate the problems through concerted efforts of all agencies of both Central Government and State Governments. The Transport and Road Safety Department in coordination with other related departments have formulated a multi - pronged strategy to address the issue of road safety based on Education, Engineering, Enforcement and Emergency Care.

It is also submitted that on account of the continuous monitoring of the Hon'ble Supreme Court the necessary institutional setup has been created in almost all the States of country including Rajasthan. In state of Rajasthan following activities/schemes have been framed and notified:

(i) Formulation of State Road Safety Policy

(ii) Setting up of State Road Safety Council and holding of meetings at least twice in a year

(iii) Setting up of a Lead Agency with adequate dedicated and professional staff to deal exclusively with Road Safety issues

(iv) Establishing a non - lapsable Dedicated Road Safety Fund by appropriating 25 percent of fines collected from traffic violators in each year

(v) Preparing a Road Safety Action Plan with annual targets for reducing road accidents and deaths

(vi) Constitution of District Road Safety Committees under the chairmanship of District Collectors.

In spite of the creation of institutional setup, there is much scope for further improving road safety measures, so as to ensure reduction in the number of road accidents, fatalities and injuries in the State. It seems that there is a necessity to draw an action plan at the level of State Government wherein simultaneous action is required to be taken on the following four issues given below:

(i) Intensive publicity for awareness of general public on traffic rules and penalties thereon payable for their violations

(ii) Strengthening of enforcement activities by extensive use of electronic monitoring for violation of traffic rules

(iii) Improvement of Road conditions by adhering to the standards specified for road engineering by Indian Road Congress

(iv) Strengthening emergency response and medical care systems

Road accidents are multi - causal and are the result of an interplay of various factors. The major causes of road accidents are lack of awareness/knowledge of traffic rules in the general public, defective road engineering, use of defective vehicles and gross violation of traffic rules. Presently the system of enforcing road/traffic discipline is mostly manual and the individuals who are violating the traffic rules are aware of the fact that in the absence of any effective enforcement mechanism they are free to violate the traffic rules. Hence, there is a necessity to create a deterrent effect in the minds of such traffic rule violators by promoting extensive use of electronic monitoring of traffic offenders.

Initiative taken by Ministry of Road and Transport and highways (MoRTH)

Looking into the road accident scenario in the country Hon'ble Supreme Court expressed its concern for road safety and directed the Central Government to formulate a committee to monitor and measure implementation of road safety laws in the country. MoRTH in 2014 under the chairmanship of retired Supreme Court Judge Hon'ble Justice J.S. Radhakrishnan notified the formulation of the above committee. As a result of the various directions given from time to time, by the above committee most of the States have established institutional arrangements to promoting road safety education and establishing adequate trauma care facilities

Publicity and Awareness Campaigns

The Ministry of Road Transport & Highways has implemented a scheme, "Grant of Financial Assistance for Administering Road Safety Advocacy and Awards for the Outstanding Work Done in the Field of Road Safety". Under the scheme, financial assistance is provided to various eligible agencies such as NGO/Trust under Indian Trusts Act/ Cooperative Society under Societies Registration Act/ Firm registered under the companies Act, 1956/ 2013 or an Academic Institutions accredited / affiliated to or recognized as a university or Deemed university by UGC Act (hereinafter referred to as 'Applicant Agency'). To create effective public awareness about road safety, the Ministry undertakes various publicity measures and awareness campaigns on road safety through social media, electronic media, and print media.

Road Safety Audits

It is mandatory to carry out the Road Safety Audit of all highway projects at all stages i.e. design, construction and operation & maintenance stages. The Road Safety Audit is being carried out as per the applicable standards laid down by the Indian Road Congress (IRC).

Pedestrian Facilities

Financial power of up to ₹25 crores for construction of Pedestrian Underpasses (PUP) and Pedestrian Subways (PSW) and up to ₹1.25 crore for construction of Foot Over Bridges (FOBs) is delegated to Regional Officers of NHAI to speed up the process. To make roads safer for pedestrians, MoRTH notified AIS 100, which contains the requirements for the protection of pedestrians and other vulnerable road users in the event of a collision with a Motor Vehicle.

Road Engineering Identification and Rectification of Accident Blackspots

High priority has been given for identification and rectification of blackspots (accidents prone spots) on National Highways. Concerted efforts towards improvement of road safety through engineering measures on National Highways have been made. The Ministry of Road Transport & Highways has identified 5,352 blackspots on National Highways based on accident and fatality data of year 2015 - 2018 in 30 states/UTs. The Ministry is taking the following steps to rectify the blackspots.

> (i) The blackspots are being rectified by providing immediate short - term measures such as cautionary road signs and markings, transverse bar markings, rumble strips and solar blinkers etc.

(ii) For long term rectification, measures such as Flyover, Underpasses, Foot over Bridges, Service roads etc. are being provided wherever required.

(iii) Traffic calming measures such as traffic warning signs, delineators, road studs, bar markings, humps at approach roads, etc. are taken at vulnerable sections of National Highways to reduce road accident fatalities.

(iv) Emergency/medical facilities for the road accident victims are provided as per the respective contract/concession agreements signed between NHAI and the contractor/concessionaire.

Vehicle Engineering

Crash safety norms: To ensure the safety of the occupants of the vehicles in an event of a crash, following standards have been notified.

(i) AIS 098: Requirements for the Protection of the Occupants in the event of an Offset Frontal Collision

(ii) AIS 099: Requirements for the Protection of the Occupants in the event of a Lateral Collision.

The applicability of these standards started from 1stOctober 2017 for new models and from 1stOctober 2019 for all existing models.

Mandatory fitment of safety technologies

To enhance the safety aspect of the vehicle, from time to time, MoRTH notifies mandatory fitment of various safety technologies in various vehicle categories. Few of the safety technologies mandated by MoRTH are as listed below:

(a) Airbags: Fitment of front airbag for driver was mandated from 01st July 2019. From 01st April 2021 for new models and 31st December 2021 for all models, fitment of co - driver airbag was also made mandatory. In this regard, the Ministry has notified GSR 148(E) dated 2nd March 2021.

(b) Anti - lock Braking System (ABS) and Combined Braking System (CBS): Mandatory fitment of ABS, applicable for 4 wheelers and for 2 - wheelers with engine capacity greater than 125 cc, was implemented from 01st April 2018 for new models and 01st April 2019 for all models. For 2 - wheelers with engine capacity less than or equal to 125 cc, ABS or CBS must be fitted.

(c) Safety Technologies: Some other safety technologies made mandatory from 01st July 2019 are seat belt reminder for driver and co - driver, over speed warning system, reverse parking sensors, and manual override for central locking door.

(d) Bharat New Car Assessment Program: The Ministry of Road Transport and Highways has issued a draft notification dated 24th June 2022, for the introduction of Bharat New Car Assessment Program (BNCAP). Under this program motor vehicles of category M1 [motor vehicles used for carriage of passengers comprising not more than eight seats in addition to the driver's seat] safety technologies in various vehicle categories.

Training and capacity building

Accredited Driver Training Centre: Shortage of skilled drivers is one of the major issues in the Indian Roadways Sector. The Ministry of Road Transport and Highways has published a notification on 7thJune, 2021, wherein the requirements to be fulfilled by accredited driver training centers have been mandated. The Centre shall be equipped with simulators and dedicated driving test track to provide high quality training to candidates. The candidates who successfully pass the test at these centers will be exempted from the driving test requirement at the time of applying for driving license, which is currently being taken at the RTO. These centers are allowed to provide industry specific specialized training as well.

To ensure good driving skills and knowledge of rules of road regulations among the drivers and to strengthen the system of driver licensing and training to improve the competence and capability of drivers, Ministry is setting up model Institutes of Driving Training and Research (IDTR) Centres, Regional Driving Training Centres (RDTCs) and Driving Training Centres (DTC) in the States/UTs. As of December 2021, a total 31 IDTRs and 6 RDTCs were sanctioned out of 31 IDTRs, 18 IDTRs are functional and the remaining are at different stages of completion.

The Ministry of Road Transport and Highways has tied up with Indian Institute of Technology (IIT) Madras to setup a Center of Excellence for Road Safety, to work on development of new products, capacity building, knowledge sharing, collaborations, research and strategic initiatives focused towards improving road safety and reducing road fatalities in the Country.

Enforcement measures

The Motor Vehicles Act, 1988 is the principal instrument through which road transport is regulated in the country. The same has been amended for the first time in a comprehensive way by The Motor Vehicles (Amendment) Act, 2019, passed by the Parliament and published in the Gazette of India on 9th August 2019. The Act is expected to bring reforms in the various segments as elaborated upon in the subsequent paras:

The Act will bring reforms in the area of Road Safety, bring citizen facilitation, transparency, and reduce corruption with the help of information technology and removing intermediaries. The Act will strengthen public transport, safeguard and protect Good Samaritan and reform the insurance and compensation regime. It will allow innovation and new technologies such as driverless vehicles, to be tested in a live environment and increase efficiency in research. The Act will facilitate Divyang by allowing motor vehicles to be converted to adapted vehicles with post - facto approval and facilitating license to drive adapted vehicles.

Electronic Monitoring and Enforcement

For provision of electronic monitoring and enforcement of Road Safety (through speed cameras, CCTVs, speed guns, dash cams, body wearable cameras etc.), rules have been notified through G.S.R. 575(E) dated 11th August 2021.

Incident Management System & Incident Management Services

The services like ambulances, patrol vehicles, cranes to be deployed at every toll plaza.

National Road Safety Board (NRSB)

The National Road Safety Board and its Rules have been notified on 3rd September 2021.

Supreme Court Committee on Road Safety

Regular review meetings are being conducted by the Supreme Court Committee on Road Safety, State Road Safety Committee and District Road Safety Committee.

The Ministry, in coordination with field offices, ensures compliance of directions of the Supreme Court Committee on Road safety.

Integrated Road Accident Database (iRAD)

Integrated Road Accident Database (iRAD) system is a central repository for reporting, management, claim processing and analysis of road accidents data to enhance road safety in the Country. The application is being developed and implemented by NIC/NICSI and the required analytics on the data is being carried out by Indian Institute of Technology (IIT) Madras under the aegis of Ministry of Road Transport and Highways (MoRTH). It is being integrated with national databases such as CCTNS, VAHAN, SAARTHI etc. Till now, the application has been rolled out in 34 States for live data entry of road accidents.

Initiatives taken by Government of Rajasthan

Measures which have been taken by the Transport department

Some of the measures which have been taken by the Transport department of the State to improve road safety so as to decrease the number of road accidents and fatalities in road accidents are as follows: -

(i) Transport department was declared as nodal department for road safety.

(ii) Following State level Road Safety Committees constituted: -

- a. High Powered Committee under the Chairmanship of Hon'ble Chief Minister of the State
- b. State Road Safety Council under the Chairmanship of Transport Minister of the State
- c. Traffic Management Committee under the Chairmanship of Chief Secretary of the State
- d. Special Task Force chaired by Principal Secretary Home/Transport and Road Safety
- e. Besides, above in each district a District Road Safety Committee under the Chairmanship of District Collector

Highlights of Road Safety Policy of Rajasthan - 2017

(i) Dedicated non-lapsable Road Safety Fund created, 25% of revenue collected from traffic violation challans in the State goes to this fund.

(ii) Road Safety War Room for immediate support of accident victims made operational.

(iii) Integrated Road Accident Database (iRAD) created.

(iv) Road safety audits of roads by the joint teams at State and District Level are carried out.

(v) Joint inspection of major road accidents by the officers of the Transport, Police and Public Works Department of the State.

(vi) Scheme for investigation of road accident cases and wayside amnesties/traffic aid posts/truck parking complexes along highways of Rajasthan

(vii) Awareness activities through IEC, FM, TV, Social media, RSRTC buses etc. are organized from time to time.

(viii) Financial Assistance to the Police department from the Road Safety Fund for regular awareness activities, reflective tape installation, establishing traffic aid posts, carrying out rescue operations, minor road repairs, establishing counseling centers for the drivers found violating traffic rules and purchase of equipment.

(ix) Automated driving testing track planned for 37 transport districts and have been made operational in 13 transport districts.

(x) Procurement of portable weighing machines/e-challan for enforcement staff

(xi) Steps taken for correcting Black spot

(xii) Mukhyamantri Chiranjeevi Jeevan Raksha Yojana - 2022 made operational which provides for granting reward of ₹5000/- and issuance of appreciation certificate for persons who carry accident victims to hospital for medical treatment.

(xiii) Mukhyamantri Chiranjeevi SadakSuraksha Yojana - 2022 made operational for free treatment of road accident victims for a period of 72 hours from the time of accident.

(xiv) Mukhyamantri Chiranjeevi Durghatna Bima Yojana - 2022 provides for compensation of ₹5 Lakh to the person who dies in road accident and ₹1.5 Lakh to ₹3 Lakh for disability caused to the victim of road accident.

(xv) Bal Vahini scheme for safe transportation of school children, establishing road safety clubs

(xvi) Carrying out capacity building programmes for stakeholders such as school going children, para - medical staff, teachers etc.

(xvii) Carrying out road safety auditors training by the engineers.

Measures which have been taken by the police department

Some of the measures which have been taken in the year 2022 by the Police department of the State to improve road safety so as to decrease the number of road accidents and fatalities in road accidents are as follows: -

(i) Constitution of Road Safety Audit Teams in each district of the State for auditing National Highways and State Highways. So far the road safety audit of 1985 Kms has been completed.

(ii) To ensure transparency in the challan system of vehicles a system of e - Challan with a facility of digital payment has been started.

(iii) The Intelligent Traffic Management System (ITMS) has been integrated with the e - Challan server of NIC for the offenses relating to Motor Vehicles Act, 1988 in the Police Commissioner Office, Jaipur. The above system enables the offenders to open the link given in the message for depositing the composition money.

(iv) To ensure uniformity in road accident data a MIS software has been developed in the department.

(v) 25 interceptor vehicles with latest technology have been allotted to different districts of the State and the e - Challan against the drivers violating the provision of the Motor Vehicles Act, 1988 are generated by using ITMS.

(vi) 40 police stations where the death rate on account of road accidents is 20 or more were monitored every day through video conferencing in the year 2022. 178 such police stations shall be monitored in the year 2023 under the above scheme.

(vii) A policy to promote use of BIS approved helmets was initiated. Special campaign was initiated to check the sale/storage of non ISI marked helmets.

(viii) Basic life saving training programme was initiated in 100 police stations located on National Public State Highways with help of NGOs in the year 2022.

(ix) Awareness programmes on traffic rules and road safety were initiated each month by Highway Mobile Teams in at least five villages located on National Highways, so far these programmes have been conducted in 2023 villages in the year 2022.

(x) 21 new traffic aid check posts were established on various national highways of the State.

(xi) Scientific investigation of the accident sites by joint teams are being carried out in those cases where the number of death(s) on account of road accidents is 4 or more.

(xii) 424 officers/subordinate police officials were accorded training to investigate on Road Safety Management and road accidents by the Rajasthan Police Academy, Jaipur in the year 2022.

The above measures have strengthened creation of an effective policy making mechanism for improving road safety, creating a robust infrastructure in terms of capacity building of stakeholders and post accidental measures which mainly relate to providing expeditious medical/financial aid to the victims of road accidents.

Intensive publicity and awareness drive through electronic, digital, and print media

The purpose of providing stringent penalties in law serves a dual purpose. On the one hand, the offender is punished for the offense committed by him and on the other hand, such penalties create a deterrent effect in the minds of persons not abiding by laws. In 2019 the Motor Vehicles (Amendment) Act was enacted wherein besides other amendments the penalties for violation of traffic laws were made stringent in the Motor Vehicles Act, 1988. The Statement of Objects and reasons of the amending act clearly states that with rapidly increasing motorisation, India is facing an increasing burden of road traffic injuries and fatalities. The emotional and social trauma caused to the family which loses its breadwinner, cannot be quantified. India being signatory to the Brasilia Declaration is committed to reduce the number of road accident fatality by 50 percent by the year 2030. Looking into the above objects the fines and penalties for the violation of provisions of the Act were increased multiple fold. It is also submitted that some new sections relating to Good Samaritans, Golden Hour, Driver refreshing training course, offenses by juveniles, framing of schemes for the transportation of goods and passengers for the promotion of development and efficiency in transportation were also enacted through the above amending Act.

The general public is not fully aware of the new provisions including the penalties payable on such violations, the impact of such violation on the driving license of the offenders, the mandatory suspension of driving license provided for committing certain offenses like jumping a red light, violating a stop sign, use of handheld communication devices while driving, passing or overtaking other vehicles in a manner contrary to law, driving against the authorized flow of traffic, the responsibility of the guardian of a motor vehicle for allowing a juvenile person to drive a vehicle, etc. are not much known to the general public. In case the above provisions are widely publicized by using social media, electronic media, and print media they will certainly create a positive effect in the minds of citizens to follow traffic rules. Many enlightened citizens may take precautions and would like to ensure that the traffic laws are followed diligently after becoming aware of the consequences of traffic violations in terms of payment of fine, disqualification for holding a driving license and the necessity to undertake driver refresher training course for becoming eligible for driving.

The provisions which require wide publicity are being listed below:

(i) Section 206(4) provides for seizing of driving license by a police officer and forwarding it to the licensing authority for disqualification or revocation proceedings under Section 19 if he has a reason to believe that an offense has been committed by a person under Sections 183, 184, 185, 189, 190, 194 - C, 194 - D or 194 - E.

(ii) Section 183 is a penal section for driving at excessive speed in case a second or subsequent offense under this section is committed then the driving license of such person can be impounded under Section 206(4) of the Act. The minimum fine under this offense is Rs. 1000 extending up to Rs. 4000 depending on the nature of the vehicle used.

(iii) Section 184 provides for a penalty for dangerous driving which includes jumping a red light, violating a stop sign, use of handheld communication devices while driving, passing or overtaking other vehicles in a manner contrary to law, and driving against the authorized flow of traffic. The minimum fine under this offense is Rs. 1000 which may extend upto Rs. 5000 and a minimum imprisonment of 6 months which may extend to one year. On committing a second or subsequent offense the fine amounts to Rs. 10000 and with imprisonment for a term which may extend to two years or both.

(iv) Section 185 provides for a fine for driving a vehicle by a drunken person or by a person under the influence of drugs. The minimum fine for the first offense is Rs. 10000 and with imprisonment for a term which may extend to 6 months or both. On subsequent offense the amount of fine is Rs. 15000 with imprisonment for a term which may extend to two years or both.

(v) Section 189 provides for the offense of racing and trials of speed and the minimum fine for the first offense is Rs. 5000 and with imprisonment for a term which may extend to 3 months or both. On subsequent offense the amount of fine is Rs. 10000 with imprisonment for a term which may extend to one year or both.

(vi) Section 190 provides for the offense of using a vehicle in unsafe condition and which has resulted in an accident then the minimum fine for the first offense is Rs. 5000 and with imprisonment for a term which may extend to 3 months or both. On subsequent offense the amount of fine is Rs. 10000 with imprisonment for a term which may extend to 6 months or both.

(vii) Section 194 - C provides for a penalty for violation of safety measures for motorcycle riders and pillion riders which is punishable with a fine of Rs. 1000 and such person shall be **disqualified for holding license for the period of 3 months**.

(viii) Section 194 - D provides for a penalty for not wearing protective headgear with a fine of Rs. 1000 and such person shall be **disqualified for holding license for the period of 3 months**.

(ix) Section 194 - E provides that failure to allow free passage to emergency vehicles is punishable with a fine of Rs. 10000 and imprisonment for a term, which may extend to 6 months or both.

(x) Section 181 provides for driving a vehicle in contravention of Section 3 or Section 4 of the Act i.e., driving a vehicle without a driving license of driving a vehicle by a person who is of an age less than the prescribed age is punishable with a fine of Rs. 5000 and with imprisonment for a term which may extend to 3 months or with both.

(xi) Section 194 - B provides for use of safety belts and the seating of children in the vehicle.

(1) Whoever drives a motor vehicle without wearing a safety belt or carries passengers not wearing seat belts shall be punishable with a fine of one thousand rupees:

Provided that the State Government, may by notification in the Official Gazette, exclude the application of this subsection to transport vehicles to carry standing passengers or other specified classes of transport vehicles.

(2) Whoever drives a motor vehicle or causes or allows a motor vehicle to be driven **with a child who, not having attained the age of fourteen years,** is not secured

by a safety belt or a child restraint system shall be punishable with a fine of one thousand rupees.

> (xii) Section 199 - A provides for offenses by juveniles. It provides that any offense under the Motor vehicles Act,1988 if committed by a juvenile then the guardians of the juvenile or the owner of the motor vehicle shall be deemed to be guilty of the contravention. The punishment prescribed for the violation of above provision is Rs. 25000 as fine and imprisonment for a term which may extend to 3 years. The registration of the motor vehicle used in the commission of the offense shall be canceled for a period of 12 months and the juvenile shall not be entitled for obtaining a learner's license unless he attains the age of 25 years.
>
> (xiii) The provision for undertaking driver refresher training courses for the revocation of disqualification of the person from holding a license. (Section 19)

Adhering to the standards specified by Indian road congress

A new section 198 - A was inserted in the Motor Vehicles Act, 1988 with the enactment of Motor vehicles (Amendment) Act, 2019. This section provides that the designated authority, contractor, consultant or concessioner responsible for the design or construction or maintenance of the safety standards of the road shall follow such design, construction and maintenance standards as may be prescribed by the Central Government from time to time. It also provides that where the above persons failed to comply with the standards for road design, construction and maintenance and such failure results in death or disability such persons shall be punishable with a fine amounting to Rs. 1 Lakh and the same shall be paid to the fund constituted under section 164 - B of the Act.

Rule 166 has also been enacted in the Central Motor Vehicles Rule, 1989 with effect from 1/10/2020 which relates to road design, construction and maintenance standards in accordance with the standards and specifications of the Indian Road Congress as may be applicable or any other instructions or guidelines issued by the Central Government from time to time.

Since over speeding is the leading cause of road accidents hence the department/agency which is responsible for maintenance of roads should display variable messages or other fixed mandatory signs relating to speed limits at regular intervals on the road and road marking using Thermoplastic Road Marking Paint due to it's hard - wearing and reflective property. Appropriate road signs such as one way, no entry, prohibition of U - turn, no parking, etc. should also be displayed on the roads so that the persons using the roads are fully aware of the road conditions and other mandatory directions to be followed by them. This will facilitate the road users while using the roads.

Auditing of roads to ensure that they are properly maintained, the road signage are being properly displayed and identification of road defects such as unauthorized construction of speed breakers, illegal encroachment on roads, illegal barricading, etc. by specialized teams.

Strengthening emergency response and medical care system

The possibility of road accidents can be minimized by adoption of various precautionary measures, even then the road accidents are bound to happen. Once the accident takes place a quick response system will ensure timely treatment of the victims that helps to minimize the fatalities on account of road accidents. In the year 2021, 9,055 fatal accidents took place in which 10,043 persons lost their lives. Majority of the deaths take place on account of delay in adequate response within the **Golden Hour** by way of providing first aid to the victims and rushing them to a Trauma Centre/hospital in the **very first hour** of the accident.

To cater to such requirements, a robust network of ambulances and hospital/trauma centers equipped with trained medical professionals would be required on different types of roads/highways. At present 73 trauma centers are operational, sanction of 3 trauma centers at Tonk, Bharatpur and Sikkar are under progress. More availability of trauma centers and ambulances equipped with robust information systems would ensure reduction in response time. Digital initiatives in terms of software applications can be adapted for different types of users such as victim/public, ambulances, hospital/trauma centers and command and control centers.

The application system that can help in quick information sharing to concerned entities through digital channels. The objective is to report any accident to the nearest ambulances and hospitals/Trauma centers easily with minimal steps by an informer. An informer of an accident can either be accident victims or the general public who intends to report it. The proposed set - up involves and ecosystem of 4 level of users having different application interface depending on their role whose details are given as under -

Applications Users -

Sn	User	Intention	Channel
i.	Public	To initiate the accident reporting	Mobile based app working over internet
ii.	Ambulance	To receive request and respond to the request	Mix set - up with internet enabled Tablet and alarm systems (sound & light)
iii.	Hospital/ Trauma Centre	To receive request and respond to the request	Mix set - up with internet enabled Tablet/ Computer systems and alarm systems (sound & light)
iv.	Command & Control Centre	To manage the entire accident reporting system	Mix set - up with computer systems, Large screens, telephones, fast internet, alarm systems (sound & light)

The envisioned accident reporting system starts in two ways namely (i) QR code based manual reporting and (ii) sensor - based auto reporting. In QR code based manual reporting, an individual would be required to install an accident reporting application in his phone and register himself by providing his personal, medical and emergency contact numbers. Individual who also happens to be a vehicle owner would also provide his vehicle details while registration. Once the registration is done, a vehicle owner would generate a QR code that would be pasted inside and outside the vehicle. Individuals who do not declare vehicle details would not be able to generate QR code but will be able to report the accident cases.

User/ Car Owner	Start → Install Application and fill up Personal details, Medical Details, vehicle details and Family contact numbers as required → Download the QR code and paste inside and outside the vehicle → Stop
Mobile Application	Validates and stores the values entered by the user → Generates QR code that has all the declared information of the user

Process steps of the end - to - end accident reporting system using QR code is given below -

Pre - requisites:

(i) QR codes are pasted inside and outside the vehicles.

(ii) Personal details such as medical history, blood group, etc. are updated in the app

(iii) Emergency contact numbers are updated in the app.

Process Flow:

(i) **Accidents** happen/occur.

(ii) Individuals (either a victim or other person) scans QR code using a mobile camera.

(iii) Scanned QR will prompt the application to open.

(iv) Application captures Geo - coordinates of the location.

(v) The application sends SOS messages to the relatives contact number including coordinates and personalized message along with contact number of the person who scanned the QR code to share the information (reporter).

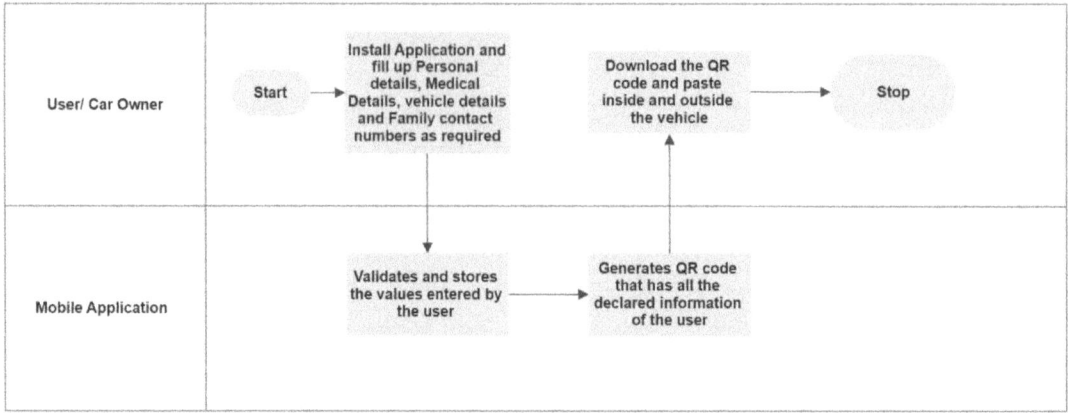
Illustrative

(vi) The application identifies nearest 3 Ambulances and 3 Hospitals/ Trauma Centres in the accident periphery and sends alerts to them including the coordinates of the accident site and appropriate message along with contact number of the reporter.

(vii) Upon getting the alert message, systems of the ambulances (all three) start alerting through sound and lights to inform the respondents.

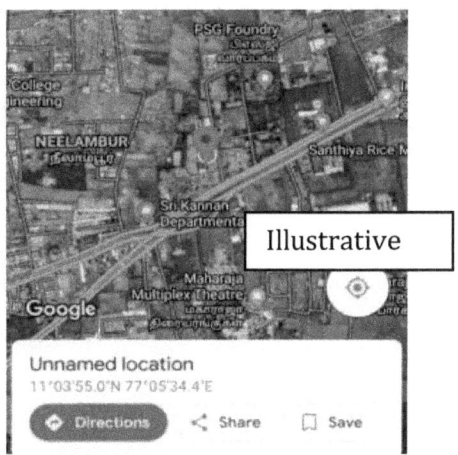

(viii) The respondents of the ambulances have appropriate time (say 5 minutes) to accept the call. The one who accepts first is booked to go to the accident site.

(ix) In case none accepts the call, the application system again looks for other 3 ambulances in the periphery to send alerts.

(x) Once accepted, the status of movement of the ambulance is displayed on the mobilescreen of the reporter (through application interface).

(xi) The ambulance rushes to the accident site with necessary equipment.

(xii) Parallelly, upon getting the alert message, Hospitals/Trauma Centre Systems alerts through alarms and lights to inform staffs about the accident

(xiii) The hospital/ Trauma centers have option to accept the call depending on availability in that hospital/ Trauma center for a given period of time (say 5 minutes)

(xiv) If during the given time period, any of the hospital/trauma center accepts the call,the system will display details of the accident, accident site on map, details of victims with their personal details and medical history.

(xv) Once the hospital / trauma center accepts the case, the location of the hospital will be displayed in the ambulance meaning that the ambulance is expected to reach that hospital.

(xvi) Once the mapping of ambulance and hospital is done, the hospital systems willdisplay the location of ambulance on geo map along with expected time of arrival of the ambulance. It carries the ambulance ID in the information.

(xvii) The interface of the hospital application shows the location of the ambulance on geo - map.

(xviii) The hospital in the meantime prepares for patient admission.

(xix) Patient(s) are brought to the hospital for treatment.

Automated accident Sensor based:

Pre - requisites:

Sensor based device is installed in the vehicle

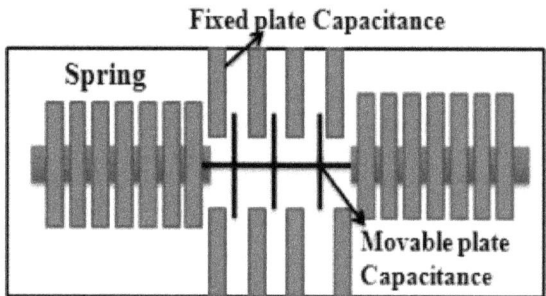

Process steps:

(i) **Accidents** happen/occur.

(ii) Sensors of the vehicles senses the accident based on impact and triggers the inbuilt application to send SOS and alert to the nearest ambulance and hospital/trauma center including coordinates and messages.

(iii) Rest of the reporting process remains the same from point no 4 of the Process flow. The only difference here would be that there would not be any contact no of reporter as the accident is reported automatically (sensor based)

Alternatively, an informer can also call the command & control center through telephone/ mobile to inform about an accident providing all required details of the accident. Respondents of the Command & Control center can register the accident in the system post which automatic information dissemination will happen to the ambulances and Hospitals/ Trauma Centres.

Process Flow: Accident Reporting Process - QR Code Based

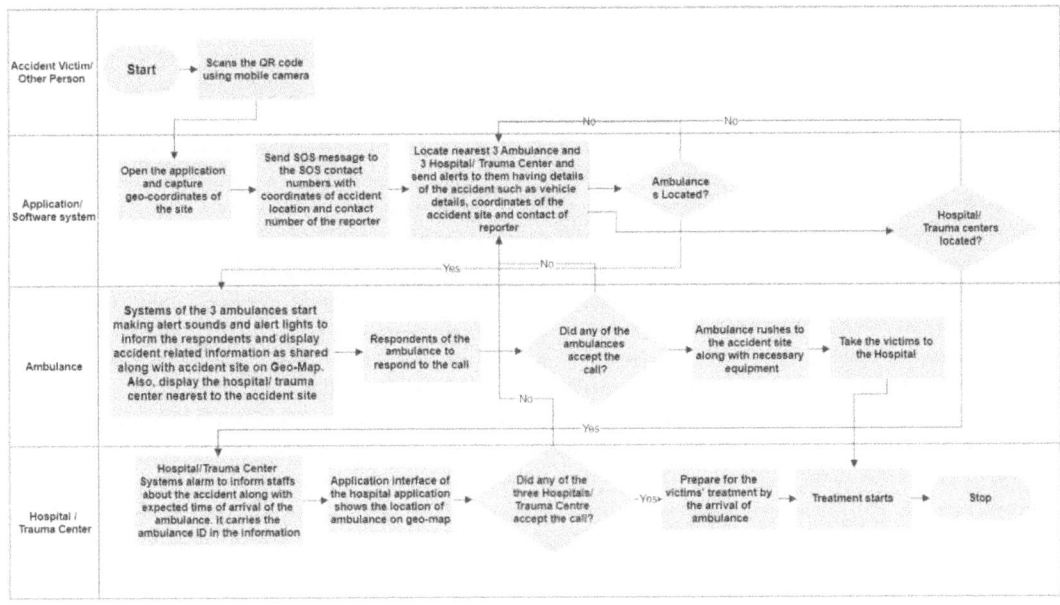

Process Flow: Accident Reporting System - Sensor Based

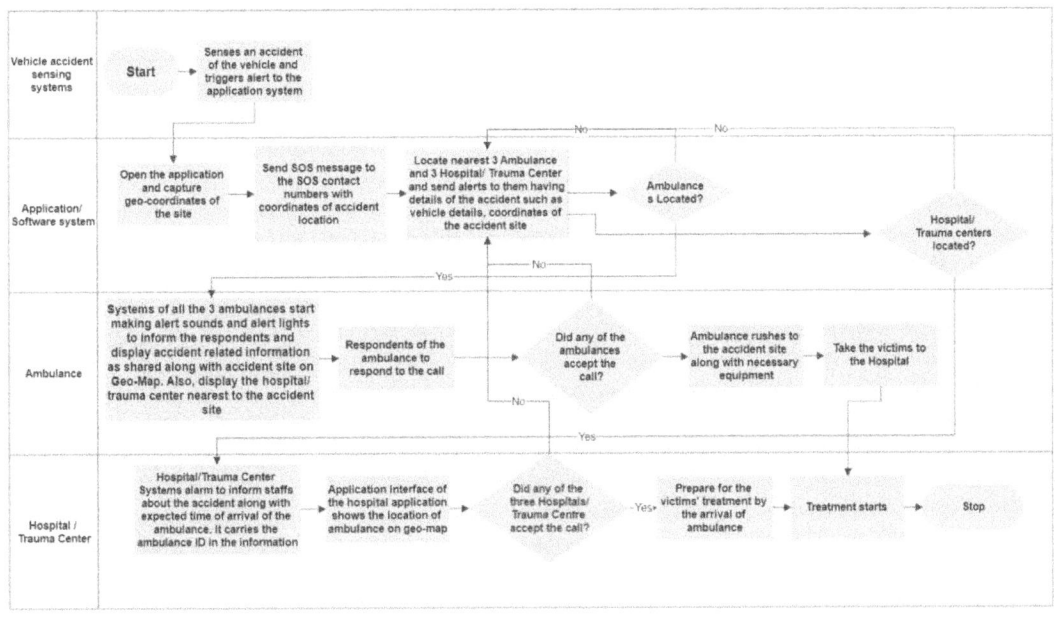

Definitions - Explanation of terms used in the Report:

Term	Definition
R^2	R - squared (R2) also known as coefficient of determination is a statistical measure that represents the proportion of the variance for a dependent variable that's explained by an independent variable or variables in a regression model.
Fatal Accident	A fatal accident is one in which one or more persons are killed a result of the accident, provided death occurs within 30 days.
Accident Severity	Number of persons killed per accident
Road Accident Risk	Number of Accidents per Lakh Population
Road Accident Fatality Risk	Number of Persons Killed per Lakh Population
Road Accident Rate	Number of Accidents Per Ten Thousand Vehicles
Road Accident Fatality rate	Number of Persons killed Per Ten Thousand Vehicles
Road Accident Density	Number of accidents per 100 Km of Road
Road Accident Fatality Density	Number of persons killed per 100 Km of Road
Vehicle Density	Number of Vehicles per Km of Road

CERAMIC BASED INDUSTRIES IN RAJASTHAN

The Ceramic Sector in Rajasthan

The Ceramic Sector in Rajasthan has abundant reserves of essential ceramic materials. These resources comprise high - quality deposits of feldspar, ball clay, fire clay, silica sand, gypsum, china clay, limestone, talcum, and dolomite. Almost all the major minerals required for the Ceramics and glass sector can be found in Rajasthan.

Notably, Rajasthan boasts deposits of Ball Clay and Fire Clay at Kolayat, Kharduja, Devikot, Baser, Silica Sand at Bundi, Feldspar at Ajmer, Rajsamand, and Bewar, Gypsum at Nagaur, Ganganagar, and Bikaner, China Clay at Neem Ka Thana, Limestone at Gotan, Talcum at Dausa, and Dolomite at Bhilwara, Alwar, and Udaipur. These deposits are renowned for their exceptional quality within the global ceramic industry.

Currently, Rajasthan is home to approximately 500 ceramic units that operate across the entire value chain. These units successfully produce various ceramic products, including tiles, sanitary ware - , insulators, tableware, refractories, and glass.

Key Ceramic Products

The ceramics sector encompasses a wide - ranging industry, manufacturing a variety of product classes such as sanitary ware (including wash basins, sinks, and toilet bowls), ceramic and ceramic ware products, electrical insulators, semiconductors, capacitors, protective wire tubes, resistors, inductors, circuit protection devices, refractories, tiles, and ceramic ware, among others.

The future of the ceramic sector is closely intertwined with ongoing economic growth and sustainable industrial development. On the global stage, the ceramic trade has undergone a series of significant transformations over the century, leading to a substantial surge in demand for high - quality ceramic goods within the globalized arena.

Analysis of Top Ceramic Products Using E-Way Bills

Upon investigating E-Way bills with a focus on ceramic - based products, it became apparent that several items are being supplied from Rajasthan, indicating their production within the state. The key products identified are

1. Ceramic flags and paving.
2. Hearth or wall tiles.
3. Ceramic mosaic cubes and similar items, whether or not on a backing.
4. Finishing ceramics.

Assessment Value (In Lakh)

FY	Export	Import	Intra State	Inward Supply	Outward Supply	Grand Total
2019 - 2020	6,481	43	32,397	1,13,154	1,37,384	2,89,459
2020 - 2021	8,863	23	36,024	1,14,752	1,37,995	2,97,657
2021 - 2022	9,364	21	35,626	1,61,088	1,63,096	3,69,196

As observed in the table above, there has been a notable increase in the export of these products, while imports have shown a gradual yet significant decrease. Moreover, there has been substantial growth in both outward and inward supplies since the fiscal year 2020 - 21. These products are primarily manufactured by large corporate entities.

Refractory Bricks, Blocks, Tiles, and Similar Ceramic Constructional Goods

Assessment Value (In Lakh)

FY	Export	Import	Intra State	Inward Supply	Outward Supply	Grand Total
2019 - 2020	13,328	7,231	4,127	15,761	44,922	85,369
2020 - 2021	7,316	7,612	3,677	12,908	22,580	54,093
2021 - 2022	1,904	8,499	3,627	19,973	13,775	47,778

An analysis of the supply trends for refractory bricks, blocks, and tiles reveals a substantial decline in inter - state outward supplies and exports to foreign countries. Simultaneously, there has been an increase in the inward supply of these products from other states and imports from international sources. Intra - state supplies have remained relatively stable.

Mineral Resources used as raw material for Ceramics in Rajasthan

Rajasthan has an abundant quantity of mineral deposits used for Ceramic industries. A district - wise list of minerals is given below:

Mineral	Districts
Silica	Karauli, Bundi
Feldspar & Quartz	Jaipur, Tonk, Ajmer, Ganganagar
Dolomite, China Clay	Alwar, Bhilwara, Udaipur
Talcum	Dausa
Ball Clay, Fire Clay	Bikaner
Gypsum, Limestone	Nagaur
Clay	Sirohi

A representation of mineral and districts on Rajasthan state map is given below:

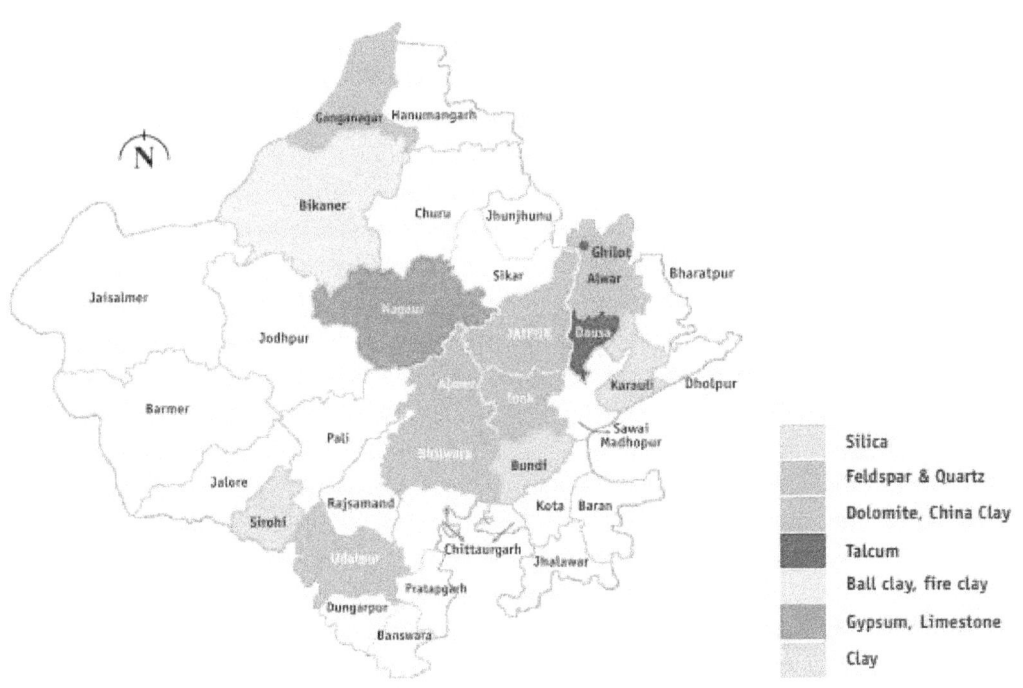

Rajasthan, India

Study on Feldspar Minerals

Feldspar minerals comprise a group of substances characterized by the presence of alumina and silica in their chemical composition. This group encompasses aluminum silicates containing soda, potassium, or lime. Feldspars find extensive applications in the ceramics and glass industries.

Rajasthan, in particular, plays a prominent role in feldspar production, accounting for approximately 90% of the total reserves and resources, with Telangana contributing 4%, and Andhra Pradesh and Tamil Nadu each contributing 2%.

State - wise Feldspar Production (In tonnes) for the years 2015 - 16, 2016 - 17, and 2017 - 18:

State Year	2015 - 16	2016 - 17	2017 - 18
Rajasthan	25,17,783	56,11,217	32,50,595
Telangana	6,73,831	6,76,811	7,98,964
Andhra Pradesh	1,52,053	1,44,646	2,17,245
Gujarat	106	2,114	3,441

State wise production of Feldspar (In tonnes)

This data presents the state - wise production of feldspar over the specified years.

Status of supply of Feldspar minerals from & into Rajasthan

(Ass Value in Lakh)

Supply	2019 - 2020	2020 - 2021	2021 - 2022	Grand Total	% of Total
Outward - Inter State	95,759	1,03,849	1,20,207	3,19,815	78%
Intra State - (Raj to Raj)	21,414	23,565	20,065	65,044	16%
Export	5,939	5,720	5,273	16,932	4%
Inward - (Other State to Raj)	3,262	2,854	3,339	9,455	2%

Feldspar supply (Ass Value in Lakh)

Based on the E-Way bill Study, it is observed that 78 % of total Feldspar is supplied to other states and there is continuous growth in outward supply for the last two years as well. In outward supply Gujarat is key recipient states approx 80% feldspar is supplied to Morbi district Gujarat. Below are top recipients district based on E-Way bill Study last three years

(Ass Value in Lakh)

District Name	Assessment Value	Count of Waybill
MORBI	23,64,82,68,594	3,82,375
BHARUCH	1,61,69,95,522	17,291
AHMADABAD	1,43,11,53,455	12,708
KACHCHH	1,35,69,70,395	9,486
SABAR KANTHA	1,01,09,66,238	15,706
SURENDRANAGAR	94,18,31,817	15,375
VADODARA	94,00,72,640	11,368

Top Feldspar recipient district (Ass Value in Lakh)

From the tables given above, it is clear that most of the Feldspar, which is the main raw material of the Ceramic industry, is supplied to Gujrat where it is used to prepare finished goods. Rajasthan has not been a prime utilizer of Feldspar by developing Ceramic based industries within the state. There are certain practical and technical reasons behind that if it is compared with Gujarat -

i. Underdeveloped Ecosystem:

ii. Unavailability of Natural Gas to run furnaces (no linkage)

iii. High cost of electricity

SWOT analysis of Rajasthan state for growth of Ceramic based industries

Strengths:

Following are identified as strengths of Rajasthan state for Ceramic based enterprises

1. Availability of high - quality raw materials and intermediate products at reasonable cost

2. Availability of low - cost labor in state

3. Land availability in core Feldspar production region such as Ajmer, Nagaur, and Jaipur

4. Rajasthan forms a considerable part of the National Capital Region which has a huge

   consuming population concerning the Ceramic & Glass Industry

5. Dedicated Land Parcel at Ghiloth for Ceramics & Glass Sector: A dedicated 750 - acre Ceramic & Glass (Industrial) Zone is notified at Ghiloth near Neemrana in Alwar district of Rajasthan. This will be a part of the Delhi - Mumbai Industrial Corridor (DMIC). Ghiloth is located approximately 100 km from the Delhi airport, off the Jaipur - Delhi National Highway (NH - 8) along the interstate natural gas pipeline.

6. To encourage investments in the ceramic, glass & allied sectors piped natural gas will be made available soon within the state.

7. Some major global companies have already set up huge manufacturing facilities in the state.

8. The Delhi - Mumbai Industrial Corridor (DMIC) passing through the state will provide excellent logistics & transportation infrastructure.

9. Skilled and relatively low - cost labor with a history of good industrial relations

10. A large domestic market

11. Investor - friendly Government which is highly supportive of private sector investment

12. Hassle - free simplified procedures through Single Window investment clearance

13. Special incentive package for ceramics & glass units

Weaknesses:

Ceramic clusters across India confront challenges with regards to energy availability, environmental issues, social issues, and raw material availability.

1. Fuel Price – Ceramics is a power - intensive industry; the manufacturing process requires natural gas to fire the kiln and after raw materials, electricity and fuel cost is the second largest cost element in the total cost of production. Frequent changes with immediate effect affect the profitability of the entities since they cannot pass on the increase in production cost immediately.

As per the data from CSO, petroleum products and clay products account for a share of 15.6% and 12.7%, respectively in the production of ceramic products. Other non - metallic minerals and mineral products, bauxite etc account for a share of 11.3%, 5.3% and 4.9% respectively.

2. Social issue – Lack of skilled manpower. Workers are prone to high risk of developing silicosis and silico tuberculosis during their working life span.

3. Environmental issues – Issues related to air pollution, wastewater and solid waste. Low awareness friendly working conditions

4. Need for Skill development: Rajasthan still has a lack of infrastructure that supports the growth of the Ceramic ecosystem. One of the major requirements is related to education and training to develop an unskilled workforce into human capital. While dedicated courses in Ceramics in the areas of R&D, Design, Marketing, etc will provide macro level boost to this sector as a whole, training & skill development institutes will upgrade the existing labor force to work more efficiently with improved quality of finished goods. Combining both the interventions, Rajasthan can be portrayed as a hub for ceramic - based industries.

5. High cost & unreliable power supply: Rajasthan has limited power generation units and depends on power purchases from other states. This causes high cost of electricity coupled with power outages. This creates an image that is not supportive to the industrial growth of Rajasthan.

Opportunities:

1. Increasing domestic and foreign demand: Introduction of vitrified and porcelain tiles which are called "Tiles of the Future" in the Indian market

2. Availability of mineral bi - products such as marble slurry that can be used in ceramics: Marble is the dominant industry in Rajasthan and has developed as a hub. There is waste material called marble slurry which is produced while marble cutting and is currently potentially un - utilized for other purposes. This slurry can be utilized as a mixture in ceramic - based products.

3. Operational SEZs and industrial parks

4. Government incentives in the RICCO scheme with attractive incentives (will be discussed in forthcoming section)

Threats:

1. Increased competition from China and Italy.
2. Dumping threats from China.

Rajasthan Investment Promotion Scheme 2019

Rajasthan has an existing scheme for the promotion of industries. The Rajasthan Investment Promotion Scheme (RIPS) 2019 is a package of financial incentives for investors who either want to invest in new businesses or expand their existing businesses .

Key features of RIPS scheme:

Benefits to manufacturing enterprises under rips - 2019

1. An eligible manufacturing enterprise shall be granted benefits and incentives as given below: -
    i. Investment Subsidy of 75% of State tax due and deposited, for seven years;
    ii. Employment Generation Subsidy in the form of reimbursement of 50% of employers' contribution towards employees' EPF and ESI, for seven years:

Provided that the Employment Generation Subsidy in the form of reimbursement of 75% of employers' contribution towards EPF and ESI shall be granted

   a) For employees belonging to Women, Schedule Caste (SC), Schedule Tribe (ST), Person with disability (PwD); and
   b) For all employees if the enterprise is providing more than 75% direct employment to persons domiciled in Rajasthan.

Provided further that the Employment Generation Subsidy shall not be granted for those employees for which the employer is receiving reimbursement under any other scheme of Government of India or Government of Rajasthan;

i. Exemption from payment of 100% of Electricity Duty for seven years;

ii. Exemption from payment of 100% of Land Tax for seven years;

iii. Exemption from payment of 100% of Market Fee (Mandi Fee) for seven years;

iv. Exemption from payment of 100% of Stamp Duty:

   a) On purchase or lease/sub - lease of land and construction or improvement on such land; and

   b) On purchase or lease/sub - lease of floor area/space in any constructed commercial building for setting up of enterprise in: -

v. IT Sector; or

vi. Apparel Sector; or

vii. Industry 4.0; and

viii. Exemption from payment of 100% of conversion charges payable for change of land use and conversion of land.

2. Notwithstanding anything contained in the Scheme, the State Government may grant a special package of incentives and exemptions, which may be over and above the benefits available to a Manufacturing Enterprise in a thrust sector.

3. Notwithstanding anything contained in the Scheme, an eligible manufacturing enterprise will be provided all the applicable benefits, as mentioned in clause 4.1 and applicable additional benefits as Thrust Sector enterprise, subject to the condition that enterprise may opt for and shall be provided either one of the following benefits, as mentioned below, namely: -

   i. Applicable Interest Subsidy; or

   ii. Applicable Capital Subsidy.

Provided that Capital Subsidy on zero liquid discharge based effluent treatment plant applicable to textile sector and apparel sector shall not be counted as capital subsidy for the purpose of this clause.

Provided further that where an eligible enterprise falls under more than one category of Thrust Sector, it shall have to opt for benefits in any one of the

Thrust sector and can avail additional benefits provided in one Thrust Sector only

Ceramic and Glass Sector

Enterprises making an investment equal to or above rupees ten crore in the Ceramic and Glass Sector shall be granted the following benefits:–

a) Investment Subsidy of 25% of State tax due and deposited, for additional three years; and

b) 5% Interest Subsidy on term loan taken by the enterprise from Financial Institutions or State Financial Institutions or Banks recognized by Reserve Bank of India, for making an investment in plant & machinery for a period of five years subject to a maximum of rupees twenty - five lakh per year.

MSME Sector:

Enterprises of MSME sector shall, in addition to benefits mentioned in clause 4.1, if applicable, be granted the following benefits: -

b) Water Conservation and Green Measures Subsidy in the form of Reimbursement of

    iv. 50% of cost incurred on water audit by any Government empanelled or Government approved agency subject to maximum of rupees two lakh;

    v. 50% of amount paid to the suppliers for the plant, excluding civil work, for establishing zero liquid discharge based effluent treatment plant;

    vi. 50% of amount paid to the suppliers for the plant, excluding civil work, for adopting Green Building Measures for the building having a minimum floor space of 2000 sq mtrs; and

    vii. 50% of amount paid to the suppliers for the plant, excluding civil work, for establishing "Reuse and Recycling of Industrial Waste Plant", subject to maximum of rupees fifty lakh and shall be one time assistance; Provided that maximum total amount of subsidy including (i), (ii) and (iii) shall be subject to maximum of rupees fifty lakh and shall be one time assistance;

c) One - time reimbursement of 50% of cost incurred on obtaining quality certification for manufacturing or processes or certification related to export, issued by any Government agency or any agency authorized by Government of India or Government of Rajasthan, subject to maximum of rupees twenty five lakh;

d) One - time reimbursement of 50% cost incurred to acquire advanced technology from premier national institutes – Indian Institute of Science (IISc), Indian Institute of Technology (IITs), National Institute of Technology (NITs), National Institute of Design (NIDs), The Council of Scientific and Industrial Research (CSIR) or any other institute set up by Government of India, subject to maximum of rupees ten lakh;

e) One - time financial assistance equivalent to the assistance provided by Government of India for obtaining Patents, Geographical Indication (GI) Tagging, and Trademark Registration.

f) One - time reimbursement of 50% of investment made on plant and machinery and testing equipments for obtaining Silver or Gold or Diamond or Platinum rating under Zero Defect and Zero Effect Certification Scheme of Government of India, subject to maximum of rupees five lakh; and

g) One - time financial assistance on raising funds (capital) through SME platform, to the extent of 50% of the investment made in the process of raising funds (capital), subject to a maximum of rupees five lakh.

Growth drivers – CERAMICS TILES Industry Key schemes launched by GoI which are expected to drive the demand for ceramic products:

Various government initiatives for infrastructure development and favorable demographics

expected to drive the ceramics, sanitary ware and bathroom fittings industry in future.

Ideal locations for developing clusters of different ceramic - based industries

In the above map, the identified area around the border of Jaipur, Ajmer and Nagar districts can be developed as cluster of different set of activities in the ceramics such as Tiles, Sanitaryware, Pottery, Terracotta, Earthenware, Dinnerware, Stoneware, Porcelain, Clay Bricks and Electrical Insulators.

The identified area is rich in Feldspar and Quartz. This will reduce the cost of transportation of the mineral as it is locally available. Additionally, there is availability of land which is well connected to highways. The area has availability of unskilled and semiskilled workforce who can be provided skill upgradation and prepared for different types of requirements in the local ceramic industries.

Suggested Initiatives and Plan for Ceramic Industry –

10. Establishment of industries

    vi. Identify scope for new ceramic - based industries on account of products made

    vii. Identify location / land in the area of border of Jaipur, Ajmer and Nagaur districts

    viii. Develop dedicated Ceramic corridor basis on road connectivity and other required facilities

    ix. Single Window Clearance for target industries

    x. Easy and accessible financing schemes for new enterprises with dedicated bank branches

11. Cluster based approach for ceramic industries

    iv. Cluster development for enhancing productivity and competitiveness as well as capacity building of micro and small enterprise

    v. Enhance competitiveness of domestic industry by providing quality infrastructure through Government and Private Partnership approach for select clusters with potential to become globally competitive

    vi. Technology up gradation of small - scale industry by providing upfront capital

12. Initiatives for Ceramic cluster improvement
    v. Established Institute of Ceramic technology for common use
    vi. Initiatives for cluster modernization and restructuring
    vii. Support to setup common facility centers
    viii. Support for setting up skill upgradation centers
13. Initiatives for Energy efficiency ceramic industry
    i. Energy efficiency programme for Small and Medium Enterprises(SMEs)
    ii. Promoting energy efficiency and renewable energy in selected MSMEs clusters
    iii. Scaling - up energy efficiency small enterprise
14. A dedicated ceramic research institute is essential for modernization as well as development of the industry.

www.ingramcontent.com/pod-product-compliance
Lightning Source LLC
LaVergne TN
LVHW070526070526
838199LV00073B/6710